TM

...For Dummies

References for the Rest of Us!®

BESTSELLING BOOK SERIES

Do you find that traditional reference books are overloaded with technical details and advice you'll never use? Do you postpone important life decisions because you just don't want to deal with them? Then our *For Dummies*® business and general reference book series is for you.

For Dummies business and general reference books are written for those frustrated and hard-working souls who know they aren't dumb, but find that the myriad of personal and business issues and the accompanying horror stories make them feel helpless. *For Dummies* books use a lighthearted approach, a down-to-earth style, and even cartoons and humorous icons to dispel fears and build confidence. Lighthearted but not lightweight, these books are perfect survival guides to solve your everyday personal and business problems.

> *"More than a publishing phenomenon, 'Dummies' is a sign of the times."*
>
> — *The New York Times*

> *"A world of detailed and authoritative information is packed into them..."*
>
> — *U.S. News and World Report*

> *"...you won't go wrong buying them."*
>
> — *Walter Mossberg, Wall Street Journal, on For Dummies books*

D0125664

Already, millions of satisfied readers agree. They have made For Dummies the #1 introductory level computer book series and a best-selling business book series. They have written asking for more. So, if you're looking for the best and easiest way to learn about business and other general reference topics, look to For Dummies to give you a helping hand.

Wiley Publishing, Inc.

5/09

Dog Health & Nutrition FOR DUMMIES®

by M. Christine Zink, DVM, PhD

Wiley Publishing, Inc.

Dog Health & Nutrition For Dummies®

Published by
Wiley Publishing, Inc.
909 Third Avenue
New York, NY 10022
www.wiley.com

For general information on our other products and services or to obtain technical support, please contact our Customer Care Department within the U.S. at 800-762-2974, outside the U.S. at 317-572-3993, or fax 317-572-4002.

Wiley also publishes its books in a variety of electronic formats. Some content that appears in print may not be available in electronic books.

Library of Congress Cataloging-in-Publication Data:

Library of Congress Control Number: 2001089293

ISBN: 0-7645-5318-6

Manufactured in the United States of America

10 9 8 7 6 5 4 3

About the Author

A dog lover all her life, **Chris Zink** got her first dog, an Irish Wolfhound, the day she graduated from Ontario Veterinary College with her DVM. From an initial interest in obedience, mainly as a survival tactic, she gradually became fascinated with all aspects of canine performance. While competing in performance events throughout Canada and the United States, Chris recognized a significant information gap. Owners and trainers wanted to know more about how canine structure and medical or physical conditions affect their dogs' performance, and how to keep their canine teammates healthy and injury-free. Yet little information was available. She therefore wrote the award-winning *Peak Performance: Coaching the Canine Athlete,* a comprehensive guide to the dog as an athlete. Her second book, *Jumping from A to Z: Teach Your Dog to Soar,* co-authored with Julie Daniels, has become the gold standard for jump training.

Chris presents Coaching the Canine Athlete seminars worldwide to rave reviews and regularly writes for dog magazines. She is also a consultant on canine sports medicine, evaluating canine structure and locomotion and designing individualized conditioning programs for active dogs. Chris has put out over 50 titles in agility, obedience, hunting, tracking, and conformation on dogs of several different breeds from the Sporting, Working, and Hound groups. Chris currently competes with two Golden Retrievers: Butterblac's For The Fun Of It MX, AXJ, AD, OAC, NGC, NJC, UDX, JH, WC (Tally) and Aureolus Alloy's Tiger Motif OA, OAJ, TD, NAC, WC (Stripe), and a Border Collie, Fate. Chris and the dogs also share their home with two Grand Champion Maine Coon cats, Petey and Topper.

In her other life, Chris is a professor at Johns Hopkins University School of Medicine, with over 100 scientific publications. There, she teaches medical and veterinary students and does AIDS research.

About Howell Book House

Committed to the Human/Companion Animal Bond

Thank you for choosing a book brought to you by the pet experts at Howell Book House, a division of Hungry Minds, Inc. And welcome to the family of pet owners who've put their trust in Howell books for nearly 40 years!

Pet ownership is about relationships — the bonds people form with their dogs, cats, horses, birds, fish, small mammals, reptiles, and other animals. Howell Book House/Hungry Minds understands that these are some of the most important relationships in life, and that it's vital to nurture them through enjoyment and education. The happiest pet owners are those who know they're taking the best care of their pets — and with Howell books owners have this satisfaction. They're happy, educated owners, and as a result, they have happy pets, and that enriches the bond they share.

Howell Book House was established in 1961 by Mr. Elsworth S. Howell, an active and proactive dog fancier who showed English Setters and judged at the prestigious Westminster Kennel Club show in New York. Mr. Howell based his publishing program on strength of content, and his passion for books written by experienced and knowledgeable owners defined Howell Book House and has remained true over the years. Howell's reputation as the premier pet book publisher is supported by the distinction of having won more awards from the Dog Writers Association of America than any other publisher. Howell Book House/Hungry Minds has over 400 titles in publication, including such classics as The American Kennel Club's *Complete Dog Book*, the *Dog Owner's Home Veterinary Handbook*, *Blessed Are the Brood Mares*, and *Mother Knows Best: The Natural Way to Train Your Dog*.

When you need answers to questions you have about any aspect of raising or training your companion animals, trust that Howell Book House/Hungry Minds has the answers. We welcome your comments and suggestions, and we look forward to helping you maximize your relationships with your pets throughout the years.

The Howell Book House Staff

Dedication

To Can. Ch Butterblac's Some Fools Dream UD, JH, WCX; Can. UD, WC "Bannor," who taught me what is important.

Author's Acknowledgments

I couldn't have undertaken this project without the generous help of many others. I would like to thank Cynthia Fox, Dee Geisert, Sue Sternberg, Debbie Van Kempen, Lauren Tapyrik, Dr. Susan Wynn, Barb Atkinson, and Elizabeth Evans for carefully reading the manuscript and making suggestions from their different doggie perspectives. I owe a great debt to Tina Moran, who cared for my dogs every afternoon for months during the writing of this book. My dogs asked me to thank Debbie Van Kempen and Lauren Tapyrik for their excellent care and companionship while I travel, and Erica Schuetz for making sure they get their exercise every day. I would like to thank Dominique De Vito for entrusting me with this project and Scott Prentzas and Elizabeth Kuball for seeing it through with patience and humor. And finally, I wish to thank Shauna, Cajun, Bannor, Tally, Stripe, and Fate for being such patient teachers.

Publisher's Acknowledgments

We're proud of this book; please send us your comments through our Online Registration Form located at www.dummies.com/register.

Some of the people who helped bring this book to market include the following:.

Acquisitions, Editorial, and Media Development

Project Editor: Elizabeth Netedu Kuball

Acquisitions Editors: Scott Prentzas and Kira Sexton

Acquisitions Coordinator:

Technical Editor: Debbie Wood

Editorial Manager: Pamela Mourouzis

Cover Photos: The Image Bank, © David DeLossy

Production

Project Coordinator: Maridee Ennis

Layout and Graphics: Brian Torwelle, Julie Trippetti, Jeremey Unger, Erin Zeltner

Special Art: Marcia Schlehr and Barbara Frake

Proofreaders: Andy Hollandbeck, John Greenough, Marianne Santy TECHBOOKS Production Service

Indexer: TECHBOOKS Production Service

Publishing and Editorial for Consumer Dummies

Diane Graves Steele, Vice President and Publisher, Consumer Dummies

Joyce Pepple, Acquisitions Director, Consumer Dummies

Kristin A. Cocks, Product Development Director, Consumer Dummies

Michael Spring, Vice President and Publisher, Travel

Brice Gosnell, Publishing Director, Travel

Suzanne Jannetta, Editorial Director, Travel

Publishing for Technology Dummies

Andy Cummings, Acquisitions Director

Composition Services

Gerry Fahey, Executive Director of Production Services

Debbie Stailey, Director of Composition Services

Contents at a Glance

Cartoons at a Glance

By Rich Tennant

"Buster and the vet have a special relationship. That's why we always try to coordinate his birthday with a worming."

page 117

"Actually, sitting on top of their doghouse during inclement weather is normal for some dogs. Catching snowflakes on the tongue, however, seems unique to our particular pet."

page 325

"Well, someone's starting to show his age. Look at how Rusty has to hold his chew-toy at arm's length now to see which one he's got."

page 301

"We're very careful about grooming. First I'll check his teeth and nails, then trim any excess hair from his ears, nose, and around the eyes. After checking for fleas and parasites I'll let Roger go off to work so I can begin grooming the dog."

page 7

Dr. Doug and his dog shared a unique companionship

C'mon Misty - scissors, scissors! That's a scalpel. You know that!

page 237

Jerry bought only one type of pet food: NASCAR Kibbles The High Performance Dog Food

page 51

Cartoon Information:
Fax: 978-546-7747
E-Mail: richtennant@the5thwave.com
World Wide Web: www.the5thwave.com

Table of Contents

• •

Introduction

• •

I confess: I am hopelessly fascinated by dogs. I discover everything I can about them. I soak up information about their anatomy, their physiology, what makes them sick, what keeps them healthy, their behavior, and how they learn. I discover new things about dogs every time I see them run, play, work, and even sleep. I used to try to keep this fanatic fascination a secret. The more I talked to people with dogs, however, the more I realized that they're curious, too. As a veterinarian, people are always asking me questions about their dogs' health, such as:

✔ Why does my dog get so many ear infections?

✔ What's the best food for my dog?

✔ My dog has vomited three times today — should I take him to the veterinarian?

✔ What should I do if my dog starts choking?

✔ How can I relieve my old dog's stiffness?

✔ Which toys are safe for my dog?

✔ Do herbal remedies really work?

Most dog people are also curious about canine behavior. They understand that their dogs' behavior is intimately linked to health, just as it is in humans. People who are depressed feel tired, they ache all over, and they have frequent headaches. Likewise, dogs with behavioral problems tend to become ill more often, they don't eat as well, and they often develop self-destructive habits that can even become life threatening. Dog people understand the need for emotional balance in the life of a healthy dog.

If you've picked up this book, you probably have some questions about how to keep your dog healthy and active for a long lifetime. This book was written to answer all those questions, and also to give you a little extra useful information you can use to impress your friends.

About This Book

In this book, I have compiled nitty-gritty information about dog health and nutrition. I haven't limited the information to bare bones details about diseases. Instead, I used a broader definition of health that includes routine health care, exercise, behavior, and training. I made this book as comprehensive as possible so there's something new and interesting for everyone, from the person who just got her first furry friend to the bona fide dog aficionado. And I slathered the book with humor, because dogs are so good at making people laugh. Whether you read this book from cover to cover or you just read a chapter here and there, I know you'll have fun finding out more about your canine companion and about how to keep him healthy and active for many, many years to come.

I'm sure you also understand that the title of this book is tongue-in-cheek. Dog lovers are not dummies at all. In fact, having a dog as your companion is one of the smartest things you can do. Many scientific studies confirm that dogs have positive effects on our physical an emotional health. People and dogs have been teamed up for over 120,000 years in one of the best partnerships of all time. There's nothing dumb about that.

How This Book is Organized

Dog Health & Nutrition For Dummies is divided into six parts. Each part, and each chapter within the parts, can be read on its own if you just want to get some quick information about a specific health- or nutrition-related question. If you want to know about the basics of canine health care and routine maintenance of your canine friend, you'll want to start at the beginning. Perhaps you want to find out more about how to feed your dog so he will remain healthy for many years to come. In that case, skip to the section on nutrition. Or maybe you have a canine senior and need to know what you can do to detect early some of those illnesses that creep up in old age. In that case, you'll want to check out the section on caring for older dogs. Feel free to start in the middle of the book and skip around as you want.

Part 1: Basic Health Care

When dogs teamed up with humans to form the most unique and long-lasting relationship in the animal kingdom, they traded in their ability to roam free and determine their own destiny for the crate-to-grave care of their human companions. Just as parents take their children to the pediatrician every year and vaccinate them to keep them safe from diseases, dog owners need to take their pets for check ups and vaccinations, too. But vaccinations are only a small part of preventive care. Proper grooming, regular dental care, flea and tick prevention, and regular exercise are all integral components of a healthy canine lifestyle. Thanks to such preventive medicine, our dogs are living much longer than ever before.

The chapters in this part describe the nose-to-toes details of doggie preventive care. You'll find explanations of when and how to clean your dog's ears, what your vet should look for in an annual check-up, and how to keep bugs from bugging your dog. I tell you how to pick a veterinarian who will become an active member of your dog's health care team, and how to get the most out of an annual veterinary check-up. Your dog needs you to read this section so that he'll have the best chance of a long, healthy life. Your dog would probably prefer that you *not* read some sections, especially the parts about clipping his nails and giving him shots — but this is one time when ignoring his wishes is definitely best.

Part II: Food, Glorious Food!

The old expression "You are what you eat" is just as true for dogs as it is for their people. Your dog is a carnivore with unique nutritional needs, and your job is to be sure that you feed him a healthy diet.

In this part, I give you everything you need to know about how to feed your dog in health and in sickness. I tell you what a dog's nutritional needs are, how to read a dog food label, and how to decide which dog food will keep your furry friend strong and healthy from puppyhood through old age. I also explain which supplements are available and how to know whether your dog needs them. If you think your dog may be too fat or too thin, I let you know how to determine whether your dog is at the right weight and what to do if he needs to beef up or slim down.

Many people today are feeding their dogs homemade meals in an attempt to provide nutrients that are lost during the processing and preserving of commercial dog food. In this part, I also discuss how to ensure that your home cookin' is providing your dog with the nutrition he needs. Finally, you'll find out how to feed dogs with special health problems, such as allergies or kidney or liver disease.

Part III: Recognizing and Treating Common Maladies

Almost every dog becomes ill at one time or another. Just like humans, dogs are exposed to infectious organisms, get injured from playing too rough, and eventually suffer the usual problems associated with old age. Your dog will stay healthier — and you will save money on veterinary bills — if you know how to identify the earliest signs of illness.

To understand disease, you must first understand your dog's body and how it works. So I begin this part by giving you a quick tour of the canine body, inside and out. Next, I explain all the nuts and bolts of canine diseases, from cancer to constipation — including their causes and cures. In this part, you'll find out what critical signs to look for so you'll know whether your hound needs to visit the veterinarian. I also tell you how to care for your ailing animal, including what to do in an emergency, how to administer CPR, and how to give pills and potions. Finally, I explain how drugs work, and I also provide information about complementary and alternative therapies such as acupuncture, massage, and botanical medicine.

Part IV: Health for the Body and Soul

Canine health involves more than just a normal body temperature and a shiny coat. After all, your dog is more than just a physical being. He also has an intellectual side, an emotional side, and even a spiritual side. In a truly healthy dog, all these facets are integrated and in balance. That's why I include in this part chapters on the canine lifestyle, from grooming to fitness, training to behavior. Your dog will better fit into your family and your lifestyle if he is clean, exercised, and well trained. He will also be an ambassador for the canine species, and will show non-dog people that a dog can be a good citizen.

Exercise is essential for overall fitness and resistance to disease, so this part has a chapter on how to provide a stimulating canine workout as well. I don't include just the basics of exercise; instead, I provide numerous ways that you can have fun while getting your dog fit and even tell you which toys can help your dog exercise his body and his mind. In addition, because basic obedience training is essential for a dog's mental health, this part gives you the tools you'll need to provide a basic obedience training program. Behavioral problems are commonly disguised as physical problems, so I help you recognize common behavioral problems and get appropriate help.

Part V: Caring for the Canine Senior

Old age: We all have to experience it eventually, but most of us dread it (even though the alternative isn't that appealing either). People can learn an important lesson from their dogs, who boldly take each step in the aging process in stride. They get gray around the muzzle but don't seek out dyes and colors to disguise their age. Their vision fades, but they still enjoy watching the birds and squirrels and don't worry about the future. Their joints begin to creak and ache, but they still carry the leash around when their people put on coats to go out for a walk. If you listen and observe, your dog can teach you to live every day to the fullest. He can teach you to appreciate the present for all its good and to put the bad behind you. Not a bad reminder to get from one of your best friends.

In this part, I explain the physical and mental changes that dogs undergo as they age and provide pointers to help keep your oldster as healthy and comfortable as possible. I also discuss the major cause of illness and death in older dogs — cancer — telling you what to look for to make an early diagnosis of cancer and how to give your dog the best chance of a cure.

Finally, I discuss the difficult subject of euthanasia, and give you tips on how to decide when it's time to ease your lifelong friend's suffering and how to say good-bye.

Part VI: The Part of Tens

The chapters in this part are jam-packed with doggie data. You can find out about the best dog health and nutrition resources on the Internet, recognize the ten signs of illness to watch for and what they may mean, identify ten ways to keep your canine companion healthy, and be aware of the ten most common household dangers — all in just a few pages.

Icons Used in This Book

In the left-hand margin throughout this book, you'll find little pictures called *icons,* which draw your attention to key pieces of information. Here's a list of the icons I use and what they mean:

The paragraphs marked by this icon highlight stories and anecdotes I share about my own dogs or other dogs (and their humans) I know.

This icon flags tips and tricks to help you keep your dog healthy or to make your life with dogs easier. I've gathered this information over the years through my own experiences as a vet and through the generosity of many dogs and dog friends. I know they won't mind if I share them with you.

This icon marks important information that's so important it bears repeating.

When you see this icon, be on the lookout for a warning about something that could be potentially dangerous for your dog.

The Dummies Man in this icon is pointing out areas where there are extra details. You don't have to read these sections to understand the topic being discussed, but they do contain a lot of fascinating stuff you may want to know, especially if you want to impress your friends at the dog park next time you visit.

How to Reach Me

Dog people are the greatest people on earth. Nowhere else will you find more sensitive, understanding people than those who enjoy the human-canine bond. I invite you to write and tell me about your experiences with your canine companions — and feel free to send me pictures, too. Who knows? I may ask you if I can use them in my next book.

You can find out more about canine health at my Web site at www.caninesports. com, where I post the latest information on canine health, especially as it relates to the canine athlete. You can e-mail me at mczink@caninesports.com, but I also love to get snail mail at: Canine Sports Productions, 6030 Daybreak Circle, Suite 150, #260, Clarksville, MD 21029

Part I
Basic Health Care

The 5th Wave   By Rich Tennant

"We're very careful about grooming. First I'll check his teeth and nails, then trim any excess hair from his ears, nose, and around the eyes. After checking for fleas and parasites I'll let Roger go off to work so I can begin grooming the dog."

In this part . . .

Here I let you know what you can do to lay a solid foundation for your dog's health throughout his life. I fill you in on the basics of canine health, let you know how you can keep your dog from developing health problems in the first place, and give you suggestions for choosing the right vet for your dog. If you want an overview of what your dog needs to be healthy, read on.

Chapter 1

Canine Health 101

*N*o one knows your dog as well as you do. You watch him play, eat, and sleep, and you pet him every day. Chances are, you will be the first one to know if something is just not right with him. Perhaps your fuzzy friend didn't eat last night. Is he just a bit off today or should you rush him to the veterinarian? In this chapter, I give you the information you'll need to make those kinds of decisions. I tell you what a healthy dog should look like, so you'll be much better at recognizing the signs of illness. I also show you how to perform a quick physical examination on your own dog, including taking his temperature and checking his pulse. Finally, I let you know how to pick a healthy puppy or adult dog when the time comes to increase the size of your canine family.

Recognizing the Signs of a Healthy Dog

The first step in taking care of your dog is knowing what he should look like when he is healthy. If you know what a healthy dog looks like, you'll be better able to know when your dog is sick and to get him the help he needs.

So, what does a healthy dog look like? The answer to this question may seem obvious, but it really isn't. Dogs vary so much in appearance that telling the difference between normal and abnormal can be difficult. Veterinarians spend a lot of time in school (and even after they graduate) learning how to recognize the signs of health in individual dogs and how to differentiate them from the signs of illness.

Determining whether a dog is healthy is difficult because dogs can't talk to us in our language and tell us how they are feeling inside. So being good observers — using all our senses to gather information about our dogs' health — is especially important. Our eyes show us the glistening coat and wagging tail of a healthy dog. Our hands tell us that the healthy dog's skin is smooth and supple. Our ears hear the deep, regular breathing of a healthy dog as he sleeps. Even our noses get involved as they smell the fresh breath of a dog with healthy teeth and gums. In the following sections, I give you some clues about what to look for (with all your senses) in assessing your dog's health.

Appetite

A hungry dog is usually a healthy dog. Most dogs consume their meals in five minutes or less. One of the first signs of illness, especially when a dog has a gastrointestinal upset or a fever, is a decreased interest in food. If your dog refuses food altogether, you need to take him to a veterinarian.

Attitude

A healthy dog exudes a love of life. His head is up, his eyes are bright, and his tail wags with the expectation of the fun that may be just around the corner. Your dog should be energetic, inquisitive, and interested in new surroundings. This very go-get-'em attitude is what endears so many of us to our canine companions. If you notice a shift in your dog's attitude that continues for more than two days, this may be a sign of other problems. Take him to a veterinarian to determine what's wrong.

Coat

The coat is one of the most variable physical characteristics of dogs — and it is also a good indicator of a dog's overall health. Depending on the breed, some dogs have long coats and others have short coats; some have double coats and others have single coats. Some dogs (like the Belgian Tervuren shown in Figure 1-1) have coats that shed by themselves, and others have coats that need to be trimmed regularly. But regardless of the breed of dog or the type of coat, a healthy dog should have a shiny, springy coat. In addition, the skin under all that hair should be soft and supple. When you pinch your dog's skin, it should spring back to its original position.

Abnormal shedding can be a symptom of a health problem. Dogs who shed have hair growth and loss in cycles that are controlled by several factors, including genetics, day length, temperature, and hormones. Each hair grows to a genetically determined length and then enters a resting phase. In time, new hairs grow in and push out the older, resting hairs. Most dogs living in temperate climates shed in the fall, when the days shorten and the temperature drops. In the spring, they again shed as they trade their denser coats for lighter summer wear. *Bitches* (the term used to refer to female dogs, regardless of their temperament) frequently shed three to four months after they have been in heat, and new mothers shed copious amounts of hair after they wean a litter of puppies.

So how do you know whether your dog is going through a normal period of shedding, or whether all that dead hair on the couch and carpet is a sign that something is wrong? First, become familiar with the months during which your dog normally sheds so you know whether your dog's hair loss is related to the usual seasonal changes. When your dog is shedding abundantly, you can accelerate the process by giving him a warm water bath, which helps remove those straggler hairs and stimulate the new batch of hairs to sprout. After your dog's bath, comb out any remaining dead hair and examine his skin. If the skin is healthy, and new, shiny hairs are beginning to appear, your canine friend is just going through a cyclical shed. If the hair still seems dull, dry, and broken, or if an area of hair was shaved but isn't growing back normally, have your dog examined by a veterinarian, especially if he is exhibiting other signs of illness.

Figure 1-1:
The Belgian
Tervuren
has an
abundant,
dense coat
that sheds
plentifully.

Ears

The ears of a healthy dog should be clean inside, with a shiny gleam to the skin that is caused by the secretion of a protective waxy substance. A healthy dog's ears should not have excessive wax, however, and the ears should never have a foul odor. If your dog's ears have a black or dark brown discharge that recurs after cleaning, they could be infected. This kind of discharge can also be a sign of a systemic illness, such as allergies or a hormonal imbalance. Take your dog to a vet to determine the root of the problem.

Eyes

A healthy dog has bright, clear, glistening eyes. The *cornea* (the outermost surface of the eye) should be transparent, and you should be able to clearly see the pupil and the tiny folds of the *iris* (the brown or blue ring that gives the eye its color).

Some dogs, particularly the Toy breeds, suffer from excessive tearing. The tears run down the side of the dog's nose and can cause brownish-red stains. This tearing is so common in Toy breeds that it is considered normal by many people. However, many people think tearing in Toy dogs is a sign of allergies, especially if it is accompanied by itchy skin or gastrointestinal upset. If your Toy dog is tearing excessively and has itchy skin or gastrointestinal upset, a change of diet is in order. You may reduce the amount of tearing by providing the dog with bottled water, and you can keep the stains from developing by daily wiping under the eyes with a damp cloth, and then drying the fur.

Gums and teeth

A healthy dog should have shiny gums that are tightly adherent to the teeth. Light-colored dogs tend to have pink gums, whereas dark-colored dogs (such as black Labrador Retrievers) and dogs that are bred to have blue tongues (such as Chow Chows and Chinese Shar-Pei) tend to have gums that are splotched with brown and black. The teeth should be white and shiny, without any buildup of brown or yellow material adjacent to the gum line. A healthy dog's breath doesn't smell particularly sweet, but neither should it be offensive.

Nose

The nose is a good barometer of your dog's overall health. We all know that a dog's nose should be cold and wet, right? But your dog's nose may become a little dry when he is sleeping, so don't panic if your snoozing canine doesn't have a slick schnoz.

Pulse

The resting heart of a healthy dog will beat anywhere from 40 beats a minute (in large breeds) to 120 beats a minute (in Toy breeds). When a dog exercises, the heart can beat at twice the normal rate or even more. Your dog's heart rate increases when he has a fever or when he is feeling pain, so if you think your dog may be feeling ill, check his pulse as one indicator of a potential problem.

Check your dog's resting heart rate when you know he's healthy so that you have a baseline to compare it to when you think he may be a bit under the weather.

Stools

The stools of a healthy dog are formed and easy to scoop. They can be any color from light to dark brown or even red, if you feed your dog food with a lot of red dye in it. Black stools, however, are not normal and may be a sign of gastrointestinal bleeding. An occasional loose stool is normal in dogs, but continued loose stools or even one episode of very watery diarrhea are reason to schedule a veterinary visit. Constipation is an uncommon problem in dogs, but it can occur. If your dog is continually straining to defecate, have him checked by a vet.

Temperature

A dog's normal body temperature is between 100.2 and 102.8 degrees Fahrenheit. Larger dogs tend to have body temperatures at the lower end of the range, and smaller dogs at the higher end.

Take your dog's temperature when he is healthy so you know what his normal body temperature is. For information on how to take a dog's temperature, see Chapter 12.

Your dog's temperature can rise several degrees during exercise, so be sure to measure his temperature when he is at rest.

Weight

A healthy dog has a slight waist and an abdomen that is tucked up higher than the level of his chest. A healthy dog should be able to trot effortlessly without the skin and *subcutaneous fat* (the fat that is located under the skin) rolling from side to side.

Even though we humans are bombarded every day by advertisements for weight-loss programs, our society's weight-consciousness doesn't carry over to our dogs. A large percentage of dogs are carrying around too much weight, and many are *morbidly obese* (a condition in which the excess weight can cause serious health problems for a dog, including early death).

To find out how to keep your dog slim and trim, see Chapter 8.

Knowing What to Look for in a Healthy Puppy

Puppies show basically the same signs of health that adult dogs do, but there are some differences, including the following:

- ✔ **Heart rate and body temperature:** Puppies' hearts beat faster and their temperatures are higher than those of adult dogs, because they are smaller and have a higher *metabolic rate* (the sum of all the body's chemical reactions, many of which generate heat).

- ✔ **Sleep requirements:** Just as human babies sleep more than adults do, puppies sleep much more than adult dogs, so don't mistake tiredness for a lack of interest in the surroundings. After a little rest, a healthy puppy is rarin' to go.

- ✔ **Development of teeth:** Puppies' baby teeth drop out and their adult teeth erupt some time between 4 and 6 months of age. At this stage, puppies' gums may bleed a little, so don't mistake this normal teething transition for gum disease.

One of the most important decisions you'll make when it comes to owning and caring for a dog is choosing a healthy puppy to begin with. All puppies are cute, but not all are healthy. Although you may be tempted to choose the weakest, sickliest pup in the litter, in the hopes of nursing him back to health, this is never a wise choice. Unhealthy puppies can be a source of great strain on any family — both emotionally and financially. You owe it to yourself, and your puppy, to choose one who is healthy right from the start.

In the following sections, I let you know what to look for when you pick a puppy, so you can be sure he'll be a good companion for many years to come.

Avoiding hereditary conditions

Every breed of dog has some hereditary problems. The most common hereditary diseases in dogs include the following:

- Allergies
- Cardiac problems
- Cardiomyopathy
- Cataracts
- Elbow dysplasia
- Epilepsy
- Hip dysplasia
- Hypothyroidism
- Progressive retinal atrophy
- Von Willebrand's disease

Ask a veterinarian what conditions are common in the breed you like best. Or turn to books that indicate the most common diseases by breed; one of those books is *Choosing a Dog For Dummies* by Chris Walkowicz (published by Hungry Minds, Inc.).Then ask the breeder you're working with to provide specific information about the genetic conditions for which her dogs have been checked and certified free. For some conditions, such as hip dysplasia, elbow dysplasia, and hereditary ocular (eye) diseases, there are organizations that keep records of dogs who have been checked and found free of these conditions. Ask the breeder to show you proof from these organizations that her dogs are clear of these problems.

You can also contact the organizations themselves to find out more about the conditions and whether the *sire* (father) and *dam* (mother) of the litter you're looking at have been certified free:

- **Canine Eye Registration Foundation,** 1248 Lynn Hall, Purdue University, West Lafayette, IN 47906; phone: 765-494-8179; Web site: `www.vet.purdue.edu/~yshen/cerf.html`. Provides information on ocular disorders.

- **Orthopedic Foundation for Animals,** 2300 Nifong Boulevard, Columbia, MO 65201; phone: 573-442-0418; Web site: `www.offa.org`. Provides information on hip dysplasia, elbow dysplasia, patellar luxation, cardiac disorders, and hypothyroidism.

- **Synbiotics Corporation,** 11011 Via Frontera, San Diego, CA 92127-1702; phone: 858-451-3771; Web site: `www.synbiotics.com/html/pennhip.html`. Provides information on the PennHip method of diagnosing and screening for hip dysplasia.

For some conditions, such as epilepsy, you'll need to rely on the honesty of the breeder to find out whether any of the puppy's ancestors have suffered from the condition. Epilepsy is disheartening for breeders and puppy buyers alike because evidence of the condition may not surface until 3 or 4 years of age — and by then, the dog may already have been bred.

The Canine Genome Project

Across the U.S., scientists are hard at work on the Canine Genome Project, a collaborative effort to decode dog DNA that has already identified many genes that cause canine diseases. For example, the genes that cause *progressive retinal atrophy,* an inherited retinal disorder that ultimately results in blindness, have been identified in several breeds of dogs. This means that males and females can be checked prior to breeding so that they don't pass on the defective genes to their offspring.

Other hereditary conditions, such as *entropion* (a condition in which the eyelids are folded inward, causing damage to the cornea), may not be evident when looking at the sire and dam of a litter of puppies, because the condition can be corrected surgically. Breeding a dog who has been surgically altered to correct or disguise a hereditary condition is highly unethical. Be sure to choose a reputable breeder who will discuss these issues with you freely and honestly.

If you are looking for a puppy to join your family, be sure to find out all you can about the genetic problems that are common in the breed you're considering. For more information on hereditary problems, turn to Chapter 10.

Paying attention to temperament

A dog's temperament is closely linked to his health. Shy, fearful, or hyperactive dogs frequently develop abnormal behaviors that can affect their health. Many temperament characteristics are hereditary. If possible, meet and interact with both the sire and the dam of your new puppy. Make sure both dogs have the temperament you're looking for in a pup. If you want a quiet dog, think twice before getting a pup whose sire is hanging from the chandeliers. If you want an outgoing dog, be wary about getting a pup whose dam does not have the courage to approach you.

Don't buy a pup who has a fearful or aggressive parent or a parent who doesn't match the expectations you have for your pet.

In addition to looking to the puppies' mother and father for clues as to how the pups themselves will turn out, what else can you do to find the pup whose personality will mesh with yours? As you sit on the floor surrounded by puppies who are climbing into your lap, chewing on your hair, and playing rough-and-tumble games with each other, you may have trouble figuring out which one is best for you. After all, they're *all* adorable. But keep in mind that at 7 to 8 weeks of age, puppies already show many of the temperament traits they'll carry with them into adulthood. By patiently and carefully observing all the pups, you can select the one whose behavior appeals to you most.

Several simple tests can assess a puppy's temperament. These tests don't have right or wrong answers, and they aren't about labeling one puppy "good" and another one "bad." Instead, they give an indication of a puppy's degree of dominance and independence, his desire to please, and his ability to cope with changes or new stimuli in the environment. Because the puppies are tested individually and in an unfamiliar location, they sometimes reveal behaviors that were not evident in the context of the litter.

Temperament tests are a way to help evaluate a puppy's natural temperament. Because temperament tests are subjective, they are best performed by someone experienced in interpreting puppy behavior. In addition, the tester should be a stranger to the puppies so the pups will have no previous associations that may affect the test results. The puppies should be awake but not tired when tested, and they should not be tested immediately after eating. Many breeders perform these tests before a puppy moves to his new home to help the breeder match each puppy to the ideal family.

Here is one example of a temperament test: The tester walks past the puppy, calling him and encouraging him to follow with happy words like, "Puppy, puppy, puppy." If you prefer a dog who is a little independent, you may choose a puppy who follows happily for a few steps and then goes off investigating, returning to the tester periodically to check back in. If you prefer an affectionate, cuddly dog, you'll want to choose the puppy who happily follows the tester wherever she goes. (No matter what you're looking for in a dog, avoid any puppy who doesn't have enough adventuresome spirit to follow at all.)

Despite such evaluations, however, a given puppy on any day can exhibit atypical characteristics because he is either tired or just not feeling his best. For more information on temperament testing, check out *Puppies For Dummies,* by Sarah Hodgson (published by Hungry Minds, Inc.). You can find lots of useful information on assessing a puppy, including a worksheet you can fill out to help you make the decision more easily. There is some controversy about exactly how well puppy temperament tests predict future behavior. However, the more time you spend with the litter, the better you will get a feel for which puppy will best fit in with your personality and your household.

The breeder can be an invaluable source of information regarding the temperament of individual puppies. Because the breeder has been observing the puppies since birth, she knows their responses to many different environmental stimuli. In addition, the breeder knows the types of temperament produced by the sire and dam.

Picking a shelter dog

If you've decided to get your next family member at an animal shelter, talk to the individuals who have been working with the dogs. Ask them to help you evaluate the temperament of each dog you are considering and to help determine his suitability to join your family. If the shelter workers can't do that, bring an experienced dog person with you to help you choose a dog who's a good fit for your lifestyle. Take your time. Leave and take some time to think. Many shelters won't let people adopt a dog the first day they see him, because they want to be sure that people don't get a dog on impulse.

Sometimes first impressions can be deceiving. I adopted a young Border Collie from a shelter a few months ago. When I first visited the shelter, I didn't like Fate at all because she was jumping up against the bars of the cage and barking frantically at the other dogs and at people who walked by. But when I took her out of that over-stimulating environment, she revealed her true nature — she loves other dogs and doesn't have an aggressive bone in her body.

Too often we get caught up in which puppy has more spots or whether a puppy is a certain color, and we forget that temperament is much more important than appearance. Remember the expression, "You can't judge a book by its cover," and concentrate on temperament first.

Giving Your Dog the Once-Over

Give your dog a quick examination every week, just to be sure that all systems are go. If you check your dog regularly, you'll be able to detect problems as soon as they appear — and sooner is always better than later.

Brushing your dog's coat

Start by brushing your dog's coat (see Figure 1-2) and examining his coat and skin. He'll be in seventh heaven as you rub your hands over his body, feeling for lumps and picking out small burrs or plant seeds he may have brought home from that romp in the woods.

One plant seed to watch out for is the *foxtail awn*. These are the seeds of common weeds that grow in fields and by roadsides throughout North America. The seed is tiny, but it has many large spikes on it that act like the barbs of a fishhook. They get enmeshed in your dog's coat and can actually drive the awn through the skin. The seed then works its way throughout the body, causing multiple infections. In some parts of California, there are so many foxtails that dog owners don't walk their dogs in fields or other open areas during the summer and fall.

Figure 1-2:
Flyer is getting his weekly once-over and brushing.

If you locate a lump during your weekly exam, part the hair and take a closer look at it. It may be a healing scab where you removed a tick several days ago or where a puppy's sharp teeth nicked the skin in play. If it is not a scab but a raised lump, take your dog to the veterinarian for an evaluation. It may require removal and microscopic examination. If the lump is small and moveable, just check it each week to be sure it doesn't change. If the lump grows or becomes attached to the tissue below, talk to your vet about having it removed.

Looking in your dog's ears

During your weekly once-over, take a peek in your dog's ears. It's kind of dark down there, so use a flashlight to see more easily. Most dogs have a little orange or brown wax in their ears. This normal secretion keeps the skin pliable and protects it from infection. If there are clumps of waxy buildup, you can remove them by moistening a cotton ball in gentle skin soap and rubbing it over the skin of the inner ear with one of your fingers. The dog's ear canal is L-shaped, so cleaning the ear in this manner poses little risk of damaging the eardrum. Just be sure you don't stick your finger deep inside your dog's ear.

When cleaning a dog's ears, don't rub the skin vigorously. This may damage the protective *epidermal* (outer) layer of skin. In addition, don't use a cotton-tipped swab to clean the ear canal because you may be able to reach far enough into the ear that you can puncture the eardrum.

During your weekly peek, if you see red skin or smell a foul odor, this can be a sign that the ear is infected. Usually a dog with an infected ear will shake his head or flinch when you touch the ear. If you suspect your dog has an ear infection, get him in to see a veterinarian right away. Ear infections are very painful, and they can spread to the middle and inner ear, causing deafness or loss of balance. In addition, prompt veterinary care helps prevent scarring, a condition that can make your dog more susceptible to subsequent ear infections.

If your veterinarian determines that your dog has an ear infection, she may anesthetize your dog and thoroughly flush the ear with a cleanser, making sure she gets the bugs out of every nook and cranny. She may culture the ear, then send your pristine-eared friend home with an antibiotic/antifungal solution for you to put in the affected ear for the next week or so. After the ear has healed, check it twice a week to make sure the infection doesn't recur.

Dogs who have dropped ears, such as Golden Retrievers and Poodles, and who enjoy swimming may be more susceptible to ear infections, probably because the insides of their ears stay moist longer. Many yeast and fungal organisms thrive in slightly damp environments. In addition, the skin of the ear canal doesn't form a tight barrier against infection unless it is dry. Dogs with allergies are also prone to ear infections. If you know your dog has seasonal allergies, or if your dog has been swimming a lot, check his ears often.

Here are a few easy steps to prevent ear infections:

- **Inspect your dog's ears regularly.** If you suspect an infection, take your dog to a veterinarian right away.

- **Gently remove excess wax and dirt.**

- **Cut away the hair around the *opening* of the ear canal.** In some breeds, such as Poodles, you should pluck the hair from *inside* the ear canal with your thumb and index finger. This allows better air circulation so the skin of the ear can stay dry.

- **Sprinkle a little foot powder designed to treat athlete's foot into your dog's ears after he has been swimming or even once a week during the spring and summer if your dog has allergies.** Athlete's foot powder contains antifungal agents that prevent overgrowth of yeast and other organisms that cause infections.

Taking a peek at your dog's toes

Canine toenails are pretty useful tools. They help your dog grip the ground when he runs, jumps, and turns. If his toenails are too long, however — and you'll know this because they'll click on the floor when he walks — they can be painful and can even change the shape of his feet.

It is a rare dog that never needs his toenails trimmed. Dogs who exercise regularly on hard surfaces such as cement wear their nails down naturally, but if they have dewclaws (the dog's equivalent of a thumb) they will need to be trimmed regularly. Most dogs, however, like the one shown in Figure 1-3, need to have their nails clipped every few weeks. The nails grow especially quickly if the dog spends a lot of time on moist, soft ground such as a grassy backyard.

Figure 1-3:
This Belgian
Malinois
is being
very good
during nail
trimming.

For many dogs, nail trimming is an unpleasant activity. You can make it easier on both you and Fido, however, by keeping in mind a few simple tips:

- ✔ Start trimming your dog's nails from the time he is a puppy.
- ✔ Make the experience as pleasant as possible by giving him treats after each foot or even after each toenail, if necessary.

✓ Learn how to clip nails quickly and accurately so you won't accidentally cut your furry friend's nails to the *quick* (the blood vessel running down the center of every nail that bleeds if you nick it).

✓ Keep your nail trimmers sharp so they cut rather than crush the nail.

You can find three types of nail trimmers. *Guillotine* nail trimmers have a hole through which the nail is inserted. A blade slides across the hole and cuts the end of the nail off. One advantage of these trimmers is that the blade can easily be replaced when it becomes dull. The other kind of nail trimmer is like a small pair of scissors with curved blades on which to rest the nail. These nail clippers need to be sharpened regularly by a professional so that they don't crush the nail. A battery-operated dremel tool can also be used to grind the nails down. Many dogs prefer this method to clippers, and the dremel tool makes it easier to avoid the quick.

Quickly and accurately clipping a dog's nails takes experience. Follow these tips and, with a little practice, you'll be fine:

✓ **Have your dog lie on his side or on his back while you clip his nails.** You can trim your dog's nails while he's standing, but have him stand on a table so that he's closer to your eye level and so he can't escape. If your dog is very fearful at nail-trimming time, slather a bunch of peanut butter on the refrigerator at nose level and cut your dog's nails while he licks at it.

✓ **With your dog's foot in your hand, hold a toe between your thumb and index finger and press on the pad.** This pushes the nail out and away from the surrounding hair. You'll see that the nail is thick where it joins to the skin, but partway down it suddenly becomes thinner. This is the part you'll need to cut off.

✓ **In dogs with white nails, hold the nail up to a light to see the quick.** For dogs with brown or black nails in which you can't see the quick, cut at the junction of the wide and narrow parts of the nail, and you should avoid the quick without any trouble.

✓ **Look at the cut end of the nail to determine whether you've cut it short enough.** If the nail is soft and has a white, crescent-shaped area on the end, it's fine. If the nail end is dry and no crescent is visible, you can shave off a little more until you see the crescent. See Figure 1-4 for an illustration of the end of a properly trimmed nail.

✓ **If the end of the nail bleeds, dip the nail in styptic powder (available from pet supply stores) or cornstarch and keep your dog relaxed and resting for about five minutes.** If he gets up and runs around, the nail will only bleed more. Don't fawn all over your dog and tell him how sorry you are. Instead, jolly him up and tell him he is a good boy. Give him a cookie if you want. That way, he'll have more pleasant associations with your minor trimming mistakes and be less stressed when it happens the next time.

✓ **Give your dog a treat for being so good!**

If they haven't been removed, be sure to trim your dog's *dewclaws,* the extra nails on the inner side of the front (and sometimes rear) legs.

If you're still uneasy about trimming your dog's nails, ask your veterinarian or professional groomer to show you how it's done.

Figure 1-4:
The end of a nail that has been properly trimmed has a white, crescent-shaped area.

While you are working on your dog's feet, check the hair between the pads. In some dogs, the hair between the toes grows very long and covers the pads. It can become matted and can accumulate mud and moisture, which is not only uncomfortable for the dog but can also increase the chance of infection. Trim the hair between the pads and around the edges of the pads. Use blunt-ended scissors to reduce the chance of accidentally cutting the skin between the toes.

Cleaning your canine's choppers

You've heard it from your own dentist: *Periodontal disease* (inflammation of the gums resulting in loosening of the teeth) is the most common dental problem in adults. The same is true for dogs, too. It is estimated that 80 percent of all dogs have *gingivitis* (inflammation of the gums) and periodontal disease by 3 years of age. If your dog's gums bleed when he chews on a bone, he probably has gingivitis. Take him for a dental checkup with a veterinarian right away.

The cause of periodontal disease in humans and dogs is the same. It starts with the adhesion of oral bacteria and food particles to the tooth, forming plaque. The plaque then becomes mineralized by calcium present in saliva, forming *calculus* (tartar). Calculus is a hard white, yellow, or brown material on the surface of the tooth, particularly next to the gum line. The calculus traps bacteria and food particles between the gum and the tooth. These bacteria produce chemicals that irritate the gums, causing inflammation (gingivitis). Eventually, the inflammation erodes the bone that holds the tooth in place. Ultimately, the tooth becomes loose and falls out (periodontal disease).

Prevention is the key to beating periodontal disease. The best preventative measure is to brush your dog's teeth regularly. You can use a toothbrush if you want, topped with meat-flavored toothpaste made specifically for dogs. You also can wipe the teeth with soft paper that contains a dental abrasive. These papers are available as discs or cuffs that you can slip onto your index finger and throw out after each use.

Dogs who chew regularly on bones, rawhide chips, or hard biscuits have significantly less plaque than dogs who don't. Many chew toys on the market reduce plaque and even remove calculus in vigorous chewers. These toys have rough surfaces that scrape the surface of the dog's teeth and massage the gums.

Follow these steps to prevent periodontal disease:

✔ **Give your dog plenty of safe chew toys.** Real bones sold specifically for dogs, Nylabones, or rawhide bones (under supervision, because dogs can choke on a soggy piece of rawhide) work well.

✔ **Brush your dog's teeth as often as possible.**

✔ **Have your dog's teeth professionally cleaned annually after the age of 3 years.**

Get your dog's teeth checked each year at his annual veterinary checkup. Any buildup of calculus should be removed as soon as possible to prevent gingivitis and the loss of teeth. Calculus usually is removed using an ultrasonic descaler with your dog under anesthesia. Your veterinary clinic may also have a veterinary technician who is an expert at removing dental calculus in unanesthetized, cooperative dogs. If your dog quickly develops new calculus buildup, you may need to schedule regular teeth cleanings more frequently.

I recommend that all dogs receive broad-spectrum antibiotics just before and for several days after the teeth are scaled. This prevents oral bacteria from replicating in small cuts in the gums and causing systemic infection. The veterinarian will give your dog an antibiotic injection before she cleans the teeth and will send you home with several days' worth of pills to follow up.

Examine your dog's mouth periodically for broken or loose teeth. If you find a broken or discolored tooth, have your veterinarian examine it and extract it if necessary. It is normal for older dogs to have brown spots on the top of worn teeth, especially their *incisors* (the front teeth). The brown spots are sites where new tooth enamel has been produced to repair the worn surface.

Sometimes older dogs have growths on their gums called *epulis*. These growths resemble tumors but are generally benign. If they grow large or are interfering with eating, they should be surgically removed.

Expressing your dog's anal glands

The *anal glands* are two small sacs located at the five o'clock and seven o'clock positions below the anus. These sacs empty during defecation or sometimes when a dog is frightened. The secretion has a distinctive odor that most people, as you may expect, find unpleasant. The anal glands are the dog's version of the scent glands of a skunk, although they don't smell quite that bad! The material in the anal sacs is clear or pale yellow-brown in color. A 40-pound dog shouldn't have more than ¼ teaspoon of fluid in his anal sacs.

If a dog has full anal sacs, he will scoot his rear on the ground, trying to empty them. If the anal glands are infected, the dog will often lick at his rear end, even to the point of creating a weeping sore next to the anus.

If your dog is scooting or licking excessively, be sure to take him to the veterinarian to have the glands emptied. If your dog has frequent anal gland troubles and if you are not faint of heart, you can ask your veterinarian to show you how to empty the glands so you can do it regularly and save yourself both time and money.

Chapter 2

Preventing Problems before They Start

*J*ust a few decades ago, in order to make it to adulthood, puppies had to avoid or successfully battle deadly diseases such as distemper, rabies, hepatitis, and leptospirosis. And fleas were a part of *every* dog's life — along with the scratching, infections, and allergies that accompany those irritating insects. But scientists and veterinarians have worked hard to develop vaccines that prevent canine infectious diseases and to design ways of keeping dogs healthy and prolonging their lives.

In this chapter, I let you know what you can do to prevent disease from hitting your dog. Following these suggestions will give your dog a better chance of living a long and healthy life, which means more time for you to play fetch, teach her tricks, run with her, let her lick your face. . . .

Vaccinating Your Dog

Today vaccinations are such a routine part of veterinary visits that most dog owners aren't aware of what a benefit they have been to dogs' health. Just a few decades ago, thousands of dogs died or were permanently disabled every year by the dreaded distemper virus, which usually attacks puppies under 1 year of age. Now we rarely hear of a dog with distemper, except in unvaccinated populations.

In 1978, canine parvovirus first appeared and began killing thousands of puppies — often entire litters — throughout the world. Veterinary scientists worked feverishly to develop a vaccine against this virus, and within a few short years, most dogs were protected by a simple vaccination.

Canine vaccinations have even contributed to the health of humans. Before the 1940s, when mass vaccination for rabies began, approximately 100 Americans died each year from rabies contracted from family pets. Now, thankfully, such occurrences are extremely rare.

Puppies should get their first set of vaccinations at 6 to 8 weeks of age, before they go to their new homes. They also need two more sets of vaccinations spaced three to four weeks apart before they are fully immunized. If you are planning to add a puppy to your menagerie, discuss with your veterinarian which vaccines your new puppy should receive and when.

Talk to your veterinarian about setting up a vaccination schedule. The vaccinations you select for your dog will depend on her age, where you live, and the chances of your dog being exposed to infected dogs or wildlife.

Many vaccines, with the notable exception of the rabies vaccines, are available through pet-supply catalogs for owners to administer to their animals themselves, but I strongly caution against this. New vaccine formulations regularly become available, and without a veterinary background or access to the latest veterinary research, you may not make appropriate decisions as to which vaccines to administer to your dog. In addition, vaccines require special storage and handling. They rapidly lose their potency during temperature changes, which can easily occur during shipping.

Table 2-1 lists the diseases you can vaccinate against, along with the symptoms they result in when a dog has the disease.

Table 2-1	Diseases You Can Vaccinate Against and Their Symptoms
Disease	*Symptoms*
Rabies	Salivation, aggression, paralysis
Distemper	Diarrhea, pneumonia, tremors
Parvovirus	Bloody diarrhea, dehydration
Infectious Canine Hepatitis	Diarrhea, pneumonia
Coronavirus	Diarrhea

Disease	Symptoms
Kennel cough	Cough, pneumonia
Lyme disease	Lameness, arthritis
Leptospirosis	Bloody urine, diarrhea, vomiting

See Chapter 11 for more details on the diseases caused by these devilish little organisms.

Getting Rid of Fleas, Ticks, and Worms

An important part of prevention is keeping your dog free of all the nasty creatures who like to use her body as their home or feeding ground. In the following sections, I let you know how to prevent fleas, ticks, and worms from bothering your dog — and what to do if they already have.

Making fleas flee

Fleas are the quintessential reproductive success story. A pair of fleas in your home can grow into a major infestation within a few weeks, and every one of those fleas is interested in just one thing: food. But not the kind of food in refrigerators, the kind in veins. And to make matters worse, these insect vampires do not care where the blood comes from — your dog, your cat, or you — and the more blood they get, the more they reproduce. If your cute little canine brings a male and a female flea home, these two fleas can populate your home with 250,000 descendants within one month!

Fleas love moist, humid weather, making the southeastern United States the flea capitol of North America. For dog lovers in warm climates, flea control requires constant vigilance. Fleas don't survive freezing temperatures, however, so in colder climes, the winter weather naturally decreases the flea population every year. In these areas, fleas are most abundant during the fall, when temperatures are dropping and fleas are moving indoors to ride out the winter months.

You first may become aware that your dog has fleas when you see her strenuously scratching her ears and neck. She also may suddenly turn and bite vigorously at her rear legs or rear end. If you see this kind of behavior, you need to check for fleas on your furry friend.

A vaccination alternative

There is increasing concern in the veterinary profession and among dog lovers about the high incidence of autoimmune disorders in dogs. In many cases, vaccines induce immunity for several years or even for a lifetime, yet most dogs get revaccinated annually. Some veterinary scientists theorize that repeated annual vaccination of dogs may overstimulate the dog's immune system, causing immune responses that attack the dog's normal tissues such as the skin or joints.

Veterinarians are reevaluating standard vaccine protocols and are studying whether annual revaccination is necessary or optimal for all adult dogs. Alternatives exist, particularly for dogs who have had an allergic response to a vaccine or who suffer from an autoimmune disease. These dogs should have their antibody levels (a measure of the immune response) against distemper, parvovirus, and other infectious agents tested each year using a blood test. If the dog is found to have a low antibody level, she can be vaccinated against that organism only.

With your dog lying down, separate the hairs around the base of her tail (a favorite flea hangout), along the backs of her legs, on her stomach, and around her neck and ears. If you see tiny black or brown irregular pieces of dirt, it may be flea dirt, which consists of dried blood and flea excrement. If you want to know whether it's flea dirt or regular old yard dirt, smear some on a damp paper towel. If the smear is reddish brown, like dried blood, you can be fairly certain it has come from fleas.

An easy way to detect fleas or flea dirt is to have your dog lie on a clean white sheet while you brush her or blow her hair with a dryer (see Figure 2-1). This may stir up a few fleas, making them jump off the dog and onto the sheet, where you can easily see them. Even if you don't see the fleas themselves, you can easily spot flea dirt on the white sheet.

You don't have to see a live flea in order for your dog and her living area to be infested. If you want living proof, however, sort through your dog's hairs some more. Fleas are very fast and jump from one place to another, so you may only get a glimpse. They are dark brown, less than ⅛-inch long, and shaped like a flat oval.

If you see even one flea on your dog, you can be certain there are at least a hundred more in one form or another (eggs, larvae, or adults) on your dog, in the carpet, and wherever your dog sleeps. It's time to go into flea attack mode! Here are the steps to take to completely free your dog and your environment of these freeloaders:

1. **Bathe your dog carefully.**

   Make sure to cover the entire dog with lather from the shampoo, keeping the shampoo on the dog for several minutes, which can suffocate fleas on the dog. Some shampoos include ingredients such as rosemary, tea tree, sage, cedar, peppermint, orange, eucalyptus, and pine needles, which can help repel or suffocate the nasty creatures as well.

2. **Gather up your dog's bedding (and your own bed linens if your dog shares your bed) and throw them in the washing machine.**

3. **Vacuum all areas of the house to which your dog has access.**

   Place the vacuum bag in a plastic bag and tape it securely shut before disposing of it outside. Otherwise, the little critters will hop out and reinfest your house.

4. **If your dog is a frequent traveler, vacuum your car for fleas.**

Figure 2-1:
You can use a blow dryer to check your dog for fleas.

If you have a severe flea infestation and these remedies aren't adequate to deal with the problem, speak with your veterinarian about the use of pesticides. Be sure to use pesticides with great care, since some pets are sensitive to them, and accidental overdose can be lethal to any pet. Pesticides sold by veterinarians frequently are more effective than those sold in pet and grocery stores. Be sure to use a pesticide that not only kills adult fleas but also prevents the maturation of eggs into larvae and adults. You can use a spray or a fogger, but in either case, be sure your now flea-free dog is out of the house while these chemicals are at work.

If you use this multi-pronged attack immediately upon seeing the first flea, you stand a reasonable chance of banishing the bloodthirsty critters from your house. But it would, of course, be better if your dog never brought one of the sneaky critters home.

Here are a few tips to prevent fleas from coming to visit in the first place:

- ✔ **Use a once-a-month topical or oral flea treatment (the best known brands are Advantage, Frontline, and Program) that kill fleas on your dog within hours.** These products are not pesticides; they are *insect growth regulators,* which prevent the development and growth of fleas. Given the time commitment and the exposure to pesticides that accompany a fight against fleas, these preventives are worth their weight in gold. Use these products during any months that don't have freezing temperatures. Although they are considered safe enough for puppies, some dogs and puppies have allergic responses to these products. If your dog experiences hair loss or other reactions, try a different flea control product.

- ✔ **Sprinkle diatomaceous earth or boric acid on the floor.** These products dehydrate fleas and flea larvae, and they don't contain any chemicals that can harm pets or children.

- ✔ **Vacuum frequently to help control the flea population in the carpet.** Place the vacuum bag in a plastic bag (so fleas can't escape), and throw it away.

- ✔ **Wash your dog's bedding weekly to reduce the chances of a flea family setting up shop there.**

- ✔ **Use "friendly" bugs called *beneficial nematodes,* which are tiny insects that eat flea larvae and can be sprayed onto your yard every 6 to 8 weeks.** They don't harm ladybugs, earthworms, or other creatures you want in your yard. You can find sources for beneficial nematodes at gardening centers that emphasize organic gardening.

Getting ticked off at ticks

Ticks are bad news: They transmit several diseases that can cause severe illness and even death in both dogs and humans.

Here are some tick-transmitted terrors:

- **Borrelia burgdorferi,** the bacterium that causes Lyme disease, is carried by the tiny deer tick and occasionally by larger species of ticks. This bacterium causes fever, lameness, meningitis, kidney disease, and chronic arthritis in both dogs and humans.

- **Ehrlichia canis** is a small microorganism carried by the brown dog tick. It causes ehrlichiosis in both dogs and humans, which is characterized by anemia, weight loss, hemorrhages, and arthritis.

- **Rickettsia rickettsii** is a microorganism carried by the American wood tick, the American dog tick, and the Lone Star tick, and it causes Rocky Mountain spotted fever. Defying its name, Rocky Mountain spotted fever is seen mainly in dogs in the southeastern U.S. from April to September when ticks are most active. The organism causes fever, rashes, and joint and muscle pain in both dogs and humans.

See Chapter 11 for more details about the effects of these bugs on dogs.

Huge numbers of tick eggs hatch each spring, and the young ticks climb onto grasses and other vegetation. Their sticky shells help them to cling to passing animals, including your adventurous canine. They quickly climb down the hair, attach to the skin, and begin to suck blood, only dropping off hours or days later when they are engorged. In the meantime, any microorganisms that were hitching a ride inside this insect traveler are transmitted to your dog through the tick's mouth.

Keeping your dog as free of ticks as possible is always the safest bet — not only for your dog, but for you as well. Here are some tick-prevention tips:

- **During the tick season (April through September), limit your dog's exposure to known tick-infested areas.** Ticks often hide in tall grasses and dense vegetation.

- **Use a tick preventive during the spring and summer months.** Several products on the market kill both fleas and ticks (and why not knock out both at the same time?). You can apply these products monthly to the skin at the back of your dog's neck. Ask your veterinarian to recommend the most effective product for your dog.

- **Examine your dog for ticks daily during tick season.** If you suspect she has been romping in a tick-infested area, examine her for ticks immediately. Be sure to check inside and behind her ears and around her eyes, all favorite tick hiding places.

- **Carefully remove all ticks and dispose of them in a sealed plastic bag.** Be sure to remove the entire tick from your dog's body.

To remove a tick, use a pair of tweezers to grasp the head of the tick where it attaches to the skin. (Wear gloves if you plan to use your fingers to remove the tick.) Apply gentle traction. In about 20 to 30 seconds, the tick's mouth will release its grasp on the dog's skin and the tick will come away cleanly. Dab some disinfectant on the bitten area. If you yank the tick away from your dog too quickly, you'll leave part of the tick's mouth behind, which can cause an infection. Kill the tick by placing it in alcohol. Save the dead tick in a resealable plastic bag, labeled with the date on which the tick was found. This may sound weird, but if your dog becomes ill, you may need to identify the species of tick that bit him.

Never remove a tick with your bare hands, and never crush a tick between your fingers. If you do, you put yourself at risk of contracting Lyme disease or one of the other tick-borne diseases.

If your dog becomes ill and you recently found a tick on her, immediately seek veterinary attention. Most tick-borne diseases can be treated successfully if a diagnosis is made immediately and appropriate treatment initiated. If the tick-borne organisms are allowed to gain a foothold, however, these bad bugs can cause serious illness or even death.

Whipping worms for good

Several kinds of worms can live in your dog's intestines and cause abdominal pain, diarrhea, or anemia. Roundworms are predominantly a puppy problem. Puppies can be infected by their mothers even before they are born. These worms can be so numerous that they cause intestinal blockage. They can also work their way up into the dog's stomach and cause vomiting. All puppies should be treated for roundworms as a part of their regular veterinary checkup.

Whipworms and hookworms can infest dogs of all ages. A dog becomes infected when she eats egg-laden feces from an infected dog. These worms attach to the wall of the intestine and gnaw away. A large infestation can cause significant blood loss, which can result in anemia.

Bring a fecal sample from your dog to each annual checkup, at least until your dog is 3 or 4 years old. A veterinary technician will check for worm eggs while the veterinarian examines your dog. If your pooch has parasites, a pill can usually put her right.

To check for worm eggs, a veterinary technician prepares a *fecal flotation*. He mixes a small sample of feces with a salt solution, which makes worm eggs float to the surface. The eggs are then trapped on a glass slide and examined under a microscope. Each species of worm has eggs of a distinctive size and shape, making specific diagnosis easy. Tapeworms and whipworms, however, may not produce many eggs, making them more difficult to detect in a fecal sample.

Knowing What to Expect from the Annual Checkup

Taking your canine companion for a thorough veterinary checkup once a year is one of the most important things you can do for her. Even though your dog may seem to be the picture of health, a veterinarian often can detect early signs of disease or organ malfunction before your furry friend shows any outward signs of problems. Your veterinarian also can help you prevent common canine conditions, treat new problems early when treatment is most effective, or institute measures to prevent a condition from becoming worse.

Before your annual veterinary appointment, make notes of any changes in your dog's health or behavior. Jot down any questions you have about your dog's care. These notes will help you provide a complete description of your dog's health history so you can get answers to your questions — and so you're not left saying, "I know there was something I was going to ask, but I can't remember what it was." Bring a pen and paper to the appointment to take brief notes about your veterinarian's recommendations — they can be hard to remember later.

Take advantage of your veterinary appointments. Ask questions and be sure you understand the answers. Use these meetings as an opportunity to work with your veterinarian to promote your dog's health and longevity. If your dog is found to be healthy at the annual checkup, don't feel you've wasted your time and money. Instead, count your blessings.

A thorough veterinary examination should contain all the components I cover in the following sections.

Health history

The veterinarian should ask whether you have observed any changes in your dog's overall health. This is your opportunity to ask questions or to express any concerns you may have with respect to your dog's health or behavior. You may want to point out any skin lumps you've found, discuss changes in your dog's food or water intake, or ask about his urination or bowel habits.

If a specific problem has prompted your visit, bring a written history of the problem. If your dog has been vomiting periodically, for example, record the date the vomiting first began, how often your dog has vomited, when (in relation to eating) he vomited, and the amount, color, and texture of the vomited material.

Physical examination

Your veterinarian has been trained to perform a detailed physical examination of your dog. As he performs the examination, he is thinking about the dog's entire body and is trying to determine whether every organ system is functioning at its peak. The veterinarian should look in your dog's mouth, eyes, and ears, and he should run his hands over your dog's body, feeling for abnormalities in the size or shape of lymph nodes and abdominal organs. He should listen to your dog's heart and lungs with a stethoscope, take your dog's temperature, and weigh her.

Don't talk to your veterinarian or rub your dog while he's listening with his stethoscope. It makes it hard for the vet to hear your dog's lung and heart sounds.

Heartworm check

Heartworms are parasites that live in dogs' hearts and cause heart failure. Mosquitoes transmit larval heartworms from one dog to another by sucking the blood of an infected dog, then regurgitating a little blood when it bites the next victim. Heartworm disease exists in most areas of the U.S. and in southernmost Canada. In some areas, such as the southeastern U.S., a large percentage of dogs who do not regularly receive heartworm preventive medication are infected. Prevention of this disease is critical because, when a dog becomes infected, treatment of adult worms in the heart requires intensive care and can be life threatening.

Several excellent products are available for preventing heartworm infection. Before a dog is placed on a heartworm preventive, however, a blood sample must be tested to make sure the dog is not already infected. This simple test can be done in your veterinarian's office while you wait. In northern areas, where temperatures reach freezing, dogs need to take a heartworm preventive only during the spring, summer, and fall — after the test shows they aren't infected. In the southern U.S., because mosquitoes are present year-round, dogs should be given a heartworm preventive year-round.

Dogs on heartworm preventive should still be tested every year, just in case the medication was forgotten or was ineffective for some reason.

Most heartworm preventives are given monthly. The pills are so tasty that you can just drop them in your dog's food bowl and she'll gobble it up. A heartworm preventive can be given to a puppy with her first set of vaccinations. And a heartworm test isn't necessary for a puppy under 3 months of age.

Blood chemistry and urinalysis

If your veterinarian notices anything abnormal during his physical examination of your dog, he may take a blood and/or urine sample to perform biochemical tests. These tests can detect infections and malfunctions of the liver, kidney, pancreas, muscle, thyroid, and other organ systems.

Vaccinations

Many vaccinations are administered annually, so having your dog vaccinated during the annual checkup makes sense. See the "Vaccinating Your Dog" section earlier in this chapter for more information on which vaccines your dog may need and when.

Deciding Whether to Neuter Your Dog

Every year in the U.S., millions of unwanted dogs — both mixed-breed and purebred — are put to death. The reason: supply and demand. More puppies are born than there are lifetime homes available. Some unwanted litters are produced by accident (many dog owners don't realize their dogs can start having puppies by 5 or 6 months of age); some litters are just the result of well-intentioned but misinformed people. A common reason given by the people who fall into the latter category is that they want their children to see the miracle of life in person, by allowing their dog to have a litter of pups. But what they may not think about ahead of time is the fact that the birth of puppies is not always a beautiful experience, especially if a puppy or the bitch dies in the process.

If you want to teach your children a wonderful lesson about the animal population, teach them the importance of spaying and neutering pets, and take them for a visit to your local Humane Society or animal shelter so they can see firsthand how many dogs are in need of a good home.

Some people who buy purebred dogs believe they can recover the purchase price of their dog by breeding it — and maybe make a little pocket change at the same time. But this is a fallacy; the cost of providing for a litter of puppies until they find new homes *always* outweighs the purchase price of the dog. It often eats up most of the profit from the sale of a litter, too.

In the following sections, I let you know exactly what is required to bring a healthy litter of puppies into the world. And I fill you in on the importance of spaying or neutering your dog as well.

Understanding how much work goes into having a litter of pups

Even when done properly, having puppies is time-consuming and costly. Frequently, you must attend to unexpected and costly details as well.

First, you have to make sure your female dog has no genetic conditions that she may pass on to her puppies. Depending on the breed, this may entail getting hip and elbow x-rays, an eye examination, and a heart examination. Some breeds require additional medical tests as well. Then you have to locate a healthy male dog of the same breed and make sure that he, too, has been tested for hereditary conditions.

After the female is bred, you need to give her proper nutrition to keep her healthy while the puppies grow inside her. (Growing puppies can be a tremendous drain on a female dog.)

Before the puppies are born — and probably before the dogs are even bred — you need to begin the tough job of finding good homes for them. This means interviewing many people and determining whether they have a safe place for the puppy to exercise (preferably a fenced yard) and whether they will provide the puppy with socialization, obedience training, and most of all, love throughout a lifetime.

About 63 days after the breeding, your bulging canine will start to whelp her puppies. You'll need to enlist the help of an experienced person to supervise the whelping. This person should know what to do if the bitch or puppies get into trouble during the birth process.

Every now and then, usually when you least expect it, the puppies just won't come out. When this occurs, they have to be taken by cesarean section. This is a costly emergency procedure that requires a skilled veterinarian and a general anesthetic.

After the newborn puppies have popped out, you need to make sure the umbilical cord is tied off and cleaned so it doesn't become infected.

During the first few hours after the puppies are born, you will be exhausted (most bitches prefer to whelp at night), but you will need to be sure the bitch is taking proper care of her puppies. She should lick each puppy until the pup is clean and dry, and she should make sure each pup gets a chance to have some milk. You need to watch all the puppies to be sure they're all strong and are nursing vigorously. Weak puppies may need to be bottle-fed every two hours. (If you thought you were exhausted before, try getting up all night long to bottle-feed a puppy. I can assure you, the fun wears off very quickly.)

Luckily, during the first ten days of the puppies' life, you won't need to clean up any messes, because the bitch takes care of this little detail by eating the feces. You do need to be very vigilant during this period, however, to make sure the bitch doesn't accidentally lie on and smother any of the puppies. Sometimes the bitch is so exhausted that she lies on a sleeping puppy and doesn't hear its distress cries underneath her.

During the nursing period, the bitch needs food of superior quality, because she will be eating for 4 or 7 or even 13!

At about 10 to 14 days of age, the puppies open their eyes. Soon afterward, they start to walk. Suddenly, the peaceful whelping box is full of action and the newly mobile family doesn't have enough room. So you need to provide the puppies with a larger pen in which they can safely explore and offer them lots of toys to play with. Spend time handling every puppy several times a day, so that they get used to the sights, sounds, and smells of humans.

Somewhere between 3 and 5 weeks of age, the puppies need to be weaned from their mother. This involves taking the bitch away from the puppies for longer and longer periods of time and introducing the puppies to solid food. You need to hover nearby with a dishrag as the puppies tromp through the food, getting it all over their faces and paws — as well as all over their littermates.

You need to puppy-proof your home, making sure nothing dangerous is within the reach of the puppies. Plus, you need to restrict the puppies' explorations to places where you can clean up their messes.

During the next short weeks, you need to teach these new little beings all about the world in which they will live. They need to experience different footing such as wood, linoleum floors, carpets, grass, and cement. Puppies, like the one in Figure 2-2, need to see as many sights, hear as many sounds, and smell as many scents as possible. They should also meet many different dogs and people. You need to teach them that people are safe and help them look to humans for comfort and leadership.

In the last few weeks before the puppies go to their new homes, you need to get them vaccinated for common infectious diseases and have them treated for worms, which most puppies have. Your prospective puppy buyers also will be visiting to meet their new canine family members. You need to prepare a packet for the puppy buyers with information on the puppies' mother and father as well as details on how to feed and care for their new puppies. Even after your puppies are gone, you probably will field many telephone calls from your puppies' new families. They invariably will have lots of questions about how to care for and train their new family members.

You also must consider the possibility that you may not be able to find homes for all the little beings you have brought into the world. You may have a few extra mouths to feed and one or more puppies to housetrain and spend quality time with over the next few months or even years.

Figure 2-2:
Puppies
need to
experience
as many
new sights,
sounds, and
smells as
possible,
well before
they go to
their new
homes.

Photo courtesy of Marcia Halliday

The bottom line? Having a litter consists of 8 weeks of intensity and a lifetime of responsibility. If you're ready for this, be sure to join your local breed club, where you will find many other individuals who will be glad to help you with all the details about making puppies. If you aren't ready for the work involved, get your dog spayed or neutered.

Neutering your dog

The only way to be sure your dog doesn't produce puppies is to get your female dog spayed or your male dog castrated. Intact male dogs and bitches in heat have an uncanny way of finding each other, and a breeding can occur in a snap.

Spaying involves the removal of both the uterus and the ovaries. *Castration* refers to the removal of a male dog's testicles. The term *neutering* is a general term to describe either spaying or castration (but you may hear the terms *neutering* and *castrating* used to mean the same thing).

In addition to preventing unwanted puppies, neutering your dog has many benefits:

- **Female dogs who are spayed prior to their first heat cycle (which usually occurs between 6 and 9 months of age) have a significantly reduced chance of developing mammary (breast) cancer compared to dogs who have had even one heat cycle.**
- **Spayed females can't develop *pyometra*, an infection of the uterus that can be quite severe and can even result in death.**

- ✔ Spayed females tend to have more even temperaments and do not go through the hormone-induced mood swings that intact bitches sometimes have.

- ✔ Neutered dogs often are better behaved than their intact counterparts. Not only are they less likely to roam (visiting neighborhood females is a major reason for roaming), they are also less likely to mark their territory by urinating in the house (testosterone is one of the major drives for this dominance-related activity). In addition, neutered male dogs are much less likely to be aggressive toward other male dogs. These behavior benefits are particularly true if you castrate your dog between the ages of 9 and 12 months, before he becomes sexually mature and develops bad habits.

- ✔ Neutering prevents the development of prostate problems often seen in older dogs.

- ✔ A neutered dog won't develop testicular cancer, a common cancer of older, intact male dogs.

Male dogs who lift their legs to urinate don't leave urine burns in the middle of the lawn, because they usually urinate on trees, fence posts, and other vertical objects around the perimeter of the yard. If you prefer that your male dog lift his leg rather than squat to urinate, wait until this habit is well established before getting him neutered.

Many people think their dogs will get fat if they are spayed or castrated, but this isn't the case. Neutered dogs frequently don't need as much food as their intact compatriots, but there is a simple solution: Don't feed them as much.

Depending on your locale and the veterinarian you select, it costs between $50 and $120 to castrate a male dog and between $75 and $140 to spay a female dog. This is an incredible bargain, given that the bill for a woman's hysterectomy is upwards of $10,000. For people on public assistance or with lower incomes and for seniors on fixed incomes, spay/neuter clinics are held in most towns and cities. These usually are sponsored by animal shelters and veterinarians as part of their ongoing effort to control the local pet population. To find out when these clinics are held in your area, contact your local animal shelter.

The gory details

Neutering a male dog involves surgically removing the testicles with a relatively simple operation. When you make an appointment to have your dog castrated, your veterinarian will ask you not to give your dog any food or water after 8:00 the night before the surgery. (Keeping your dog from eating or drinking decreases the likelihood of the dog regurgitating during surgery.) The veterinarian will anesthetize the dog and make a tiny incision in the skin just in front of the testicles. The testicles are then slid up under the skin and removed through this little slit. The skin is sutured with three to five sutures. Your dog is then allowed to wake from the anesthesia and to rest overnight — either at the veterinarian's office or at your home — after the surgery.

Spaying a female is more involved than neutering a male, because it involves opening the abdomen. As with any general anesthetic, the veterinarian will ask you not to give your dog food or water after 8:00 the night before the surgery. After your dog is anesthetized, the veterinarian will make an incision in the center of her abdomen. He will find the uterus and ovaries and cut them out, first making sure that all the blood vessels are clamped off so they don't

bleed. In a young dog, the blood vessels are tiny and are easy to clamp off. After a female has been through a heat cycle, however, the vessels are larger and require special attention so they don't bleed. This is why spaying a dog after her first heat is usually more expensive. If a bitch is pregnant, the vessels are very large and are full of blood to feed the growing puppies; therefore, some veterinarians refuse to spay a pregnant bitch (sometimes requested to prevent the birth of puppies) because of the danger of postoperative bleeding. After removing the uterus and ovaries, the veterinarian sutures the abdominal incision and the dog wakes up. She then may stay overnight at the clinic to make sure she rests and doesn't stress the incision in the early stages of healing.

For the first couple of days after surgery (whether for castration or spaying), your dog should rest and should only go outside to the bathroom. For the next week, mild exercise such as on-leash walking is all right. About ten days after surgery, the veterinarian will check to make sure the incision is healing properly and remove the sutures (or check on self-dissolving sutures).

Chapter 3

Working with Your Dog's Vet

*O*ne of the most important things you can do to keep your dog healthy is develop a relationship of mutual respect with a veterinarian. Knowing that you and your veterinarian are partners in maintaining your dog's health and in caring for your canine companion when he has problems can be a tremendous relief. In this chapter, I show you exactly how to establish this kind of relationship — from choosing a vet to making your dog feel good about going there. I also give you some great suggestions for tackling the often-expensive costs involved with keeping your dog healthy.

Choosing the Right Vet for You and Your Dog

You should choose a vet for your dog in the same way you choose a doctor for yourself. Just as you probably wouldn't have much luck choosing your physician from the Yellow Pages, there are better ways of finding a veterinarian than turning to the phone book.

Personal references from friends and acquaintances or your dog's breeder, if she lives nearby, can be very helpful in making your selection. Ask your friends whether their veterinarians have been able to make a diagnosis when their dogs haven't been well. If their dogs had surgery, find out whether the recovery was uneventful and complete. Also find out whether their veterinarians discussed the dogs' illnesses and treatments and whether they answered questions thoroughly.

When you've compiled a short list of possible veterinarians, call and make an appointment to see each of them without your dog. Tell them you would like to meet them, tour their clinics, and discuss your dog's care. Look for the following qualities when choosing a veterinarian for your dog:

- **Someone with several years' experience.** Your veterinarian should usually be able give you a diagnosis after she has examined your dog and performed the necessary tests. She may not always come up with a single diagnosis, but she should have a list of possibilities and a plan for how to differentiate between those possibilities. And if your veterinarian doesn't know the diagnosis or she can't answer the questions you have, she should at least be able to offer you an explanation of her thought processes and plans for further evaluation.

- **Someone you can communicate with easily.** Your veterinarian should be willing to answer your questions and should be able to explain, in terms you understand, both your dog's diagnosis and her recommendations for treatment and follow-up care. Your veterinarian should be willing to listen to you and should not ignore your observations regarding your dog's health. She should work with you as a partner, as someone who can help her work to improve your dog's health.

- **Someone who works in a modern facility.** Your veterinarian should have a modern, clean facility (approved by the American Animal Hospital Association), with capable veterinary assistants and access to a diagnostic lab that can provide the results of most tests within 24 hours. She should have staff on the premises 24 hours a day to care for seriously ill dogs, or she should be able to move seriously ill dogs to a 24-hour emergency facility for overnight care and observation. Your veterinarian should be available during emergency hours or should be able to refer you to an emergency clinic for problems that occur at night or on weekends.

- **Someone who is willing to make referrals.** Your veterinarian should be willing to refer your dog to a specialist for further evaluation. She should not be threatened if you ask for a referral to obtain a second opinion about your dog's condition.

- **Someone who has specific interests and specialty training.** Every veterinary professional has areas of special interest. Perhaps your veterinarian is especially interested in working with dogs. Maybe she has a particular interest in your breed of dogs. Not all veterinarians enjoy or are equally talented at performing surgery. And that's okay. But, because many dogs need surgery at some time in their lives, you need to know how comfortable your veterinarian is with surgery — what surgical procedures she performs and what kinds of cases she refers to a specialist. Ask her about the surgeons she refers to. Do the surgeons work in the same practice? If not, do they visit the practice to perform surgery, or would you have to transfer your dog elsewhere?

Don't wait until your dog is ill to find a vet; get the facts and start developing a working relationship with a veterinarian while your dog is healthy.

When you visit a veterinary clinic, watch the staff. It always is a good sign when the receptionist and technical staff enjoy being with dogs and work well together.

Don't choose a veterinarian on the basis of the prices she charges for her services. Veterinarians have a great deal of time and money invested in their education, clinic, and equipment. A veterinary clinic has very high overhead because of the cost of maintaining all the same equipment as a human hospital (the building, the surgical and anesthetic equipment, an x-ray machine, ultrasound equipment, and so on) and the cost of top-notch personnel to care for your dog and to assist with surgery. A veterinarian who consistently charges less for her services than other vets in the same area is probably cutting corners somehow, perhaps in a way that can affect your dog's care. To get the best health care for your dog, expect to pay for it.

Above all, when choosing a vet, trust your instincts. If you feel uncomfortable talking freely with a veterinarian, if you are concerned about the care your animal receives, or if for some reason your dog takes a strong dislike to a particular vet, search for another veterinary partner.

Helping Your Dog Enjoy His Trip to the Vet

Many dogs hate visiting the vet's office. And it's really not surprising, given the fact that their associations usually are negative. Think how a routine veterinary checkup (see Figure 3-1) must appear to your dog. First, he has to wait in a small room full of dogs, cats, and other animals, most of whom are extremely fearful. Then he is led into a tiny room and is placed on a cold, slippery table. Next, a stranger who smells like a mixture of soap, chemicals, and other animals touches him all over his body, looks in his mouth and ears, and sticks a cold glass thermometer up his rear end. To top it all off, the stranger usually pokes him with at least one needle, often more.

But you can take some steps to ensure that your dog's veterinary experiences are good ones. Here are some ways to prevent your dog from developing a fear of his trips to the vet:

 ✔ **Occasionally drop by the vet's office with your dog when you don't have an appointment.** Bring your dog into the office and have the receptionist give him a cookie or two. Chat for a while and then leave. This way, your dog will learn to view the vet's office as a fun place, instead of a place where he only gets poked and prodded.

✔ **Make sure your dog gets experience riding in the car just for fun.** If he only rides in the car when he has to see the veterinarian, he soon will become fearful as soon as he gets in the car.

✔ **Schedule your veterinary appointments for a time when there are fewer dogs in the office, if you can.** This reduces the social stresses on your dog and reduces your time in the waiting room. If your dog is particularly worried while he's in the waiting room, stay with your dog in the car until the veterinarian is ready to meet with you (you can run in and let the office staff know you're in the parking lot and have them come get you when they're ready).

✔ **Bring an ample supply of treats with you.** Give your dog a treat for entering the door and another for sitting with you quietly. This is a good reason to train your dog in the basics of obedience — he'll feel more secure if he is asked to do something familiar (like sit and stay) during this stressful period. During your office visit, ask the veterinarian to give your dog some treats periodically, especially just before she examines your dog or before she does something stressful such as inserting the thermometer.

✔ **Don't mistakenly praise your dog for being stressed.** Many people make the mistake of trying to comfort their dogs when they act fearful in the veterinary office. But your dog may interpret this as you praising him for his worry. You're better off ignoring him when he acts worried and praising him and giving him treats for even small acts of boldness.

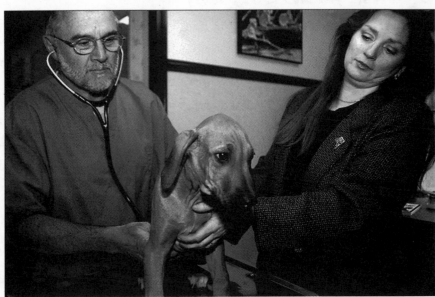

Figure 3-1:
Visiting the vet can be a difficult experience for many dogs, so make an effort to find a vet who is kind and caring and who obviously enjoys working with your pet.

© Mary Bloom

Start these preventive measures from the very first visit. Don't wait until your dog shows signs of fear.

Covering the Costs

If your dog gets sick, will you be prepared to pay the bill? Treating a simple infection can cost hundreds of dollars, and cancer treatment routinely costs thousands. Of course, you want to provide the best treatment possible for your furry friend, but top-notch veterinary care comes at a price. Before an accident or a sudden illness has you emptying your savings account or, even worse, opting for euthanasia because of a lack of funds, consider the alternatives in the following sections and see if there's an option that's right for you.

Personal savings plans

The best way to make sure you'll always have funds available to pay veterinary bills is to set up a canine cash reserve. If you deposit $30 to $50 a month in a savings account in your pet's name, you'll be surprised at how much you can save. In a year or two, you'll have enough to pay the bill for most serious illnesses. Save the spare change you collect at the end of the day, and you'll have all your dog's health care covered.

You can use your canine cash reserve to pay for _all_ your veterinary bills, or you can set it aside for any expenses over a certain amount (such as $200). The money will continue to grow throughout your dog's life, and you will have a substantial sum accumulated when your dog is older (when he's more likely to require more expensive treatments).

The only disadvantage of this system is that you have to have the discipline to make it work.

Don't wait until the last minute to come up with funds to pay your dog's medical expenses. If you put $2 of change a day into a savings account, at the end of three years you'll have saved several thousand dollars — enough to pay for just about any catastrophic illness.

Pet insurance

Obtaining pet insurance is one way to ease veterinary sticker shock. Insurance companies charge annual premiums between $150 and $300 for a healthy adult dog. Basic coverage for puppies is slightly less, and when your dog reaches 8 years of age, the cost of coverage rises incrementally as your dog gets older. Basic plans usually don't cover routine preventive care, although such coverage may be available for an extra charge. The basic plans are designed to cover a percentage of the veterinary charges for unexpected illnesses. They don't cover preexisting conditions or hereditary diseases. So if your dog has hip dysplasia, for example, surgical or medical treatment to ease his pain would not be covered. But if your furry friend were hit by a car or decided to eat a dish towel (yes, I knew a dog who did that once), the costs of veterinary care would be covered (after payment of a deductible) up to a maximum amount for that condition.

Making sense of the deductions, maximums, exclusions, and other insurance lingo can be tough, so be sure to read the insurance company's literature carefully before signing on the dotted line. If you have any questions about what will and will not be covered, speak to an insurance company representative. Don't hesitate to ask whatever questions you have about the coverage you're considering. Think about some of the illnesses your dog (or one of your previous dogs) has suffered and ask what percentage of the charges would be covered. Using a real-life example will help you understand exactly how much you will be responsible for and determine whether the cost of the insurance is worth it.

If you keep good financial records, you can add up how much you spent on veterinary care during the last five years and calculate how much you typically spend on veterinary care every year. Take a look also at how much you have saved to deal with a catastrophic illness. This will help you determine whether you may benefit from pet insurance.

Clinic-based HMOs

For a number of years, individual clinics have offered *well-care plans,* in which clients pay a monthly fee and receive discounts on routine care and preventive maintenance such as annual checkups, vaccinations, fecal exams, deworming, and heartworm checks. Some programs also offer member discounts on dental cleaning and surgical spaying or castrating.

Prepaid health care programs offer a way of spreading out (and perhaps reducing) the costs of routine veterinary care, but they generally do not cover hereditary diseases, preexisting conditions, or catastrophic illness. In addition, they cover your pet only for care provided in that specific practice. So if your pet gets ill while you're on vacation, or he requires the care of a specialist not in that practice, you're on your own.

If you are considering taking advantage of a comprehensive preventive care program, do a little math to figure out whether it's right for you. Make a list of all the preventive care services you would normally avail yourself of in a year, and add up the cost of those services. Then compare that number with the cost for the services offered by the clinic's well-care plan. Clinic-based plans often provide a significant discount to those clients who want to provide the most complete preventive care for their furry friends.

Pet-care credit companies

Several credit companies offer credit to cover unexpected veterinary fees. If your dog suddenly becomes ill or has an accident and you're short on funds, this option can save your dog's life. Unlike pet insurance, credit companies do not require you to sign up ahead of time (although your veterinarian must be registered with the company), and there are no exclusions or deductibles.

To take advantage of this service, you just fill out a credit application, which your veterinarian transmits to the lender. If the application is approved, your veterinarian is paid within 48 hours, and a payment schedule is established for repayment of your loan.

Of course, all this comes at a price. These companies generally charge 18 to 24 percent interest (similar to what you may pay in interest on a credit card debt), making this an expensive prospect if you have to make payments over a long period of time. Nonetheless, this option is available if the only other choice is euthanasia.

Another option, which gives you more power over the interest you pay, is to keep a major credit card with no balance in order to ensure that you have enough money to pay for emergencies.

Part II
Food, Glorious Food!

The 5th Wave   By Rich Tennant

Jerry bought only one type of pet food: NASCAR Kibbles The High Performance Dog Food

In this part . . .

Here I fill you in on everything you need to know about your dog's nutrition. You get the basics of what your dog needs and find out how to choose the right dog food for your dog (from the myriad options before you). I also help you decide whether to supplement your dog's diet, and I give you some great suggestions if you decide to make your dog's food yourself. Finally, I provide special help if your dog has special needs (ranging from overweight to cancer and everything in between).

If your dog is looking at you with that longing, hungry look, she's really telling you to read the chapters in this part. And how can you say no to a face like that?

Chapter 4

The Building Blocks of Good Nutrition

Dogs are carnivores. Their teeth are shaped for biting, tearing, and grinding flesh, and their intestinal tracts are short, with enzymes that are good for digesting proteins (but aren't very good at breaking down and absorbing plant material). So it only makes sense that your dog's diet should be meat-based.

Dogs are also opportunists, which means they'll eat whatever comes their way, including the trash in your kitchen and the grass in your yard. They do gain nutritional benefits from vegetables, fruits, and grains, but they still need meat in their diets as their main source of nutrition.

This chapter covers the eight building blocks of nutrition. All these building blocks are required in a well-balanced diet, regardless of the dog. But the *amounts* of each of these nutritional elements that each dog needs depends on that dog's unique situation — puppies and adults need different amounts, as do spayed and pregnant females, and active and inactive dogs.

To find out more about special situations in which your dog's diet may need to change, turn to Chapter 8.

Proteins

Proteins are the most critical component of food for your canine carnivore. They are also the most abundant element in your dog's body. Your dog needs proteins to produce hair, nails, tendons, cartilage, and all the connective tissues that support the rest of the tissues and organs in her body. So adequate protein is important for your dog's growth and proper development, for her muscle development and strength, for a functioning immune system, for the production of functioning hormones, for the proper volume of blood, for injury repair and prevention, and much, much more (see Figure 4-1). You can see why protein is the most important of all the nutrients in a dog's food!

Besides being a major structural component of your dog's body, your dog's body can also use proteins to produce energy if necessary. Fats and carbohydrates are much more readily available sources of energy, but proteins can be broken down and converted when necessary, for example during times when there is a low food supply.

Proteins are made up of amino acids that are linked in a chain. When your dog eats protein, enzymes secreted by the pancreas into the intestine break the proteins down into short chains of amino acids called *polypeptides,* which are small enough to be absorbed by the intestine. There are 20 different amino acids — some are considered *essential amino acids* and others are considered *nonessential amino acids.* As the name implies, the essential amino acids are required by your dog, so she needs to have those amino acids supplied in her food. Food that contains all the essential amino acids is referred to as a *complete protein source.* The nonessential amino acids are . . . drumroll, please . . . not essential, which means that if your dog doesn't get them in her diet, she can convert some of the other amino acids into those that she's missing.

Figure 4-1:
This dog, Fate, was abandoned at a shelter in terrible condition, but after just two months of proper nutrition, her coat is rich and glistening.

Your dog can get proteins from both animal and plant sources. But only animal-source proteins are complete protein sources, and not all of them are complete. Examples of complete protein sources that come from animals are eggs, whole milk, and lean meat. Grains are another important source of proteins in dog foods, but they are incomplete protein sources because they don't contain some of the essential amino acids your dog needs. Plant protein sources that are frequently used in dog foods include soybeans, wheat, and corn.

Your dog's major source of protein should be animal products, not grain. Don't buy a dog food in which soybean meal, soy flour, or corn gluten meal is the primary, or even the secondary, source of protein. Dogs don't have sufficient enzymes to digest them and use them properly as sources of protein.

The American Association of Feed Control Officials (AAFCO) is the organization that sets guidelines as to what specific nutrients dogs need in their foods and how much of those nutrients are required for their health. They have determined that foods for adult dogs should contain no less than 18 percent protein, and that foods to be eaten by lactating females or puppies should have a minimum of 22 percent protein. Military or police dogs, mushing dogs, and other dogs who are working hard every day or under a lot of stress may need more protein. Dogs who are recuperating from injuries or surgery may need more protein as well, so that they can build new proteins and repair muscles, tendons, and ligaments.

Not all complete protein sources are created equal. For example, a cow's hoof and a filet mignon may both have all the essential and nonessential amino acids, but your dog can get the amino acids she needs more easily from the filet mignon than she can from the cow's hoof. Some proteins are just more digestible than others; digestible proteins can be broken down and absorbed by your dog's gastrointestinal tract, giving her the nutrients she needs. So how do we know in which form the proteins are digestible and in which form they aren't? To measure digestibility, nutritionists measure the amount of protein in a food, feed it to dogs, and then measure the amount of protein in the dogs' feces. (I never said it was a pretty job.) The difference between how much was in the food to begin with and how much the dog excretes tells us how much of the protein the dog actually absorbed, and that is the digestible protein. It stands to reason that a protein isn't very useful to your dog if it ends up fertilizing your lawn instead of nourishing her body. Hair and feathers are a cheap source of protein — but they're also indigestible, so even if your dog wanted to eat a pile of feathers, she wouldn't get much protein from her meal. Eggs, on the other hand, are highly digestible, but they're also expensive. Not surprisingly, the more digestible the protein, the more expensive the dog food. So, as with many things in life, you get what you pay for.

Beware of foods that advertise over 90 percent digestibility. The highest quality dog foods are 82- to 86-percent digestible, whereas economy foods (like the inexpensive foods you can get in grocery stores) are around 75-percent digestible. The percent digestibility of a dog food is not stated on the label, although most dog food manufacturers will provide you with that information on request.

If your dog's feces are voluminous, this may be a sign that her food isn't highly digestible.

Fats

Fats are the major source of energy for dogs. All dogs need an energy source to help them be able to chase squirrels or beg at the dinner table. Dogs who live outdoors in the cold need enough fat to supply them with the energy to keep warm. And police dogs and working dogs need enough fat to prevent them from having to get their energy from their carbohydrate or protein supplies.

But fats do more than provide your dog with energy. They also help keep your dog's skin and foot pads supple and her coat healthy. Supplying an allergic dog with the proper amount and type of fats can make a huge difference in how much she scratches. Fats also carry fat-soluble vitamins into the body from the intestine. These vitamins are essential for health, and the only way your dog can absorb them is if she has enough fat to carry them into her body. Plus, just as with our own food, fat makes a dog's food tastier, which can be important in helping dogs who are ill eat enough to provide the nutrients they need for healing.

Fatty acids are the major component of fat. Dogs really only need omega-6 fatty acid (often referred to as *linoleic acid*), because they can't make it on their own. Linoleic acid keeps your dog's skin supple and pliable, and keeps her pads and nose leather flexible. Dogs with deficiencies of linoleic acid have scruffy, dry coats and dry, cracked pads. Luckily, dogs don't need a lot of linoleic acid. Good sources are beef, pork, chicken, and the oils from corn, safflower, and soybeans.

Omega-3 fatty acids can also help dogs with allergies by controlling the inflammatory responses in their skin. Omega-3s can improve dry skin and have been reported to decrease stiffness from arthritis. But omega-6 and omega-3 fatty acids have some opposing functions, so you need to be sure your dog is getting a balance between these two components. Shoot for a ratio of omega-6 to omega-3 fatty acids of about 5 to 1.

Your dog is better off if her food has the correct ratio of omega-6 to omega-3 fatty acids than if you try to provide it in supplement form to balance it out. So look for dog foods that have safflower oil or corn oil to provide the omega-6 fatty acids and fish oil or fish meal to provide the omega-3 fatty acids.

The ratio of omega-6 to omega-3 fatty acids is listed on the bags of some of the better quality foods, so especially if your dog is having skin problems, opt for a higher-quality food — and one that has the correct ratio of omega-6 to omega-3.

Although your dog needs fat in her diet, too much fat can contribute to obesity, the number one nutritional problem in dogs. Excessive fat can also slow down the digestive process and may cause nausea, diarrhea, and even vomiting. High-fat diets also play a role in the development of *pancreatitis*, an inflammation of the pancreas that can result in very severe vomiting and sometimes even death. So you need to be sure to control the fat levels in your dog's diet. Feeding a high-quality dog food (and not giving your dog lots of extras), watching your dog's weight, and making sure she gets enough exercise is the best way of ensuring that she won't become obese.

On the other hand, just because less fat is better for humans doesn't mean that a low-fat diet is good for our dogs. Too little fat can lead to dry, flaky skin; dry, cracked pads; and a dull, broken hair coat.

Be sure to read the dog food label before choosing a diet for your dog (Chapter 5 tells you all about dog food labels), and observe your dog's response to the food. If you don't like the appearance of your dog's coat and skin on one diet, try a different one. Your dog's food should include good-quality animal fats and can be supplemented with cold-pressed oils such as linseed, wheat germ, or soybean oil. Growing puppies and pregnant or lactating bitches need a minimum of 8 percent fat in their diet. Adult dogs need a minimum of 5 percent fat. High levels of fats (above 16 percent) are not needed for most dogs, except hard-working dogs such as stock dogs, police dogs, and sled dogs.

Carbohydrates

Every cell in your dog's body needs a continuous supply of carbohydrates, particularly in the form of glucose, in order to function properly. In fact, it is so important for cells to have glucose that the body produces a specific hormone called *insulin*, which drives glucose into the cells. Glucose is especially important in the function of your dog's brain and muscles. Carbohydrates also assist in the digestion of other nutrients, especially fats. Your dog's carbohydrate requirements vary according to her level of activity, her health, and her overall energy needs.

Carbohydrates come in three basic forms: sugars, starches, and cellulose. Sugars and starches are called *simple carbohydrates* because they are readily available as glucose or are readily broken down into glucose. Good sources of simple carbohydrates are rice, oatmeal, corn, and wheat. Simple carbohydrates are easy for your dog to digest when they've been properly cooked; they also add texture and mouth feel to the food, making it more palatable for your dog. Cellulose, the main carbohydrate found in the stems and leaves of plants, is a *complex carbohydrate*. Dogs don't have the enzymes necessary to digest cellulose, so when cellulose is present in a dog food, it is usually serving as *fiber*, which helps regulate water in your dog's large intestine and aids in the formation and elimination of feces (see the following section for more information on fiber).

The best foods use the carbohydrates that come in grains; there should be no need to add extra sugar to food, although some manufacturers do this to make a food taste better. The AAFCO has no recommended minimum or maximum levels of carbohydrates in dog foods. Carbohydrates make up the remainder of the bulk of the food after the fats, proteins, fiber, and vitamins and minerals have been added.

Fiber

Fiber is an important component of dog food. It provides bulk to the food and helps the intestinal contents absorb water, which results in formed stools that are readily expelled. If a food has too little fiber, the dog may have loose stools, because there is nothing to help the stools form. If a food has too much fiber, it will pass much more quickly through the gastrointestinal system, making digestion less efficient and the stools hard and compacted.

Beet pulp is an excellent source of fiber. It is the dried residue from sugar beets, which first have been cleaned and freed of crowns, leaves, and sand, and then used to extract sugar for human foods. Dried tomato pomace is another good source of fiber. It is the dried mixture of tomato skins, pulp, and crushed seeds that is a by-product of the manufacture of tomato products.

Most maintenance, puppy, and performance dog foods contain between 3 and 6 percent fiber. Weight reduction diets may have between 8 and 25 percent fiber. (For more details on diets for weight reduction, see Chapter 8.)

Water

Water is the most plentiful molecule in your dog's body (your dog's body is two-thirds water), and it is essential for every one of her functions, from digesting food to dashing across the yard. In the gastrointestinal tract, water dissolves nutrients to prepare them for digestion and helps transport the nutrients across the intestinal wall.

Your dog loses water by several routes, through salivation and respiration and in her urine and feces. If your dog loses more water than she takes in, she will suffer from dehydration, which, if severe and untreated, can be fatal. Because water is such an important component of your dog's diet, she should be given free access to clean water at all times.

Enzymes

Enzymes play a role, often in conjunction with vitamins, in just about every body reaction. They are like the keys that unlock the doors to chemical reactions. Each enzyme is the catalyst for one specific reaction, which is why there are so many different enzymes. The pancreas secretes several kinds of enzymes that assist in digestion. In addition to enzymes secreted by the pancreas, enzymes are also present in fresh foods.

In most dogs, the pancreas produces sufficient enzymes for digestion. However, in some dogs, pancreatic function is not optimal. This is often the case in older dogs, who frequently have trouble fully breaking down their foods for optimal absorption of nutrients, and in dogs with pancreatitis (inflammation of the pancreas) or pancreatic cancer. For these dogs, supplementing the diet with pancreatic enzymes, which predigest the food, is helpful.

Vitamins

Dogs require 14 different vitamins. With only a few exceptions, dogs don't make the vitamins themselves, which means the vitamins must be supplied in the food. Vitamins participate in numerous chemical reactions that help to release the needed nutrients from the dog's food and help the dog's body to put those nutrients to use. Vitamins can be either water-soluble or fat-soluble.

Water-soluble vitamins

The water-soluble vitamins have to be supplied on a daily basis, because they are continually broken down and excreted. They include the following:

- **Thiamin (vitamin B1):** Promotes a good appetite and normal growth. Required for energy production.

- **Riboflavin (vitamin B2):** Promotes growth.

- **Pyridoxine (vitamin B6):** Important in the metabolism of proteins and in the formation of red blood cells.

- **Pantothenic acid:** Required for energy and for protein metabolism.

- **Niacin:** A constituent of many enzymes that process carbohydrates, proteins, and fats.

- **Vitamin B12:** Necessary for normal DNA synthesis and intestinal function.

- **Folic acid:** Works together with vitamin B12 and in many of the body's chemical reactions.

- **Biotin:** A component of several important enzyme systems.
- **Choline:** Required for proper transmission of nerve impulses and for utilization of sulfur-containing amino acids.
- **Vitamin C:** Participates in the formation of bones, teeth, and soft tissue.

The daily requirements for each of these vitamins are supplied in premium dog foods. Generally, an excess of these water-soluble vitamins is harmless because they are readily excreted in the urine. But as long as your dog is eating a high-quality complete and balanced commercial diet and is completely healthy, you don't need to worry about supplementing her diet with water-soluble vitamins.

Fat-soluble vitamins

The fat-soluble vitamins don't have to be supplied in the food every day because excess levels are stored in your dog's body's fat. Because they are stored for months in the body, these vitamins can accumulate to toxic levels. However, this is very rare.

Here are the fat-soluble vitamins your dog needs:

- **Vitamin A:** Necessary for proper vision, especially night vision. Important in bone growth, reproduction, and maintenance of tissues such as the lungs, intestines, and skin.
- **Vitamin D:** Critical to the dog's ability to use calcium and phosphorus for bone and cartilage growth and maintenance.
- **Vitamin E:** An antioxidant that protects the cells (and dog food) from oxidative damage. Especially important for muscular and reproductive function.
- **Vitamin K:** Essential for normal blood clotting.

Minerals

Minerals are present in small amounts in the tissues of all living things. Teeth, bones, muscles, and nerves have especially high mineral content. Although the AAFCO provides guidelines for the minimal amounts of minerals necessary for canine growth and development, each dog's mineral requirements depends on her current nutritional state. For example, if a dog is iron deficient, she will need and absorb more iron from the intestinal tract. In addition, working dogs and dogs who are ill or stressed may also have higher requirements.

The controversy over vitamin C

Possibly the most controversial water-soluble vitamin is vitamin C. Many breeders and dog owners claim that vitamin C helps reduce the incidence and severity of bone and joint problems such as hip dysplasia in large, fast-growing breeds of dogs, but there is currently no scientific research to confirm this. Unlike humans, dogs synthesize their own vitamin C, so many nutritionists believe there is no reason to add it to a dog's food.

On the other hand, there may be circumstances in which dogs are not able to synthesize sufficient vitamin C, either genetically or in cases of severe illness. For example, in one study, racing sled dogs supplemented with vitamin C were able to run farther and remain more stress-free than their partners who received a placebo. So, in growing, ill, or hard-working dogs, supplying vitamin C as a supplement may be helpful.

The only problem is we don't know how much vitamin C a dog requires for health and how much a healthy dog is able to synthesize. If you decide to give your dog vitamin C, don't feed her megadoses. A dose of 500 milligrams a day is fine for small dogs and 1000 milligrams a day will suffice for large dogs.

Minerals can be divided into two groups: the major minerals and the trace minerals. The major minerals are required in gram amounts each day, whereas the trace minerals are required in milligram or microgram amounts per day. Of the trace minerals, there are several that are known to be required for canine health, and others whose role in growth and health are less understood.

Your dog's body needs to maintain a delicate balance between the levels of various major and trace minerals. In addition, for several of the trace minerals, there is a very narrow window between the level that is required and the level that is toxic. So supplementing an already balanced dog food with minerals can create more problems than it solves.

Table 4-1 lists the different minerals your dog needs and which foods are good sources of these minerals.

Table 4-1	Sources of Minerals
Mineral	*Source*
Calcium	Dairy products, poultry, and meat bone
Phosphorus	Meat, poultry, fish
Magnesium	Soybeans, corn, cereal grains, bone meals
Sulfur	Meat, poultry, fish

(continued)

Table 4-1 *(continued)*

Mineral	Source
Iron	Organ meats
Copper	Organ meats
Zinc	Beef liver, dark poultry meat, milk, egg yolks, legumes
Manganese	Meat, poultry, fish
Iodine	Fish, beef, liver
Selenium	Grains, meat, poultry
Cobalt	Fish, dairy products

Major minerals

The four major minerals are calcium, phosphorus, magnesium, and sulfur. Calcium and phosphorus are the most important minerals in all dogs' diets, but especially in the diets of growing puppies. Calcium is needed for muscle contraction, for nerve transmission, and for blood coagulation. It is also required to activate numerous enzymes that affect virtually every process in the cell. Phosphorus plays a part in nearly all chemical reactions in your dog's body. Working together, calcium and phosphorus strengthen your dog's bones and teeth.

Although the ratio of calcium to phosphorus in a dog food is important, recent studies suggest that the total amount of calcium ingested may be more important. Excess calcium is thought to contribute to the development of hip and elbow dysplasia, *osteochondrosis dissecans* (degeneration of the joint cartilage), and other bone and joint problems. (For more on these studies, see Chapter 8.) Deficiencies of calcium frequently occur in dogs who are fed all-meat diets. A severe deficiency of calcium can cause rickets and bone malformations. A moderate deficiency can cause muscle cramps, impaired growth, and joint pain.

As of this writing, all premium-quality adult maintenance dog foods produced by major manufacturers have enough calcium to support the healthy growth of puppies, including those of giant breeds. Resist the urge to provide extra supplementation of vitamins and minerals, particularly those containing calcium, to your growing puppy if she is on a high-quality complete and balanced dog food.

Never add bone meal to a complete and balanced diet. Not only are you likely to alter the critical calcium to phosphorus ratio, you also risk decreasing your dog's ability to absorb and utilize many of the other minerals she needs.

Magnesium is essential for many of the cells' enzymatic reactions. It also helps promote the absorption and metabolism of many other vitamins and minerals, including vitamins C and E, calcium, and phosphorus. Like calcium and phosphorus, magnesium is important in bone growth and development. In fact, 70 percent of the magnesium in your dog's body is present in her bones. Magnesium is rarely deficient in complete and balanced diets. However, its absorption can be impaired when the diet is too high in calcium and phosphorus.

Your dog needs sulfur for the synthesis of a variety of components in her body, most notably proteins. Sulfur is also an important constituent of joint fluid and cartilage and, thus, is important for proper joint health.

Trace minerals

Your dog needs only very small amounts of the trace minerals in her diet. Trace minerals can be found in meat and grains, and they also are provided as a supplement in complete and balanced premium dog foods. A balanced diet is still the best source for all the vitamins and minerals required for optimum health.

The trace minerals include the following:

- ✔ **Iron:** Iron is present in every cell in the body. It is particularly important, along with protein and copper, for the production of red blood cells, which are responsible for transporting oxygen from the lungs to every part of the body. Dogs with iron deficiency develop anemia. But remember, iron is needed in only small amounts, so it is important that you not supplement with iron unless you have a prescription.

- ✔ **Zinc:** Zinc is important in the metabolism of several vitamins, particularly the B-vitamins. It is also a component of several enzymes needed for digestion and metabolism, and it promotes healing as well. Your dog needs zinc for proper coat health. Some breeds of dogs, particularly the northern breeds such as Siberian Huskies, appear to have problems with absorption and/or utilization of zinc. These dogs develop poor hair coats and dry, scaly skin with sores particularly on the nose and mouth, and stiff joints unless they are supplemented with zinc.

- ✔ **Copper:** Copper is a trace mineral that has many different functions. It is needed for the production of blood and for the proper absorption of iron. It is also involved in the production of *connective tissue* (the cells and extracellular proteins that form the background structure of most tissues) and in healing. Copper is found in fish, liver, and various grains. The amount of copper in a grain is related to the level of copper in the soil where the grain was grown. A copper deficiency can result in anemia and skeletal abnormalities. Some breeds of dogs, such as Bedlington Terriers and Doberman Pinschers, can have a genetic problem that interferes with the metabolism of copper. In these dogs, copper is stored in the liver to toxic levels, resulting in hepatitis.

✔ **Iodine:** Iodine is critical for the proper functioning of the thyroid gland, which regulates the body's metabolism and energy levels and promotes growth. Iodine is found in high levels in fish. It is added to most dog foods to make the levels sufficient for canine health.

✔ **Selenium:** Selenium works with vitamin E to prevent oxidative damage to cells. It is needed in only minute amounts in the diet of dogs. Meats and cereal grains are good sources of selenium. In dogs, an excess of selenium results in death of the muscles of the heart as well as damage to the liver and kidney. Deficiency results in degeneration of the heart and skeletal muscles.

✔ **Manganese:** Manganese is a component of many different enzyme systems in the body. Most importantly it activates enzymes that regulate nutrient metabolism. It is found in legumes and whole-grain cereals; animal-based ingredients are not a good source of manganese.

✔ **Cobalt:** Cobalt is a part of vitamin B12, which is an essential vitamin. Cobalt does not appear to have any function independent of vitamin B12.

In addition to these trace minerals, other trace minerals that are known to be important in laboratory animals but have an unclear role in dogs include molybdenum, cadmium, arsenic, silver, nickel, lead, vanadium, and tin.

As scientists discover more about the nutritional needs of dogs, they are beginning to recognize that our canine companions may need different nutrient levels for optimal health than they need to just prevent deficiencies. The next few years will likely see significant changes in the composition of dog foods. So keep your eyes and ears open for new information. Be sure to discuss any nutritional questions with your veterinarian. And if you have a question about a specific dog food, don't hesitate to call the manufacturer. I have found them to be very helpful.

How dog food is made

How do some cows or chickens and a pile of grains turn into your dog's dinner? First the animals are slaughtered and the body parts not used for human consumption are put into bins according to which parts of the body they do or do not contain. These are either shipped directly to the dog food manufacturer or they are rendered and the meal (what remains after the fats are removed) is shipped to the manufacturer. Similarly, grains may be shipped directly to the dog food manufacturer or the meal (what remains after the oils have been extracted for use in human foods) may be shipped. The manufacturer then grinds and separates the whole grains into their different components. For example, wheat may be separated into wheat flour, wheat germ meal, wheat bran, and wheat middlings.

The ingredients are then mixed in their proper proportions and added to the *extruder,* a large tube containing a screw that mixes the ingredients with steam and water under pressure and then squirts the mixture out through holes at the end, kind of like a pasta-maker squeezes out spaghetti. A knife cuts the ribbon into small pieces, which are then moved along a conveyor belt through a dryer/cooler until the right amount of moisture remains. The food is then coated with fat, vitamins, and flavorings.

The high temperature at which dry dog foods are processed means that proteins are broken down and may be changed in their structure and quality. In addition, any enzymes that were in the food components are destroyed by the heat. Vitamins that have been destroyed during processing have to be sprayed back onto the food after it cools. But we're not sure whether the components that are added back are really the same as those that were present in the unprocessed food components, and this is why some people prepare foods for their dogs at home (see Chapter 7 for more information). As a trade-off, however, processed dog food is virtually sterile. None of the common bacteria that are present on beef and poultry such as *Salmonella* and *E. coli* remain after the food is processed.

The major difference between dry and semi-moist foods is that semi-moist foods are not dried as much, and they have more preservatives and sugar added. Canned dog foods are heated but not sent through an extruder. Thus, they tend to retain more of the natural proteins, fats, vitamins, and enzymes.

Chapter 5

Feeding Your Hungry Hound

*I*f you're like most people, when you look at the shelves of dog food in the store, you're bewildered by the choices available to you. There are puppy foods and senior foods; foods for large dogs and foods for small dogs; diet foods for pudgy pooches; foods that claim to be all-natural; foods that make promises about how they'll improve your dog's coat; foods that make their own gravy; and foods shaped like little bones.

How can you possibly pick the best food for your furry friend — a food that will give him all the nutrients he needs and help him to live a long and healthy life? Worry not. In this chapter, I describe the meat and potatoes of feeding your dog. You find out how to read dog food labels — and how to read between the lines. The bottom line: The information in this chapter will help you make better choices when you're buying dog food.

Identifying the Main Types of Dog Food

Many different forms of dog food are available today. *Dry food* usually contains less than 10 percent water; *semi-moist foods* contain 25 to 40 percent water; and canned food contains 75 to 80 percent water.

You may also have heard the terms *premium* or *super-premium* to describe dog foods, but these terms don't have a legal definition (which means they can be used by anyone who wants to use them). *Premium* is a term frequently used to describe high-quality dog foods generally sold in pet supply stores rather than grocery stores. *Super-premium* is generally used by some when referring to the highest quality foods that are prepared using the best ingredients available. Likewise, there are no legal definitions for the terms *gourmet* or *natural* when referring to dog food.

A brief history of dog food

Prior to the late 19th century, there was no such thing as prepared dog food. Lucky dogs owned by the well-to-do ate the leftovers from their owners' dinners, and street dogs aplenty canvassed the alleys, scrounging for what food they could find in the trash. In the 1870s, a time when transportation literally used horse power, a European entrepreneur devised a unique way to solve the problem of what to do with the carcasses of the many horses that died every day in the cities: He decided to package and sell the horsemeat as dog food. The idea caught on, particularly among the wealthy, who appreciated the convenience of having a ready-made food for their dogs.

The first commercial dog foods in North America were made by Ralston-Purina in 1926. Their foods were tested on dogs kept by the company in large kennels on their property near St. Louis, Missouri. Ralston-Purina dog food was given the ultimate test when it was fed to the sled dogs on Admiral Byrd's expedition to Antarctica in 1933. Although this was a punishing test for a dog food, it also was an early precursor to the celebrity endorsements that are a major part of the advertising budgets for many large companies today.

In the decade after World War II, the idea of prepared dog food really caught on. The economy was booming and people didn't mind spending a little money for the convenience of having a ready-made dog food for their canine companions. Besides, the companies producing these dog foods were performing studies on the nutritional needs of dogs, and their foods were billed as containing everything a healthy dog needed.

At that time, most dog foods were canned. This method of preserving food was familiar to Americans, who enjoyed the convenience of canned human foods that could be stored for months or even years on their shelves. In 1956, dog food companies began to utilize the *extrusion process,* in which nutrients in dried form are mixed with water, steam and pressure-forced through an opening, and the extruded material is cut into small pieces. The food pieces are then cooled; coated with vitamins and other components that are lost in the process of heating; flavored; and packaged.

Dry dog food allowed the consumer to more easily carry large amounts of dog food home from the grocery store. In addition, people found pouring food from a bag more convenient than cranking open a metal can. Plus, dry foods were advertised as helping keep dogs' teeth cleaner. As a result, since the late 1960s, the majority of dogs have been fed dry dog food, although canned food is still widely used, especially for smaller dogs.

In the early 1970s, the National Research Council (NRC) published the first recommendations listing the minimal nutritional requirements of dogs. Dog food companies now had a standard by which they could measure the nutritional value of their foods and parameters by which they could claim their foods to be complete and balanced. (The term *complete* indicated that all the required nutrients were present in their foods, and the term *balanced* indicated that these nutrients were in the correct proportions.) The NRC nutrient requirements for dog foods were supplanted in 1992 by nutrient profiles established by the American Association of Feed Control Officials (AAFCO). Throughout the late 20th century, as the dog population continued to grow, so did the dog food industry. By 1999, the pet food industry was an $11-billion-a-year industry — and very competitive. Today, dog foods are advertised and marketed every bit as competitively as human foods, highlighting the importance of being aware of what you're buying.

Most veterinary nutritionists agree that semi-moist dog foods offer very little nutritional value. These foods contain dyes and other nonessential additives so that they can be shaped into little bones, steaks, or other shapes. The additives may make the food visually appealing to the consumer, but dogs don't care or even notice what their food looks like. Semi-moist foods also are preserved with sugar, which contributes to obesity and periodontal disease in dogs.

Who's in charge around here?

Several watchdog groups oversee various parts of the dog food manufacturing and marketing process. Here is a rundown of the regulatory agencies and what they do:

✔ **The Association of American Feed Control Officials (AAFCO):** The AAFCO consists of animal food officials from the U.S. and Canada who have joined to develop minimum standards for dog foods (and other animal foods as well). In 1992, the AAFCO published its standardized nutritional guidelines for dog foods, which most dog food manufacturers use as their nutritional standard. The AAFCO has also established specific guidelines for what should and should not be included on dog food labels. Although the AAFCO does not have any powers mandated by law, reputable dog food companies willingly comply with its guidelines — which allows them to state on their dog food labels that they meet or surpass AAFCO guidelines. You can contact the AAFCO at P.O. Box 478, Oxford, IN 47971, or visit its Web site at www.aafco.org.

✔ **Pet Food Institute (PFI):** PFI has been around since 1958 and is the national trade association for pet food manufacturers. It monitors legislation that affects the pet food industry and lobbies for the interests of pet food manufacturers before federal legislative bodies, such as the Food and Drug Administration (FDA), the U.S. Department of Agriculture, the Federal Trade Commission (FTC), the AAFCO, and Congress. As a way of self-policing, PFI has established the Nutrition Assurance Program, which provides specific guidelines for the feeding trials that are used to test the nutritional quality of dog foods. Dog food companies that have complied with these guidelines in their food trials can state on the label that their food provides complete and balanced nutrition according to AAFCO procedures. For more information, contact PFI at 2025 M Street, NW, Suite 800, Washington, D.C. 20036, or visit its Web site at www.petfoodinstitute.org.

✔ **National Research Council (NRC):** The National Research Council's Committee on Animal Nutrition was the first group to establish minimal requirements for canine nutrition. First published in 1974, the minimal requirements are similar to the recommended daily allowances (RDAs) you see on packages of human foods. The NRC requirements for dogs were updated in 1985, and they plan another update in 2001. The new 2001 report will be based on a comprehensive review of the scientific literature on canine nutrition and will contain information on the impacts of physiologic status, temperature, breed, age, environment, and physical activity on the nutritional requirements of dogs. The Canine Nutrition Expert Subcommittee of the AAFCO currently recommends that dog foods use its nutrient profiles rather than those of the NRC. The NRC, however, provides an important and independent source of information on the nutritional requirements of dogs for the consumer. You can access the NRC publications by going to www.nas.edu/nrc/.

Avoid foods that don't have complete nutritional information on the label (see the "Reading a Dog Food Label" section of this chapter for more information). Foods that are produced and sold within the same state aren't required to have complete nutritional information the way foods that are sold across state lines are. These foods may be nutritionally sound, but without complete information, you can't be sure. Steer clear of dog foods that haven't been tested in feeding trials using real live dogs as well.

Reading a Dog Food Label

The first place you need to look when trying to decide on a food for your furry friend is the label on the bag, box, or can. Reading a dog food label really isn't very different from reading the nutritional label on your cereal box. A certain amount of nutritional information must be included on the label, but there is a certain amount of leeway in exactly how the dog food company presents that information.

You can divide the label up into two parts: the *product display panel* (on the front of the package) and the information panel (usually on the back of the package).

The product display panel

The product display panel is the place where the dog food company hopes to catch your eye. So it makes sense that it appears on the front of the package. You'll typically find a few key pieces of information on the product display panel, primary among them the dog food company name, the product identity, the product use (whether it's dog food or cat food, for example), and the net weight of the package. You may also find a banner statement, which is where the dog food company makes claims about the quality of the food. I cover each of these parts of the product display panel in the following sections.

Dog food company name

The dog food company (for example, Ralston Purina or Iams) usually displays its name prominently on the front of the dog food bag.

Product identity

The product identity section states the name of the product, such as Big Bart's Beefy Dinner.

Any terminology regarding the meat or meat flavor used in the product identity statement has to comply with a list of specific definitions. Here are some examples of common phrases and the standards that need to be met in order for the dog food company to use the phrase:

- **Beef for dogs:** The food must contain 95 percent beef by weight.

- **Beef dog food:** The food must contain 70 percent beef by weight.

- **Beef dinner, beef entrée, or beef platter:** The food must contain 25 percent beef by weight.

- **Dog food with beef:** The food needs to contain only 3 percent beef.

- **Beef-flavored:** The food doesn't need to contain any beef; it just needs to taste like beef (using artificial flavors).

The same rules for terminology apply to any meat source in dog food, such as chicken, lamb, and so on.

Product use

The product use statement just indicates which animal the food is formulated for (dogs or cats, for example).

Net weight

The product display panel also includes the net weight of the package contents.

Just as with human foods, dog food manufacturers frequently change the size of containers without changing the price. For example, a can that looks to be a standard 6-ounce size may actually contain 5.5 ounces (but stay at the same price). Be sure to read the label carefully.

Banner statement

The front of the package may also have a *banner statement,* which is where the manufacturer makes specific claims about the dog food. The content of banner statements is regulated by the AAFCO. For example, if a label says that dogs prefer the taste of that food, it must also tell you what other dog foods were tested to arrive at that conclusion. An example of a correctly worded statement regarding preferred taste would be, "Preferred by dogs over the leading premium brand."

There also are rules regarding what defines a *light/lite, low-calorie,* or *less fat* dog food. If a manufacturer states that its food is *light* or *low-calorie,* that food must have 15 percent fewer calories than the average of other dog foods in the same category. If the manufacturer claims that a certain dog food has "less" of a component, the claim must state how much less and tell the consumer less than what. For example, a dog food claiming to have *less fat* must state the percentage reduction in fat (on the basis of weight, not volume) and must state that this is less fat than other dog foods in the same category (dry, semi-moist, or canned, for example).

Dog foods using the terms *lean* or *low-fat* must meet yet another set of standards. They must have a maximum fat content that is 30 percent less than the industry average for dog foods. In addition to the required statement listing the minimum amount of fat in the food (see the "Guaranteed analysis" section later in this chapter), these foods must also state the maximum amount of fat, because these diets are used for weight loss.

The information panel

The information panel is where the dog food manufacturer tells you the nitty-gritty details of what's in the food. You'll usually find it on the back of the package. The information panel should provide a guaranteed analysis of what's in the food, an ingredient list, a nutritional adequacy statement, feeding guidelines, and the manufacturer's contact information. I cover each of these in the following sections.

Guaranteed analysis

Legally, dog food labels are only required to state the minimum levels of protein and fat and the maximum levels of moisture and fiber in the food. These are only minimums and maximums, so keep in mind that the dog food may have more than the minimum amounts or less than the maximum amounts of components stated on the label.

If your dog is ill, small differences in the amount of these important nutrients may make a difference in his health, so if you have any questions about what's in your dog's food and whether you're giving him everything he needs, talk with your vet.

The AAFCO nutrient profiles for dog foods let you know the minimum requirements for protein and fat for both adult dogs and puppies. But the AAFCO protein and fat levels are listed on a dry-weight basis, whereas the proteins and fats on a dog food label are listed on an as-is basis, which includes water. This difference can lead to some confusion when you try to determine whether a given dog food has the levels of nutrients your dog needs. It can also be confusing when you compare one dog food to another, because each dog food may have a different level of moisture (which affects how much of the nutrient is actually there on a dry-weight basis).

To make accurate comparisons between two foods, you need to do some math, so get out your calculator and follow these steps (I use protein as an example, but you can do the same equation for other nutrients as well):

1. **Find the percentage of protein in the dog food.**

2. **Find the percentage of moisture in the dog food.**

3. **Subtract the percentage of moisture from 100 to get the percentage of dry.**

4. **Divide the number you got in Step 1 by the number in Step 3 and multiply by 100.**

   This gives you the percentage of protein on a dry-weight basis.

So, for example, if you're looking at the label of a dry dog food (see Figure 5-1), and it says that the food contains 26 percent protein and 10 percent moisture, you would take that 10 percent moisture and subtract it from 100, which gives you 90 percent dry. Then take the 26 percent protein and divide it by 90 percent dry, then multiply by 100, and you get 29 percent protein on a dry-weight basis.

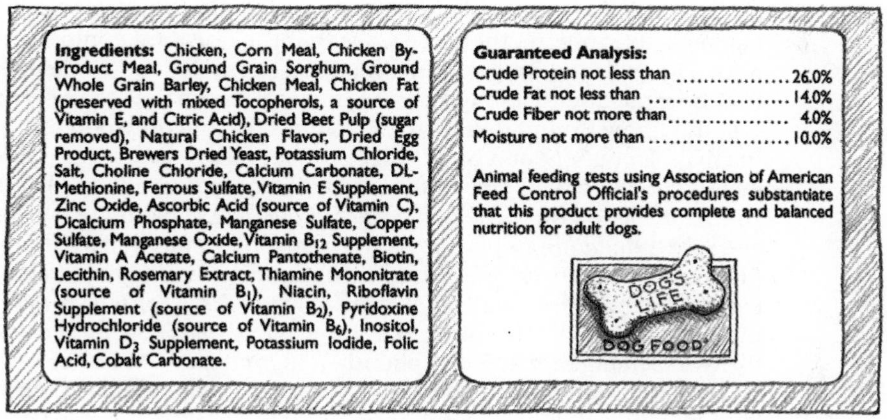

Figure 5-1:
A dog food label can tell you exactly how much protein (on a dry-weight basis) is in your dog's food, but you may need to do a little math to get that number.

Ingredients: Chicken, Corn Meal, Chicken By-Product Meal, Ground Grain Sorghum, Ground Whole Grain Barley, Chicken Meal, Chicken Fat (preserved with mixed Tocopherols, a source of Vitamin E, and Citric Acid), Dried Beet Pulp (sugar removed), Natural Chicken Flavor, Dried Egg Product, Brewers Dried Yeast, Potassium Chloride, Salt, Choline Chloride, Calcium Carbonate, DL-Methionine, Ferrous Sulfate, Vitamin E Supplement, Zinc Oxide, Ascorbic Acid (source of Vitamin C), Dicalcium Phosphate, Manganese Sulfate, Copper Sulfate, Manganese Oxide, Vitamin B_{12} Supplement, Vitamin A Acetate, Calcium Pantothenate, Biotin, Lecithin, Rosemary Extract, Thiamine Mononitrate (source of Vitamin B_1), Niacin, Riboflavin Supplement (source of Vitamin B_2), Pyridoxine Hydrochloride (source of Vitamin B_6), Inositol, Vitamin D_3 Supplement, Potassium Iodide, Folic Acid, Cobalt Carbonate.

Guaranteed Analysis:
Crude Protein not less than 26.0%
Crude Fat not less than 14.0%
Crude Fiber not more than 4.0%
Moisture not more than 10.0%

Animal feeding tests using Association of American Feed Control Official's procedures substantiate that this product provides complete and balanced nutrition for adult dogs.

If you're looking at the label of a canned dog food, the formula is exactly the same, but you'll find significantly different results. If the label says that the food contains 9 percent protein and 80 percent moisture, you would take that 80 percent moisture and subtract it from 100, which gives you 20 percent dry. Then take the 9 percent protein and divide it by 20 percent dry, then multiply by 100, and you get 45 percent protein on a dry-weight basis.

So what does all this math tell you? If you just compared the labels of the food, you would have easily thought that the dry food had more protein (because the dry food label said the food contained 26 percent protein and the canned food only contained 9 percent). But when you do the math, you discover that the canned food actually has 45 percent protein (on a dry-weight basis), compared to 29 percent in the dry food.

If all this math seems to be more trouble than it's worth, here's a quick rule of thumb to help you compare dry and canned foods. For a dry food, to determine the level of protein, fat, or fiber on a dry-weight basis, add 10 percent to the level that is listed on the label. For a canned food, take the amount of protein, fat, or fiber and multiply it by four. This timesaving tip makes it easier to compare dry and canned foods while you're standing in the store trying to make up your mind.

As this exercise demonstrates, canned foods typically have much more protein than dry foods. A major reason for this is because grains are needed in dry foods to help them hold their shape after extrusion. Thus, canned and dry foods made by the same manufacturer for the same life stage usually have radically different percentages of protein.

Ingredient list

Dog food manufacturers are required to list the ingredients in each dog food in descending order by amount, on a dry-weight basis (refer to Figure 5-1 for an example). Every ingredient must be listed. Even though your canine companion is a carnivore, there are ways that the dog food company can actually have a grain as the most abundant ingredient in its food while making it *look* like the most abundant ingredient is a meat. Here's how they do it: Let's say that the Chow Hound dog food company is making dog food using wheat as the main ingredient and poultry by-product meal as its second most common ingredient. Instead of just listing *wheat,* the company can break down wheat so that it's listed on the label as *wheat flour, wheat germ meal, wheat bran,* and *wheat middlings.* This allows the company to put *poultry by-product meal* first on the list, because the food contains more poultry by-product than it contains wheat flour, wheat germ meal, wheat bran, or wheat middlings. The four wheat ingredients can be put lower on the list, making the wheat seem like a less important and less abundant ingredient. What does this mean for you and your dog? Don't just look at the first ingredient; scan down the list of ingredients, and if the second, third, fourth, and fifth ingredients on the list are all something other than meat, keep in mind that your dog may be getting more of that than he's getting of meat.

In general, a good-quality dog food will have two quality animal protein sources listed in the first few ingredients. Look for a food that also has two different sources of fat in the ingredient list, for adequate energy and to provide all the essential fatty acids. Poultry, turkey, or chicken fat are higher in quality than animal tallow, because they have more unsaturated fatty acids and are more digestible. Sources of *linoleic acid,* which is an important omega-6 fatty acid, include most vegetable oils soybean, lecithin, corn oil, wheat germ oil, sesame seed oil, and linseed oil, so look for these on your dog food label as well. (***Remember:*** The right balance of animal fats and plant oils is important for a glossy hair coat and soft, pliable skin.) In addition, look for whole grains, vegetables, and other real-food ingredients on the label.

Dog food companies frequently change the composition of their dog foods, so the label on the food you purchased yesterday may not be the same today. Keep the ingredient list from your current dog food label in your wallet and periodically check it against the labels on the dog foods you're buying, just to make sure you're buying a food with the same nutrients in the same proportions as you thought you were.

TIP

Vocabulary 101

If you're confused by some of the lingo on dog-food bags, you're not alone. Here are some of the definitions for the food terms you'll see in the ingredient list:

- **Animal by-product meal:** This consists of rendered animal tissues that don't fit any of the other ingredient definitions. It still can't contain hair, horns, hoofs, hide trimmings, manure, or intestinal contents or extraneous materials.

- **By-products:** Meat by-products are non-human-grade proteins obtained from animal carcasses. They can vary greatly in their digestibility, and there is no way for the consumer to determine their digestibility.

- **Meat:** This is the clean flesh of slaughtered cattle, swine, sheep, or goats. It must come from muscle, tongue, diaphragm, heart, or esophagus.

- **Meat and bone meal:** This is rendered from mammal tissues, including bone. Other than that, it is similar to meat meal.

- **Meat by-products:** This consists of fresh, non-rendered, clean parts of slaughtered mammals. It does not include meat but does include lungs, spleens, kidneys, brains, livers, blood, bones, fat, stomachs, and intestines. It cannot include hair, horns, teeth, and hoofs.

- **Meat meal:** This is a rendered meal made from animal tissues. It cannot contain blood,

hair, hoofs, horns, hide trimmings, manure, or intestinal contents or extraneous materials. It may not contain more than 14 percent indigestible materials. Lamb meal is made from lamb parts. Meat meal is made from cattle, swine, sheep, or goats.

- **Poultry (or chicken or turkey) by-product meal:** This consists of ground, rendered, clean parts of the carcass of slaughtered poultry such as necks, feet, undeveloped eggs, and intestines. It cannot contain beaks or feathers.

- **Poultry (or chicken or turkey) by-products:** This consists of non-rendered clean parts of slaughtered poultry such as heads, feet, and guts. It must not contain feces or foreign matter.

Rendering is a process by which animal parts are heated slowly over a long period of time to liquefy the fat so that it can be removed. What remains is mainly dry proteins and is called *meal*. (You partly render your bacon when you put it on a paper towel before putting it in the microwave. The heat liquefies the fat, which drips onto the paper towel. The bacon comes out dry and crispy.) If you see the term *meal* in reference to plant sources, it means that the oils have been extracted from the plant or grain and the meal is what remains.

Nutritional adequacy statement

Dog food manufacturers can determine the nutritional adequacy of dog foods in two ways. The best way is for the dog food manufacturer to conduct *feeding trials,* in which it feeds its foods to real live dogs and sees whether they like to eat it, whether they gain weight at the proper rate, and whether their blood and bodies have the right composition of proteins and fats. AAFCO requirements state that dogs in feeding trials must be fed the dog food for at least six months. If a dog food has been tested in feeding trials, the label will say so, usually in a statement something like this: "Animal feeding tests using Association of American Feed Control Officials' procedures substantiate that this food provides complete and balanced nutrition for maintenance." Try to choose a food that makes this kind of claim on its package.

Dog food manufacturers can also sell dog foods that have been formulated according to the AAFCO nutritional profiles for dogs but have not been tested on dogs in feeding trials. To make a formulated food, the manufacturer adds an amount of protein that is at least 18 percent for adult dogs, an amount of fat that is at least 5 percent for adult dogs, and the required amounts of all the other required nutrients. If you feed your dog a food that has been formulated but not tested on dogs, then your dog essentially becomes the test subject. There are numerous examples of formulated dog foods that looked good on paper but when fed to dogs resulted in nutritional deficiencies — that's why I recommend that you stay away from foods that have not been tested in dogs.

There is, however, a loophole in the regulations regarding feeding trials for dogs. After a dog food manufacturer has proven by feeding trials that a given food is nutritionally adequate, the manufacturer may state that formulated foods have been tested by feeding trials, as long as the formulated foods are in the same *family*. Unfortunately, there are no guidelines as to the definition of a *family* of dog foods. In this matter, therefore, we are left to trust the dog food manufacturer's word.

Feeding guidelines

Every dog food label must have recommendations regarding how much to feed dogs of different sizes. The feeding guidelines on the label, however, usually *overestimate* the amount of food a typical dog needs to eat every day. Cynics say that this is a ploy on the part of the dog food manufacturers to sell more food. The dog food manufacturers indicate that these guidelines are based on calculations of what typical dogs in their feeding trials needed to satisfy their energy requirements. The dogs in these feeding trials get a great deal of exercise, however, so this may be true. But few dogs fit the mold, and most need much less food than the amount listed on the bag.

See the "Figuring Out How Much to Feed Your Dog" section, later in this chapter, for more information.

Manufacturer's contact information

Manufacturers are required to list the address and telephone number of their customer service departments on every dog food label. In addition, many dog foods now also provide Web site addresses.

Take advantage of this resource. In my experience, the customer service departments of dog food manufacturers are very helpful. If they don't know the answer to a question, they will hunt it down and call you back. If you call a dog food company and they cannot or will not provide the information that you need, don't feed that food to your dog.

Figuring Out How Much to Feed Your Dog

You have your dog's food bowl in hand and the dog food on the counter in front of you. But how do you decide how much food to put in the bowl? If you're just starting to feed a new food, and the label tells you how many calories the food contains, you may want to start with the information in Table 5-1, which lists the calorie requirements of dogs depending on the dog's weight and activity level. For the purposes of the table, an *inactive* dog is one who rarely gets more than a jaunt around the yard, a *moderately active* dog is one who gets 15 to 30 minutes of continuous exercise every day, and a *highly active* dog is one who gets at least several hours of exercise every day.

If the label doesn't provide information on the caloric content of the food, you have to use the manufacturer's recommendations as a starting point. But instead of feeding the amount recommended on the bag, start by feeding 25 percent *less* than the manufacturer recommends, and then increase or decrease the amount as necessary.

If your dog gains weight, decrease the amount of food he's getting. If he loses weight, increase the amount.

Table 5-1	The Caloric Requirements of Dogs		
Caloric Requirements (Based on Activity Level)[1]			
Dog's Weight (In Pounds)	**Inactive**	**Moderately Active**	**Highly Active**
10	234	303	441
20	373	483	702
30	489	633	921
40	593	768	1117
50	689	892	1297

(continued)

Table 5-1 *(continued)*

Dog's Weight (In Pounds)	Caloric Requirements (Based on Activity Level)[1]		
	Inactive	Moderately Active	Highly Active
60	779	1008	1466
70	863	1117	1625
80	944	1222	1777
90	1022	1322	1923
100	1097	1419	2064

[1]*Figures represent the average number of calories required daily to maintain the dog's weight.*

The figures in Table 5-1 include calories from all sources during a given day, including treats and snacks.

As dogs exercise more, they need more calories to maintain their weight. But as dogs get larger, they require relatively fewer calories to maintain their weight. This is because larger dogs generally have slower metabolisms than smaller dogs. Age can affect caloric requirements, too. As a dog goes from 1 to 7 years of age, his energy requirements drop by an incredible 24 percent.

Dogs' metabolisms vary so greatly that the best way to know exactly how many calories your dog needs each day is by trial and error. Feed the amount of food that will maintain your dog's weight. If he loses weight, feed more. If he gains, feed less.

Choosing the Best Food for Your Dog

So how do you make that final decision in terms of what food to provide for your dog? As a general rule, start by feeding a name brand, good quality, commercial balanced diet that has been tested by feeding trials in dogs.

Put more trust in companies that have been around for a while, because they have their own internal quality controls in addition to those imposed on them by the regulatory agencies. They also have more nutritional information on which to base their decisions about which ingredients to use and how to mix them for the best results.

Preservatives and antioxidants in your dog's food

Antioxidants are preservatives that are added to foods to help protect the fats, oils, and fat-soluble compounds such as vitamins from breaking down. Unsaturated fats readily mix with oxygen in the air and become rancid. Rancid fats are not just a problem because they smell bad; they also cause the food to lose its flavor and texture. More importantly, rancid fats can affect a dog's health. When a dog eats rancid fats, he may end up suffering from a relative deficiency of vitamin E, a natural antioxidant that the body uses to combat rancid fat.

Because all dog foods contain *some* unsaturated fats, they all require some sort of antioxidant preservative. Many foods are preserved with preservatives, including BHA, BHT, and ethoxyquin. Ethoxyquin has been especially controversial, because there were concerns that it caused cancer. However, studies in dogs and puppies have not shown an increase in cancer due to ethoxyquin. Still, because of consumer preferences for more natural ingredients, most dog foods are now preserved with vitamin E and vitamin C instead of BHA, BHT, or ethoxyquin. Ironically, the vitamin E and vitamin C that are used in dog food are manmade, too — so they're not exactly "natural."

If you're feeding a dog food that has been preserved with vitamins E and C, be sure the food is less than six months old when you give it to your dog. To determine how old your dog's food is, you need to understand the date codes on the labels. Dog food manufacturers use a variety of codes on the bags to mark the freshness of their foods. Most use a production code that indicates the date and even the time and the plant where the food was made. Other manufacturers use a *best used by* code, which indicates the time by which the food should be consumed. To determine how fresh your dog's food is, call the manufacturer and ask them to explain their code. They will tell you what each number and letter means so that you will always be able to pick the freshest food at the store.

Finally, a food's antioxidant powers are depleted more rapidly during hot humid weather, so in the warm summer months, use food that is less than six months old. Always store your dogs' food in a cool, dry place, and don't buy more than a month's supply at a time.

As a rule, the best quality foods are not the cheapest. However, the reverse isn't necessarily true: Paying a lot for your dog food won't *guarantee* its quality. As you search for the best food, don't hesitate to experiment. Be a good observer. Talk to your veterinarian and other dog people like your breeder. Over time, you will gather more information and be able to make better decisions based on fact as well as experience.

When you have selected a quality food for your furry friend, your job isn't done. You still need to keep close track of your dog's response to the food. Watch his body condition. Your canine companion should maintain a correct weight on his new food. If he gains some weight but looks and acts healthy and full of energy, it may be that the nutrients in the new food are more digestible than those of the previous food, so you don't need to feed as much. If your dog loses weight on his new food, start looking for another. Your dog's coat should grow and glisten on his new food and his skin should be pink and supple, with no sores. A dog's coat is often a reflection of his general health, although it isn't the only monitor you should use. For example, during the spring in temperate climates, most dogs' coats look dry as they shed their heavy winter garb for a lighter spring coat.

One of the best criteria you can use to monitor your dog on a new food is to observe his stools. Stool quality is determined by the ingredients in the food, the relative amounts of different ingredients, the type and amount of fiber, and the digestibility of the ingredients. Small, firm stools indicate a food that is highly digestible. Your dog should not, however, be constipated or straining to defecate. Large stools, particularly if they are somewhat loose, may indicate a food that contains less digestible nutrients and/or a high fiber content. Your dog's stools will vary from day to day. But if your dog often has small, hard stools, consider changing to another food. Those stools may be easy for poop pick-up but they may also mean that your dog is chronically constipated.

What's not on the label

Unfortunately, dog food labels give you no indication of the *quality* of the ingredients used in the food. For example, the label isn't required to say whether grade I or grade V corn is used, even though the quality of corn can make a major difference in the nutritional quality of the dog food. In fact, in the mid-1990s, there was a great deal of rain during one growing season and thousands of acres of farmland were flooded in the midwestern U.S. The quality of grains that year was very low and many stored grains were damaged by fungus. Whether knowingly or not, some of the low-quality and damaged grains were used by dog food manufacturers, resulting in illnesses in dogs.

On dog food labels, there is also no indication of the digestibility of the food. Digestibility is quite a significant issue, however, because nutrients in the food are of no value unless they can be absorbed and used by the dog. For example, iron in the form of rust can't be absorbed by a

dog's body, whereas ferrous sulfate can, yet they both may appear on a dog food label as just *iron.* Where digestibility is concerned, we are at the mercy of the dog food companies. Dog food manufacturers benefit from using digestible ingredients, because they result in smaller stools, which the consumer appreciates and desires. On the other hand, digestible nutrients are more expensive, so this is always a balancing act. If you're interested in knowing the digestibility of your dog's food, you can call the customer service number for the manufacturer.

Dog food manufacturers also don't have to provide specific information on the *palatability* (tastiness) of their foods. They frequently do comment in the banner that their food is highly palatable, but there are no specific guidelines as to what exactly that means. But most dog foods *are* highly palatable. After all, the dog food company won't sell much dog food if dogs turn their noses up at it.

Monitor your dog's attitude and energy level. If you feed your dog a good-quality food, he will have lots of get-up-and-go. He will have the energy and endurance to play all you want. And most of all, he will have that joy for life that we all appreciate in our canine companions.

What's the best dog food for your dollar? Most people find that they save money by buying good-quality, premium foods for their dogs — the kind of food that is sold at pet supply stores rather than grocery stores. This is because dogs need to eat much less of a good quality food to take in their required nutrients. In addition, dogs on high-quality foods probably have fewer health problems and when they do, they heal faster. The icing on the cake is the easier cleanup in the yard.

Paying attention to your dog's special dietary needs

Dogs are considered *facultative carnivores*, which means that their basic carnivorous nature has been modified a bit because they have lived with people and eaten human food for over 120,000 years. Some people theorize that each breed of dog should eat the foods that breed was fed by the people in the countries from which those dogs arose. So Portuguese Water Dogs, who helped the Portuguese fishermen on their boats, would need to have fish as their major source of protein, and Australian Cattle Dogs would need to eat a lot of lamb. Luckily, there doesn't seem to be any foundation for this theory, but if there were, people with dogs of African origin such as Basenjis or Salukis would spend more time shopping for their dogs' dinners than for their own!

Even so, some breeds or lines of dogs do have genetic alterations that result in specific dietary needs. For example, vitamin B12 deficiency occurs in some lines of Giant Schnauzers. Some dogs of the Northern breeds, such as Siberian Huskies and Alaskan Malamutes have difficulty absorbing zinc and therefore need higher levels of zinc in their diets. Bedlington Terriers can have trouble with the metabolism of copper,

causing them to store copper in the liver and eventually suffer from hepatitis, so they need foods that are low in copper. Some Dalmatians metabolize *urea* (a byproduct of the breakdown of proteins) differently from other dogs and get bladder stones, so they need to eat food that is low in *purines* (molecules such as ammonium urate that can form bladder stones). Most of these genetic alterations are well recognized, however, and reputable breeders are working to eliminate these problems in their lines.

Your dog doesn't need to have one of these genetic mutations, however, to have difficulty absorbing nutrients or to be sensitive to certain components of a food. For example, dogs with inflammatory bowel disease may have difficulty absorbing vitamins and often need to be supplemented, particularly with the water-soluble vitamins such as the B vitamins. Dogs also may have different needs depending on their age, activity, body condition, stress levels, and temperament. Even the climate can make a difference in what your dog needs to eat. That's why feeding your dog is really largely dependent on your dog and his unique needs.

Paying Attention to How You Feed Your Dog

Many people *free-feed* their dogs, which is the practice of keeping your dog's bowl full and letting him eat whenever he wants. Although this may seem like an easy approach to feeding, there are many reasons why it is best not to free-feed:

- ✔ **Dogs who are free-fed are more likely to be overweight.** This may not have been true in the past, but with today's highly palatable foods, your dog will enjoy eating long past the point where he is full. The result is that he will likely take in more calories than he needs and carry the fat to prove it.

- ✔ **You can't tell exactly how much your dog is eating.** In fact, you may not recognize your dog is ill until you suddenly notice you haven't been adding much food to his bowl in the past few days. Food intake is one of the best indicators of health, so you should always be in a position to monitor your dog's intake accurately.

- ✔ **Medicating dogs who are free-fed is more difficult.** If you have to give your dog pills, such as heartworm preventive and your dog is free-fed, you will have to make sure you pop it down his throat and he swallows it. If, however, he gets fed two square meals a day, you can just add the pill to his food and it will go right down the hatch!

- ✔ **Free-feeding is difficult in multi-dog households.** Frequently, one dog hogs the food and gains weight while the other dog is deprived of the food and loses weight. Plus, free-feeding is impossible if your dogs require different kinds of food.

So how many times a day should you feed your dog? Puppies should be fed four times a day until they are 3 months of age, when they can be moved to feedings three times a day. At 6 months of age, dogs can be fed twice a day, and this is probably the best feeding schedule for a dog to stay on for life. Some dogs are fed just once a day and get along fine. Occasionally, however, dogs who are fed once a day vomit a little fluid or bile 12 to 18 hours after their last meal. If they are fed twice a day, this problem goes away.

No two dogs are exactly the same. They have different metabolic rates, they have different metabolisms, and they may need to eat different diets. If you have more than one dog, even though it is more convenient to feed all your dogs the same food, make sure you monitor each dog's response to the diet you are feeding and change the food if an individual dog needs it.

Give your dog a quiet place to eat. If there are other dogs in the house, don't feed them from the same bowl. Feed them at a distance from each other so they don't feel threatened that the other dog will come and steal their food. The best solution is to feed your dog in a crate, so he can enjoy his meal in the privacy of his den. After you put the bowl down, give your dog 15 minutes to eat. If he hasn't finished in that time, you are either feeding him too much or he isn't motivated to eat. By removing the bowl, you can be assured that he will be much more motivated to eat at the next meal. Don't be held hostage by a picky dog. If you try to encourage him to eat by talking nicely to him and giving him delectable treats, he will soon up the ante, demanding better and better treats until he's not consuming his dog food at all.

Many veterinary nutritionists believe that we should be rotating our dogs' diets — feeding them one food for three to six months, then switching to another diet. They theorize that abnormal proteins may be formed during the processing of food or that individual foods may have undetectable deficiencies or small differences in the availability of certain nutrients. By rotating your dog to a new food every three to six months, you prevent too much exposure to the abnormality in any given food.

The fresh factor

Giving your dog fresh vegetables and even some fresh fruit on a regular basis is a good idea. Wolves (from which our dogs are descended) eat the greens and grains from their prey's stomach and also eat grasses and berries at times. Dogs enjoy fresh vegetables and benefit from the vitamins and fiber they provide. The only vegetable to stay away from is raw onions (cooked onions are fine).

Feed your dog the leftovers from your preparations for dinner in addition to other vegetables, especially the meats and vegetables. That way both you and your dog benefit. Just make sure that vegetables aren't the major component of your dog's food.

If you give the vegetables in large pieces, they provide mostly fiber because dogs don't have the enzymes to digest *cellulose,* the major component of the cell walls of plants. If, however, you put the vegetables through a juicer or a super-blender that breaks down the cell walls and turns the vegetables to mush, your dog will also benefit from the nutritional content of the vegetable. It's your choice!

Chapter 6

Supplementing Your Dog's Diet

*B*elieve it or not, there really is no one accepted definition of what a nutritional supplement is, which means that just about anything that can be put in your dog's mouth can be sold under the name *supplement*. The problem is that you don't want to be putting just anything in your dog's mouth.

The American Veterinary Medical Association (AVMA) defines supplements as micronutrients, macronutrients, and other nutritional additives that are used as therapeutic agents. The concept of supplements being used for *therapy* is important: It implies that supplements should be used to improve your dog's health. That, in turn, implies that supplements should be standardized and rigorously tested for their therapeutic effects, their correct dose range, and their toxicity, just like medicines are.

Unfortunately, more often than not, supplements for dogs (and often for humans, too) have not been tested at all. They frequently are plants or minerals or combinations of products obtained from nature for which there has been some professed benefit. Many nutritional supplements are, indeed, beneficial when used properly. But some are not. In fact, some supplements may even be harmful.

In this chapter, I explain what supplements are, how they can be used, which ones have been found to be beneficial, and in which circumstances. I also provide some warnings about the use of supplements and describe guidelines as to how you can figure out whether to supplement your dog with a given product.

Let the Buyer Beware

Although there are government regulations about truth in advertising, particularly about making medical claims that are not proven in scientifically controlled trials, supplements themselves are largely unregulated. So you can go to the pharmacy and see ginkgo biloba for sale, but no matter how closely you read the label, you won't find a statement anywhere as to why you may want to take ginkgo biloba.

The Food and Drug Administration (FDA) has strict regulations as to what health claims may be made on a label. Companies have ways of getting around these regulations, however. For example, in their advertisements they frequently imply the benefits of their products rather than state them specifically. They show people giving testimonials rather than specifically stating the benefits their product is alleged to provide. In addition, you will notice that they rarely give guarantees. With the burgeoning supplement industry, the federal government just doesn't have enough staff to monitor the many supplements on the market, let alone to police the companies and ensure even minimum standards of quality control. In fact, as of this writing, the United States Department of Agriculture (USDA) has only two people who regulate the supplement industry for the entire U.S.

Given that the supplement industry is largely unregulated, here are some of the potential problems with the production and marketing of supplements:

- ✔ **There are no standards for quality control in the production of supplements.** One manufacturer of an herbal supplement may be careful to select organically grown plants only from farmers who use natural methods to control weeds and pests. But another company may buy herbs that have been treated with toxic pesticides and herbicides, or even herbs that are left over from other undefined manufacturing processes. And both products may appear identical when you read the labels. For example, both manufacturers can use the term *natural* on the label, even though the first is clearly more natural than the second.

- ✔ **Supplements can interfere with essential components of your dog's basic diet, with medications your dog may be taking, and with other supplements.** Be careful to supplement only with specific nutrients that your dog needs. For example, some Siberian Huskies (and other breeds) do not efficiently absorb zinc from their foods. They develop thickened, crusty skin with scabs and lose their hair. If your dog has this problem and you give her a zinc supplement to combat it, and if you also add abundant calcium to her food, your dog won't be able to absorb the supplemental zinc, because calcium interferes with the zinc's absorption.

✔ **Just because a supplement is a normal constituent of many dogs' diets, it isn't inherently safe.** Although reports about supplements' toxicity are quite alarming, they also have several inherent problems. The FDA's adverse event-reporting system for dietary supplements is both voluntary and anonymous, making it vulnerable to error.

So how can you know what you're really getting when it comes to supplements? Buy from companies that have been in business for a number of years and that have a reputation to uphold. Companies that produce supplements start up and go under just about every day, so purchasing from a company that has a long-term commitment to its product is essential.

You can also investigate whether you're purchasing a quality product by going to one of the Web sites that report the results of independent tests on supplement quality. One such site is ConsumerLab.com (`www.consumerlab.com`), which purchases large numbers of supplements and sends them out for independent testing to measure the products' purity and to determine whether the products contain the amounts of active ingredients that are listed on the labels. These reports are posted on the ConsumerLab.com Web site. Another excellent Internet source of information on supplements is SupplementQuality.com (`www.supplementquality.com`), which includes information on standards and regulations for supplements, safety issues, and how to read the labels.

Before giving your dog any supplement, discuss it with your veterinarian or with a veterinary herbalist or nutritionist.

Sharks as cancer-fighters?

An example of supplement misinformation was the proposed use of shark cartilage to prevent cancer in humans. In the early 1990s, a book was published stating that sharks don't get cancer and implying that shark cartilage contained cancer-preventive components. Because cancer is something that all of us are familiar with and many of us live in fear of, the media latched onto this subject and soon everyone was talking about shark cartilage as a cure for cancer. As a pathologist who has performed postmortem examinations on many different species of animals from zoos and aquaria, including sharks, I can tell you that sharks *do,* in fact, get cancer. In fact, they actually can get cancer that begins in the cartilage (the very part of the shark that was touted as having cancer-preventive substances). Nonetheless, I was surprised to see a booming cottage industry begin, with various companies selling shark products to prevent cancer.

Calcium: It doesn't always do a body good

My first dog as an adult was an Irish Wolfhound, Shauna. I had gone for so long without a dog as I went through college and veterinary school that when I finally had the time to spend with a dog I just wanted to get the biggest dog I could. My puppy's breeder told me to be sure to supplement her diet with lots of bone meal (essentially calcium and phosphorus), because she was a giant breed and needed lots of calcium to grow. So I faithfully supplemented her with what we now know was much more calcium than she should have received.

Shauna developed hip dysplasia, elbow dysplasia, and cervical vertebral instability (Wobblers syndrome), and she died of bone cancer at the tender age of 5 years. Based on scientific studies on growing dogs, I now know that the high levels of calcium I fed her caused or at least contributed significantly to those problems.

Determining Whether Supplements Are Necessary

So why supplement your dog's food? The truth is that most dogs don't require supplements if they are eating a complete and balanced premium-quality dog food and are healthy. But just as dogs' metabolic needs differ, so may their nutritional requirements. Your dog may not have exactly the same nutritional requirements as the dogs in which her food was tested. If you give your dog an excellent quality food, but she isn't looking and acting first-rate, she may need her diet supplemented with additional nutrients.

If you're thinking about supplementing your dog's diet, start with a visit to your veterinarian. He will give your dog a complete physical examination and will take blood and urine samples to determine whether all systems are go. He may recommend supplementation with specific dietary or herbal products. If you want more information or disagree with your veterinarian's assessment, you can always ask for a referral to a veterinary nutritionist or herbalist.

Don't just supplement your dog because your neighbor is supplementing his. You need to have a specific reason for supplementing your dog's diet.

Here are three rules for intelligent supplementation:

✔ **Give a supplement only if your dog needs it and only in the amount that she needs.** Supplement only with the amount recommended by your veterinarian or a veterinary nutritionist or herbalist. Many of the minerals, for example, have a very narrow range between an effective level and a toxic level. Where supplements are concerned, more is not necessarily better.

✔ **Feed only a supplement that lists its exact makeup on the label.** A supplement that says it contains ground abalone shells, organically grown barley, and kelp, but doesn't tell you exactly how many milligrams of calcium, phosphorus, magnesium, and other minerals are in the product is keeping important information from you, the consumer. The manufacturer knows the exact composition of the product, and it should provide that information to the consumer.

✔ **If your dog has no response (or a negative response) to the supplement after six to eight weeks, stop feeding it.** Observation is the key here. Many people feed one supplement and then another and then another. After a while, they don't really know what their dog is being fed and why. I frequently talk to people who are feeding upwards of six to eight different supplements to their dogs. They generally are uncertain as to why they are feeding the supplements, except that someone, usually a salesperson, told them it would help their dogs. Remember to have a healthy distrust of advertised claims where supplements are concerned, just as you have in other aspects of your life.

There is one exception to this last rule. If your dog has been diagnosed by a veterinarian as having degenerative joint disease, such as hip dysplasia, she will probably benefit from supplementation with a joint-protective nutraceutical (covered in more detail later in this chapter) even if she appears to show no response. Sometimes people who supplement their dogs with joint-protective nutraceuticals report that their dogs seem to show no signs of improvement in comfort or mobility. However, when they cease to supplement, the dog becomes very stiff and painful. I believe that many such dogs, before being given the supplement, are stoic, living with the pain of arthritis without much complaint. They may not, therefore, reveal that they feel better upon supplementation. But when the supplement is removed, they really do notice the difference, and they show that in their behavior.

The contents of your dog's supplement can change without warning. Always carry a copy of the label in your wallet and check it against the label on the replacement product you are about to buy.

Being Aware of the Benefits of Supplementation

Despite the warnings and cautions that I start this chapter with, supplements can be a benefit to your dog under the right circumstances. In the following sections, I highlight three key areas of your dog's health that can be improved by the use of supplements.

Always discuss supplementation with your vet before venturing into these often muddy waters.

Boosting your dog's nutrition

Nutrients assist the body in healing from an illness or injury. When your dog is healthy, the basic nutritional components are sufficient to maintain her health. But when your dog is ill, she may need additional specific nutrients to promote healing or she may need the basic nutrients in different proportions than are required just to maintain her health.

Antioxidants

Antioxidants are helpful molecules that may help to decrease your dog's risk of developing cancer. In addition, antioxidants can be helpful in reducing the tissue damage associated with allergies and other inflammatory diseases or infections.

There are a number of natural antioxidants, including vitamins C and E, *carotenoids* (antioxidants found in orange and green vegetables that also can be converted by the body into vitamin A), and *bioflavonoids* (antioxidants found in fruits and vegetables that have vitamin C-like activity). Antioxidants are abundant in fresh foods but they are killed during the high-temperature processing of dog foods. So they are added back to processed dog foods, usually in the form of vitamins C and E. Providing antioxidants to your dog in the form of fresh foods, especially vegetables and fruits, is a good idea.

Although dogs do make their own vitamin C, they don't make large amounts of it, and they don't increase their production during times of stress when it may be helpful to have increased levels of antioxidants. I recommend, therefore, that dogs be given additional vitamin C and other antioxidants such as vitamin E and carotenoids during times of stress, such as when they are ill. Antioxidants can be helpful for dogs who are suffering from allergies or cancer. And growing puppies may benefit from additional vitamin C as well.

In addition to vitamins C and E, other natural antioxidants are present in fresh foods, including the enzymes *superoxide dismutase* and *catalase.* Because these also are destroyed during the processing of dog food, providing them to your dog during times of illness can be helpful.

The presence of natural antioxidants is just one of many reasons why I recommend that every dog be given fresh vegetables and fruits even if they are fed a complete and balanced dog food. Mixed bioflavonoids are antioxidants that are found in fruits (particularly citrus fruits), seeds, and other plant material.

Fish oil

Fish oil provides essential fatty acids, particularly omega-3 fatty acids, which have natural anti-inflammatory benefits (see Chapter 4 for more information). Fish oils, therefore, can be helpful for nutritional therapy in the treatment of cancer, allergies, kidney disease, heart disease, and diabetes.

Some people are concerned about the feeding of fish oils to dogs, however, because fish may be contaminated with heavy metals from pollution. Flaxseed oil is the best nonanimal substitute for fish oil; the active ingredient in flaxseed oil is linoleic acid. Many veterinary nutritionists believe that flaxseed is an acceptable source of essential fatty acids for healthy dogs. It may, however, be important for sick animals to receive their essential fatty acids in the form of fish oil as opposed to flaxseed oil, because it is a natural animal source of omega-3 fatty acids.

Helping your dog battle joint diseases

Arthritis, or *degenerative joint disease,* is one of the most common and most difficult to manage problems in dogs, especially older dogs. It arises whenever there is an abnormality in the fit of the bones that form joints. In hip dysplasia, for example, the ball of the femur does not fit tightly into the socket of the hip, so when the dog walks, the ball of the femur rubs against the socket, creating friction. Whenever there is friction in a joint, the bones respond by creating scar tissue and new bone. And this eventually results in arthritis. As anyone who suffers from arthritis will tell you, the constant grinding of bone against bone is extremely painful — and the same is true for our canine companions with arthritis. For many years, veterinarians thought that degenerative joint disease was irreversible and that the best that we can do is give the dog anti-inflammatory drugs (to try to reduce the development of scar tissue) and painkillers (to try to dull the pain). Now that assumption has been challenged.

In the last decade, many supplements have hit the market claiming to not only protect joints from continuing injury, but also to repair injured joints. These products are derived from naturally occurring substances such as the green-lipped mussel or the tracheas of cattle. These naturally occurring therapeutics are called *nutraceuticals* (to differentiate them from man-made drugs, or *pharmaceuticals*). These products are sold singly and in combination with other nutraceuticals and sometimes with vitamins, minerals, and antioxidants under a multitude of names. New products come out every month.

Being aware of everything that you're putting in your dog's mouth is important, so this growing number of products can be very confusing. As with other nutritional supplements, nutraceuticals are not regulated by federal agencies as pharmaceuticals are, which places even more responsibility on you, the consumer.

One of the first nutraceuticals used in the treatment of degenerative joint disease was in an injectable form called Adequan. This product was shown to reduce the inflammation and pain of arthritis in horses and to promote healing of damaged joint cartilage. These same effects have been seen in dogs, and the product remains an excellent anti-arthritis treatment for our canine companions. One major advantage of Adequan is that, because it is injectable, it acts immediately.

All the other nutraceuticals are designed for oral supplementation. Because some of these molecules are broken down and digested in the stomach, it may take as long as six to eight weeks for the oral products to reach effective levels.

Because nutraceuticals are naturally occurring substances, they don't have the same potential for toxicity as pharmaceuticals. But neither are they totally harmless. There is thought to be some risk of bleeding in dogs who are fed high levels of nutraceuticals, particularly if the dog has a pre-existing blood-clotting problem.

So how do you know whether your dog may benefit from joint-protective nutraceuticals? If your dog has been diagnosed by a veterinarian as having a problem that results in less than ideal joint conformation or fit, she will probably benefit from supplementation with a mixture of nutraceuticals. The most common such problems are hip dysplasia, elbow dysplasia, cervical vertebral instability, patellar luxation, degenerative disk disease, and osteochondrosis dissecans (OCD). In addition, if your dog has had an injury to any component of a joint, such as damage to the anterior cruciate ligament of the knee, any other torn or ruptured ligament, or a fracture involving the joint, she also will benefit from nutraceutical supplementation. Discuss your interest in using joint-protective supplements with your vet. He may have experience with a supplement that has been particularly effective in other dogs with the same problem.

Because our dogs are active throughout their lives, they have a certain amount of wear and tear on the joints. So I recommend giving all canine seniors joint-protective nutraceuticals starting at about 8 years of age. By that age, they probably have a few joint-related aches and pains.

I don't recommend supplementing healthy adult dogs or growing puppies with joint-protective nutraceuticals, because you risk covering up the pain associated with acute joint damage and thus missing the opportunity to make a correct diagnosis and treat the problem more appropriately at the time it happens.

As with other nutritional supplements, be sure to purchase nutraceuticals only from a reputable company. With the huge increase in the use of these products, not only in dogs but in humans, too, many fly-by-night companies have arisen to feast on the profits from unsuspecting buyers. Many of these products have less than the advertised amounts of product and some have even been found to have none. So be a wise consumer and buy from companies that have a reputation to uphold. You may need to experiment to see which product most benefits your dog.

Making digestion easier for your dog

A healthy dog's intestinal tract is perfectly capable of supplying the enzymes needed to digest the starches, lipids, and proteins in her food. But dogs who are ill may need a little help getting the most out of the food they eat.

Digestive enzymes

If your dog has chronic diarrhea of unknown cause or suffers from a lot of flatulence, digestive enzymes may help her digest her food. They may also help animals with excessive shedding, dry flaky skin, brittle haircoat, and other abnormalities of the skin and hair by making nutrients, especially fats, more available for absorption. Thin animals or those who seem unable to gain weight despite eating, will probably benefit from added enzymes as well. Older animals, especially, can benefit from the addition of digestive enzymes to their food, because older animals may lose the ability to produce sufficient enzymes on their own. There is also some evidence that adding digestive enzymes to a dog's food may help reduce chronic inflammation such as in dogs with arthritis, allergies, or autoimmune diseases.

There are many different enzyme formulations on the market. Some have to be added to the food 20 to 30 minutes before feeding, whereas others don't, so be sure to check the label of the enzymes you buy. Some formulations also contain vitamins, minerals, and/or fatty acids, but I recommend avoiding these and adding specific nutrients only as necessary.

Probiotics

Probiotics are live, beneficial bacteria that are normally present in the gastrointestinal tract and help to maintain the proper environment for digestion. They help to digest certain food components that your dog isn't able to break down on her own. This allows your dog to absorb all the nutrients she requires for robust health. Probiotic bacteria also may prevent bad bacteria such as *Salmonella* from gaining a foothold and replicating in the intestine.

If your dog commonly suffers digestive upsets such as frequent gas or bouts of diarrhea, she may have an imbalance in her intestinal bacteria. Try giving her probiotics. Probiotics are also helpful when your dog is being treated with antibiotics, because the antibiotics may kill the natural beneficial bacteria in the intestine in addition to the harmful bacteria at which they are targeted. Even stress can alter your dog's normal gastrointestinal bacteria, making your dog more susceptible to gastrointestinal upsets. Addition of probiotics during times of stress may help prevent diarrhea or gas or even gastrointestinal discomfort that your dog doesn't visibly complain about.

A recent study of the viability of commercial probiotics showed that only 2 of 13 products matched their label specifications. Some contained no viable bacteria at all. Because probiotics are *live* bacteria, they don't have a very long shelf life so get them fresh from a health food store, keep them refrigerated, and give your dog lots of them.

Although yogurt may be a good source of *Lactobacillus acidophilus* (a species of beneficial bacteria), it frequently doesn't contain large quantities of live bacteria. In addition, if your dog's digestive upset is caused in part by lactose intolerance, yogurt may actually exacerbate the problem rather than get rid of it.

Chapter 7

Good Ol' Home Cookin'

*T*he majority of dogs today are fed commercially prepared dog food, and they're doing pretty well on it. Dogs today are healthier and live longer than at any other period in their history. Of course, they also have the benefit of excellent veterinary care, vaccinations to prevent fatal infectious diseases such as rabies and distemper, and confinement in homes and yards to protect them from traffic.

But all is not perfect in the canine kingdom. Many, many dogs suffer from allergies and other disorders caused by an overreaction of the dog's immune system. Many dogs also die from cancer, a condition that is partly related to the inability of the immune system to detect and destroy abnormal cells. But there is an ongoing debate about whether more dogs have allergies and cancer today than in the past, or whether we're simply better at diagnosing these problems. Maybe the increased rate of allergies and cancer is just a result of the fact that dogs are living longer and are exposed to more pollutants and toxins, so they have a greater chance of developing these problems. Or maybe we're inadvertently breeding lines of dogs with an increased susceptibility to cancer, and that explains the numbers. These interactions between genetics and the environment are very difficult to dissect, so the debate rages on, and food is at the heart of it.

The Argument against Processed Foods

A growing body of people believe that we are not serving our dogs well by feeding them processed dog foods. There is an increasing concern that prepared dog foods, particularly those that are produced by the extrusion process, may have been altered in such a way that they're somehow contributing to some of the immune-related health problems of dogs.

How may the extrusion process alter dog food? First, extrusion requires that the food be heated to between 80 and 200 degrees for up to an hour and a half. This heat may destroy natural enzymes that the original food ingredients contained. It may also break down vitamins and natural antioxidants that are present in the food. The dog food manufacturers attempt to compensate for the lost nutrients by adding them back after the extruded food cools. But do we really know enough about what all those nutrients are, their correct form, and the balance between them to correctly replace what was lost? And wouldn't it be better if the original nutrients were just retained in the first place?

Some canine nutritionists are also concerned that the high temperatures used in the extrusion process alter proteins in the foods, causing them to change shape and appear foreign to the immune system. This may be a particular problem when there is a break in the lining of the intestinal tract that forms a barrier between the intestinal environment and the body. For example, a viral or bacterial infection may damage the cells that line the intestinal tract; treatment with non-steroidal anti-inflammatory drugs such as aspirin can also cause breaks in the intestinal lining. Those altered proteins can then be exposed to the immune system, which identifies them as foreign and mounts an immune response. Over time, if the body is continuously exposed to such proteins, the dog may develop an immune response to that component in his food. And this may be one way that food allergies develop.

The Pros and Cons of Homemade Diets

Homemade diets — just like any other diet — have advantages and disadvantages. So before you jump on the home-cooking bandwagon, be sure that it's right for your dog. The following sections are a great place to start.

Come and get it!: Considering the advantages to homemade meals

Veterinarians are seeing increasing numbers of dogs with allergies that improve significantly or recover completely when put on homemade diets. We're discovering that there is more to feeding dogs than just providing them with the essential nutrients at levels that prevent deficiencies. In fact, dogs may be healthier if they are fed *natural foods* (that is, foods that are not altered by chemical processes). In addition, individual dogs may need certain nutrients that are outside the nutritional guidelines provided by the AAFCO. These concerns have led people to reexamine what they are feeding their dogs and to look for a better way. As one solution, many people are feeding their dogs homemade diets.

Perhaps the biggest advantage to homemade diets is what I call the *health factor*. If your dog has food allergies, persistent skin problems, or frequent gastrointestinal upsets, he will likely improve significantly on a properly formulated homemade food. If your dog is a canine athlete, particularly if he is a working stock dog or competes in some of the tougher canine sporting events such as mushing, field trials, and herding trials, he may have more strength and endurance if he is fed a nutritionally complete and balanced homemade diet, or if his diet is supplemented with substantial amounts of protein and fats.

By preparing a homemade diet, you are able to feed your dog healthy, natural nutrients. The foods you give your dog will retain their vitamins, enzymes, and antioxidants. In addition, you will have the flexibility to tailor your dog's food to his specific needs. You also have the advantage of knowing the quality and freshness of the foods that comprise your dog's diet.

Dogs are not vegetarians. They need protein, preferably animal protein, to live a long and healthy life. If you are a vegetarian, you probably don't like to handle meat. But keep in mind that your dog will do much better if you don't impose your way of life on him.

Being sure to look at the drawbacks

If you're thinking about feeding your dog a homemade diet, you need to be aware of some of the drawbacks. First, and probably most important, unless you are a canine nutritionist, you probably don't know how to formulate a complete and balanced diet for your dog, so you have to get good advice on what to feed. I provide several examples of complete and balanced diets later in this chapter. But you should also buy books, get on the Internet, and talk to other dog people. Dog lovers are passionate about nutrition, and they will be glad to share their opinions! Be sure not to believe *everything* you read, however. In addition, always talk with your vet about the diet you have chosen to feed.

Some of the published homemade diets are now out of date because new nutritional information has become available. This is of particular concern for homemade diets in books that were published prior to the mid-1990s, when scientists found that growing dogs did not need the high levels of calcium previously recommended.

Recently, veterinarians at Tufts University Veterinary School and the University of Pennsylvania Veterinary School performed a study in which they tested the nutritional content of three popular homemade and two commercial raw diets. A nutritional analysis showed that the majority of the diets had deficiencies or excesses of calcium and/or phosphorus, and that their calcium-to-phosphorus ratios, which should be 2-to-1, were also abnormal. This means that growing dogs fed these diets would be at high risk for the development of bone and joint deformities. Low levels of potassium, magnesium, iron, manganese, and zinc were also found, whereas vitamin D, which can be toxic at high levels, was very high in all the diets.

But you *can* stack the nutritional cards in your dog's favor while feeding a homemade diet. Make sure that you feed a diet that is complete and balanced. (Several complete and balanced diets are provided in this chapter.) If you get a recipe for a homemade diet from another book, be sure that the diet is listed as being complete and balanced. As an alternative, you can contact a canine nutritional service and get the nutritional content of your dog's diet estimated. To locate a veterinary nutritionist, call the American College of Veterinary Nutrition at 540-552-3988, or visit its Web site at www.acvn.org. A veterinary nutrition service will ask you to weigh and measure everything that you feed your dog. For a moderate fee, they will estimate the levels of proteins, fats, carbohydrates, vitamins, and minerals that your dog is eating. If your dog's diet is imbalanced, they will make suggestions as to how you can modify it. Using a service like this can help you be a little more confident that you're feeding your dog what he needs.

The very best way to ensure that the homemade diet you are feeding is complete and balanced according to our most up-to-date nutritional knowledge is to send a sample of your dog's food to a nutrition laboratory to be tested. Just send 1 to 2 pounds of food that is representative of what you feed your dog to the NY DHIA, Forage Analysis Lab, 730 Warren Road, Ithaca, NY 14850-9877 (or call them at 607-257-1272), and for less than $50, the lab will give you a report that tells you exactly what levels of protein, fat, carbohydrates, calcium, phosphorus, and other minerals and vitamins are in your dog's diet. This is the best way to be sure that your dog is being fed for health and longevity.

What About Raw Diets?

Raw diets based on feeding raw, meaty bones to dogs, have become popular in the last few years. Raw meat is what wolves eat, and wolves are our canine companions' ancestors. Feeding raw food avoids the potential loss of nutrients associated with cooking. The bones provide a source of calcium and other minerals and are excellent for keeping dogs' teeth clean. Proponents of feeding raw meaty bones also claim that the bones don't pose any risk to dogs' health, and many dogs do well eating them.

Sadly, however, at veterinary clinics across the country, dogs fed raw diets have been treated for fractured teeth, intestinal obstructions, perforations, and bacterial infections of the abdomen (a result of intestinal perforation), and some have even died.

Another disadvantage of raw diets is the public health hazard associated with the handling and feeding of raw beef and poultry. Most of us are aware of the high incidence of contamination of meat and poultry with bacteria such as *Salmonella* and *E. coli.* Every few weeks you hear another report in the media of people becoming seriously ill and even dying from eating poorly cooked meats that were contaminated with these bacteria. (I know how ill *Salmonella* can make a person, because when I was in veterinary practice I contracted it from a horse with diarrhea. I became so dehydrated that the skin on my face and fingers sloughed off and I was hospitalized for over a week. *Salmonella* is not something to be blasé about.) In a scientific study, feces from nearly 1,000 sled dogs in Alaska were tested for *Salmonella.* Most sled dogs that are run long distances are fed raw diets because of their incredible need for immediately available high-quality proteins and fats. An alarming 70 percent of the dogs were found to be shedding *Salmonella* in their feces. Thus, feeding raw foods to dogs constitutes a significant public health hazard, especially to children, elderly people, and others whose immune systems may be compromised.

There is one final myth about raw diets that I feel I must dispel: the concept that dogs do not become ill from *pathogenic* (disease-causing) organisms in raw meats. I recently read a letter from a woman who had been feeding her Great Dane raw beef. The dog had suddenly become very ill; he was disoriented and unable to keep his balance. Over the next two days, the dog became totally blind and paralyzed. A complete work-up at a veterinary hospital showed that the dog's brain was infected with *Neospora caninum,* a parasite that is common in raw beef. Despite aggressive antiparasitic treatment, the dog will never recover his sight and it is unlikely that he will ever walk normally again. Because of this and other similar studies and reports, I do not currently recommend feeding raw foods to dogs. We just can't trust our raw meat to be free of contamination with pathogenic organisms.

So, if cooking kills vitamins and enzymes, but raw, meaty bones are not a healthy choice, what alternative is there if you want to feed a healthy, fresh homemade diet? In my opinion, the best approach is to cook your dog's meat gently, to medium well done. Sure, you'll lose a few nutrients, but the tradeoff in your dog's health is huge. And don't forget, by using fresh vegetables and fruits (see Figure 7-1), you will be providing your canine companion with lots of healthy vitamins, enzymes, and antioxidants as well. Don't feed bones to your dog. Instead, supply your dog with the exact amount of calcium he needs through supplementation.

Figure 7-1:
Vegetables are a great source of vitamins, enzymes, and antioxidants for your dog.

Complete and Balanced Homemade Diets

For the recipes in this section, I consulted with a board-certified veterinary nutritionist to provide you with the best nutritionally complete and balanced homemade diets for your dog. In this section, I provide three recipes for homemade dog foods — one for puppies, one for adult dogs, and one for canine senior citizens. I also give you a breakdown of the nutritional components of each diet.

Even though these diets were formulated to be complete and balanced, they aren't necessarily ideal for *your* dog. Always observe your dog to be sure that the food you're feeding is providing him with what he needs. If he is maintaining his weight without getting fat, and has strong muscles, a shiny coat, healthy skin, a sparkle in his eyes, and the energy and attitude to run and play any time he wants, you'll know the diet is working.

If your dog has allergies, use sources of protein and/or carbohydrate that he isn't allergic to (see Chapter 8 for special diets for dogs with allergies). For example, you can substitute turkey for chicken or pasta for rice.

Homemade diets vary quite a bit in their nutritional profile depending on the ingredients used and the methods of preparation. Be sure to watch your dog to see that he is active and alert, with lots of zest, sparkling eyes, and a shiny coat. If your dog lacks energy, has frequent gastrointestinal upsets, loses weight, or has a dull coat, make an appointment to discuss your dog's diet with your veterinarian.

Nutritional formulations for all recipes were provided by Veterinary Nutritional Consultations, Inc., at www.petdiets.com.

Quick 'n Nutritious Adult Dog Diet

This recipe makes enough to feed an average 50-pound dog for one day. You can cook enough food for a week, freeze half, and refrigerate the rest to feed over the next three days. Dogs differ greatly in the amount of food they need to maintain their body weight, however, so you may need to feed more or less than the amount listed. If your dog is bigger or smaller than 50 pounds, just adjust the recipe accordingly. Feed only the amount of food that your dog will consume in 15 minutes at each feeding. *Remember:* Because this food has no preservatives, always refrigerate the food and do not store more than three days' worth of food in the refrigerator. Also, you can find the Theragran-M Advanced and calcium carbonate (for example, Tums) at grocery stores and pharmacies.

2⅛ cups large-grain brown rice, cooked

5 ounces roasted chicken (dark meat), roasted turkey (dark meat), beef, or fish

1 teaspoon corn oil

½ teaspoon light salt

2100 milligrams calcium carbonate

2 caplets Theragran-M Advanced

2 cloves crushed garlic (optional)

Lettuce, broccoli, or carrots, washed (optional)

1 Cook the rice until light and fluffy.

2 Bake the chicken, beef, fish, or turkey at 325 degrees for 30 minutes.

3 Crush the calcium carbonate and Theragran-M tablets.

4 Mix all ingredients.

5 Add 2 cloves crushed garlic, if desired for flavor. Add washed, low-calorie vegetables such as lettuce, broccoli, or carrots for extra flavor and fiber, if your dog likes them.

6 Feed warm (heating gently in the microwave if necessary) for better flavor.

Nutrition at a glance (per day, or 2 servings, on a dry-matter basis): calories 875, protein 26%, fat 12%, fiber 4.3% (minimum), linoleic acid 3.8%, calcium 0.5%, phosphorus 0.36%

Healthy, Happy Puppy Diet

This recipe is enough to feed a medium- to large-breed, 25-pound, 2- to 9-month-old puppy for one day. Depending on the size of your puppy, he may eat more or less than the amount in this recipe, so you can adjust the recipe accordingly. Feed only the amount of food that your dog will consume in 15 minutes at each feeding. *Remember:* Because this food has no preservatives, always refrigerate the food and do not store more than three days' worth of food in the refrigerator. Also, you can find the Theragran-M Advanced and calcium carbonate (for example, Tums) at grocery stores and pharmacies. Feed this diet to your puppy up to 9 months of age. After that, switch your pup to the Quick 'n Nutritious Adult Dog Diet.

1½ cups large-grain brown rice, cooked

5 ounces roasted chicken (dark meat)

¾ cup cottage cheese (4% fat)

1 teaspoon corn oil

⅔ teaspoon light salt

3100 milligrams calcium carbonate

3½ caplets Theragran-M Advanced

2 cloves crushed garlic (optional)

Lettuce, broccoli, or carrots, washed (optional)

1 Cook the rice until light and fluffy.

2 Bake the chicken at 325 degrees for 30 minutes.

3 Crush the calcium carbonate and Theragran-M Advanced tablets.

4 Mix all ingredients.

5 Add 2 cloves crushed garlic, if desired for flavor. Add washed, low-calorie vegetables such as lettuce, broccoli, or carrots for extra flavor and fiber, if your dog likes them.

6 Feed warm (heating gently in the microwave if necessary) for better flavor.

Nutrition at a glance (per day, on a dry-matter basis): calories 865, protein 35%, fat 15%; fiber 3% (minimum); linoleic acid 3%, calcium 0.8%, phosphorus 0.4%

Senior Citizen Sustenance

This recipe is enough to feed a 50-pound senior dog for one day. Your older dog will benefit from this food if he is showing signs of aging such as stiffness, graying of the face, or reduced tolerance for exercise. Your dog may eat more or less than the amount in this recipe, so you can adjust the recipe accordingly. Feed only the amount of food that your dog will consume in 15 minutes at each feeding. ***Remember:*** Because this food has no preservatives, always refrigerate the food and do not store more than three days' worth of food in the refrigerator. Also, you can find the Theragran-M Advanced and calcium carbonate (for example, Tums) at grocery stores and pharmacies.

2 cups large-grain brown rice, cooked

2 ounces roasted chicken (dark meat)

1 medium egg, cooked

1 teaspoon corn oil

½ teaspoon light salt

1700 milligrams calcium carbonate

1½ caplets Theragran-M Advanced

1 Cook the rice until light and fluffy.

2 Bake the chicken at 325 degrees for 30 minutes.

3 Crush the calcium carbonate and Theragran-M Advanced tablets.

4 Mix all ingredients.

5 Add 2 cloves crushed garlic, if desired for flavor. Add washed, low-calorie vegetables such as lettuce, broccoli, or carrots for extra flavor and fiber, if your dog likes them.

6 Feed warm (heating gently in the microwave if necessary) for better flavor.

Nutrition at a glance (per day, or 2 servings, on a dry-matter basis): calories 728, protein 21%, fat 12.5%, fiber 4.6% (minimum), linoleic acid 4%, calcium 0.5%, phosphorus 0.36%

Chapter 8

Meeting Your Dog's Special Nutritional Needs

....

In This Chapter

▶ Watching your dog's weight

▶ Making sure your large-breed puppy grows at the right rate

▶ Helping your dog through cancer and heart disease

▶ Changing your dog's diet when her stomach is upset

....

*W*hen you were a kid and you stayed home from school sick, did your mother give you chicken soup? If she was anything like my mom, she told you that her chicken soup had special healing powers. And if you were anything like me, you figured she was just teasing you and that what really made you feel better was the love with which the soup was prepared and offered. But studies show that chicken soup really does contain healing ingredients. So although your mom's recipe wasn't any more magical than the mom next door, she wasn't completely off her rocker when she told you that her soup would make you feel better.

In fact, if you really think about it, the fact that food is important for healing makes perfect sense. Proteins supply amino acids, which the body needs to heal wounds and repair tissues that have been damaged by infections, inflammation, or cancer. The immune system relies on proteins and fats for the production of antibodies and to fuel immune cells, which attack infectious organisms and destroy tumor cells. And when your dog has a fever, her body's energy demands are increased by 5 to 7 percent, so she needs more calories and nutrients to prevent her body from falling into a negative energy balance.

By modifying your dog's diet, you can reduce the severity of the disease from which she's suffering, just like your mom's chicken soup did for you. By tweaking her diet just a bit, you can help a dog with allergies stop scratching so much, help a pooch with congestive heart failure live longer, see that a canine with kidney disease can catch her ball for a few more years, and even make a dog with cancer more comfortable. Food is pretty powerful stuff!

In this chapter, I cover the power of food. I provide some important information on how to prevent the two most common diseases that result when dogs get too much food or too much of certain nutrients: obesity and arthritis. Then I let you know how you can use food to help heal your hurting hound.

Helping Your Overweight Dog Shed Those Extra Pounds

Estimates suggest that 40 to 50 percent of dogs in North America are overweight. In this age of abundance and leisure, more Americans are overweight than ever before — and dogs (much to their delight but ultimately to their detriment) are sharing in this overabundance of food and gaining weight right along with their owners.

Dogs don't put food in their bowls — *we* do. And, more often than not, we are giving our dogs too much!

Overweight dogs have a higher risk of musculoskeletal problems and suffer from many of the same illnesses that overweight people do — heart disease, liver disease, kidney disease, arthritis, and shortness of breath. Fat dogs don't live as long as dogs of a healthy weight — and dogs already don't live long enough! (Who doesn't want his dog to live forever?)

Knowing what causes obesity

So why are so many dogs overweight? In the following sections, I cover some possible answers to this difficult question.

Following the recommendations on dog food labels

Even the most active dog doesn't need as much food as most dog food companies recommend. The best way to determine how much food your dog needs is to feed her the amount that maintains her weight. Figuring out what this amount is requires a little patience and some trial and error. Two dogs of the same breed and size may require vastly different amounts of food to maintain their weight. So get your dog weighed regularly at your vet's office and compensate for any fluctuations in weight by changing the amount of food you feed your dog.

Feeding adult dogs the same amount of food they were fed as adolescents

This is a common mistake among dog owners. Growing puppies and young adult dogs eat a lot of food! But just as most of us eat less now than we did as teenagers, adult dogs need less too. A dog's metabolism slows down with maturity and adult dogs need less food to maintain their weight. As your dog ages from 1 year old to 7 years old, her energy requirements decrease by 24 percent.

To make matters worse, being overweight encourages a dog to exercise less, thus perpetuating a vicious cycle of overeating and lack of exercise. The best way to feed your dog is to adjust her food intake to her activity level. Every time you go to the dog food bag, think about how much exercise your dog has had (not how much exercise she may get tomorrow if you get around to taking her for a walk), and dole out the food accordingly. And when you're calculating her daily intake, don't forget to include all the delicious treats you give her for being so good!

In the winter, your dog may not get as much exercise, so decrease her intake accordingly.

Not knowing how to determine whether a dog is overweight

Dog owners typically have no idea how much their dogs should weigh, so if you fall into this category, you're not alone! Dogs vary in height, bone structure, and muscularity, so there is no one "right" weight for a dog of any given breed. Although many people claim that a dog is not overweight if you can feel her ribs, this method of determining weight is too easy to cheat with — after all, you can feel the ribs of even a fat dog if you push your fingers in hard enough.

The best way to determine whether your dog is at the best weight for her is to examine her overall body condition. Dogs of a correct weight should have a tucked up abdomen, and you should be able to see a narrowing at the waist when you look down on her from above. In addition, you should be able to see indentations where the last few ribs are.

Worrying that dogs won't get enough nutrients if they get less food

Premium dog foods are packed with nutrients. If your dog is overweight, unless she has a hormonal problem, she is getting *too much* nutrition. Cutting back will not put her in nutritional jeopardy. Remember that, just like humans, individual dogs vary in their metabolic rate, and some dogs just need less food than others do.

Going to a vet who won't tell you when your dog is overweight

I have asked many vets why they don't tell clients that their dogs are overweight, and I always get the same response: "I've lost so many wonderful clients because they were offended when I told them their dogs were overweight. So I just don't tell them anymore."

You *want* a vet who will tell you when your dog is overweight, because obesity is a serious health problem for dogs. So please, don't be offended if your vet tells you that your pooch has put on a few too many pounds — it doesn't reflect on you personally. And if you suspect that your dog may have gained some weight and your vet isn't saying anything about it, ask.

Not ignoring a dog who begs for food

When you have faced up to the reality that your dog needs to shed a few pounds, you need to decide on a plan. To peel the pounds off your pooch, you need to decrease her caloric intake and increase her exercise. But how can you reduce your dog's caloric intake without having to look into her sad brown eyes that tell you how much she's suffering?

You can decrease the caloric content of a diet in one of two ways: reduce the fat and/or carbohydrates, or increase the fiber. I like the second option best, and so do most of the dieting dogs I know. Doggie diet foods that have *both* lower fat and higher fiber contents than maintenance diets occasionally cause dry, flaky skin. So I like to create my own doggie diet food by keeping my dog on the food that she's already doing well on, but adding fiber. I call this the Veggie Diet, and here's how to do it: Reduce your dog's regular food by 25 to 30 percent, and add back twice that volume of fresh vegetables. You can use just about any green vegetable, but stay away from peas, corn, and potatoes, which are too high in digestible carbohydrates to help with weight reduction. Personally, I like to use canned pumpkin — not the kind with sugar and spices, ready-made for pies, just solid packed pumpkin. It has a texture similar to canned dog food, is easy to dish out, adds fiber and a few vitamins, and makes dogs feel full so they don't go foraging in the yard for leftovers. Plus, dogs love it!

Here's an example of how to feed the Veggie Diet using real numbers. If you're currently feeding your dog 2 cups of dog food a day, you would reduce the amount of dog food to 1½ cups, and then add in 1 cup of canned pumpkin or green vegetables. Here's the math: 2 cups × 0.25 = 0.5 cup. So you reduce the dog food by ½ cup to 1½ cups. Then you feed in vegetables twice the amount of dog food you've taken out — so 0.5 cup × 2 = 1 cup of vegetables.

The Veggie Diet can really take the weight off dogs, especially when you combine it with an exercise program. And your dog won't feel hungry because of the extra volume of food she's eating. When your dog has lost the weight, you can gradually increase her intake of dog food until she stops losing weight but maintains her slim figure — the specific amount depends on the dog's metabolism. Don't, however, return to feeding the amount she ate when she became overweight.

When you're trying to help your dog lose weight, be sure to measure your dog's food exactly — don't guess at the amount. And don't forget to give your dog regular exercise (see Figure 8-1). Not only will the exercise help her lose excess fat, but also the muscle mass she'll gain will burn more calories, even when she's lying on the couch! That will help maintain her svelte figure over the long haul.

Figure 8-1:
This
Whippet
is fit, not
fat. Look
at him kick
up the dust
as he runs!

Train your furry friend that begging for food is not a viable option any more. (This will help you keep her weight under control, because you won't constantly have to look the other way when she begs.) How do you do that? The best way is to modify your own behavior first. Don't ever feed your dog when she begs — not at the table and not when she hangs around under your feet while you're making your own dinner. Put your dog's dinner in another room and close the door until you're finished cooking and eating. Or have a mat on which your dog must lie when you're cooking dinner and eating (see Chapter 17 for tips on how to teach your canine Einstein to do this).

Paying Attention to Your Large-Breed Puppy's Special Needs

How big is a *large-breed dog?* Many people define a large-breed dog as one that weighs 65 pounds or more when fully grown. That would include all dogs the size of a Labrador Retriever or larger. But it also includes some dogs who, as adults, will be small in stature but big in weight, such as Basset Hounds and Clumber Spaniels.

Be careful about the nutrition of your growing puppy. Several studies have clearly demonstrated that overfeeding and oversupplementing puppies, especially rapidly growing large-breed ones, can have disastrous effects on their bones and joints. In one such study, litters of puppies were divided into two feeding groups. Group A puppies were allowed to eat as much as they wanted of a good-quality puppy food, and they were supplemented with vitamins and minerals. Group B puppies were fed 75 percent of the amount their littermates chose to eat and were *not* supplemented with vitamins or minerals. The dogs who were fed as much they wanted and supplemented had a significantly higher incidence and severity of hip dysplasia, elbow dysplasia, osteochondrosis, bone deformities, and a number of other bone and joint abnormalities than their littermates whose diets were limited. A high level of total energy (essentially, fat and carbohydrates) and excess calcium were the factors that contributed to the bone and joint abnormalities in these growing pups.

The goal in feeding fast-growing large-breed pups is to optimize skeletal growth as the body weight increases. You want to avoid increasing your pup's total body mass faster than her skeleton can carry it. This kind of growth (in which the skeleton can't keep up with the body mass) occurs most commonly in some of the obesity-prone breeds such as Labrador Retrievers and Golden Retrievers, and also in the Giant breeds as well, but other breeds are susceptible, too.

Unfortunately, dog food labels currently aren't required to state energy levels. Some dog foods, however, *do* provide this valuable information. When comparing two foods, if one has more energy per gram, you'll know to feed less of that food.

As important as the total energy in a dog's diet is the level of calcium. A few years ago, nutritionists believed that the calcium-to-phosphorus ratio was more important than the total amount of each mineral. We now know that this isn't true and that the level of calcium in a growing dog's diet is a very significant factor in bone and joint health. In fact, the data confirming the role of calcium in growth is so overwhelming that the AAFCO changed its recommended nutrient profiles to include not only a minimum recommended level of calcium, but also a maximum. Its recommendations are that puppies and lactating bitches have 1 percent calcium in their diet and that adult dogs have 0.6 percent, but that, for either group, the level not be higher than 2.5 percent.

Currently the best way to grow puppies is to feed them a large-breed puppy food (even if the pup isn't a large breed) or an adult-maintenance dog food that has been shown to be adequate for all stages of a dog's life. The food should contain not more than 1 percent calcium on a dry-weight basis.

Be sure to monitor your pup's body condition and not let her get roly-poly. You should be able to see a tucked up abdomen, a waist, and a hint of ribs. Don't concentrate on how much your pup weighs, but instead monitor her body condition. In most cases, this means you will feed less than the amount of food recommended on the dog food label. If your pup starts to get too thin, just increase her food a bit. If she is getting a bit chubby, decrease it. Veterinary nutritionists recommend feeding your puppy this way until she has achieved 80 percent of her anticipated adult weight, then change to an adult maintenance food.

Many dog breeders and owners, myself included, have been feeding premium adult foods with the correct level of calcium to puppies for decades, raising happy, active puppies that grow into strong, well-proportioned, healthy adults.

Controlling Skin Problems

Allergies are very common in dogs, just as they are in people. Although most dog allergies are caused by inhaled allergens, such as pollen and dust, some dogs are allergic to certain components in their food.

An allergy is caused by an extreme hypersensitivity to a substance that most dogs aren't sensitive to at all. Your dog's body sees the allergen as foreign and produces antibodies to it. When the allergen is ingested or inhaled, the antibodies bind to it, resulting in the release of *histamines* (chemicals that cause blood vessels to dilate) from cells. If the histamine is released in the skin, it causes the skin to be itchy. When the dog scratches, more histamine is released and the dog gets itchier, creating a vicious cycle. If histamine is released in the intestine, it causes diarrhea.

If your dog has itchy skin or chronic diarrhea, she should be examined by your veterinarian. The vet may recommend that your dog see a canine allergist to determine exactly what the offending allergens are. Most allergies in dogs are caused by allergens other than those in food, such as pollen and dust. But the most common foods to which dogs are allergic are beef, milk, wheat, soy, and artificial food additives.

If your veterinarian feels that your dog may be allergic to a component in her food, he will probably suggest that you try to alleviate her symptoms with a change in diet. The first step is to go up one notch in food quality. For example, if you're feeding a grocery store food, you may change to a premium diet (sold at pet supply stores). Make the switch over a period of three days, and put your dog's food in a ceramic or stainless steel bowl. Plastic bowls are porous and may retain food residue even after washing. Don't give your pooch any snacks, rawhide bones, or other toys to chew on during this test period. Keep a daily record of your dog's comfort level. How much is she scratching? Where is she licking? It may take as long as six to eight weeks for you to see a reduction in these symptoms.

If you're already feeding a premium diet, and your dog has signs of allergies, you can move up to a hypoallergenic diet. A *hypoallergenic diet* is one that contains forms of protein and carbohydrates that your dog has not been exposed to, such as fish and potato.

Therapeutic diets

Several companies, including Hills, Waltham, Eukanuba, and Purina, manufacture prescription or therapeutic diets for sale by veterinarians for the nutritional therapy of specific illnesses. These diets may not be complete and balanced because of the special needs of dogs with specific diseases, so don't feed them to healthy pets. Because they have very specific nutritional components, these diets should be used only under the guidance of a veterinarian, who can ensure that the dog has been examined and diagnosed as having the specific illness for which the diet was made.

The term *hypoallergenic* doesn't have an agreed-upon definition in the world of dog food manufacturing. What is hypoallergenic for one dog may not be for another. As a result, the AAFCO and the FDA do not permit dog food manufacturers to use the term *hypoallergenic* on dog food labels.

If your dog still suffers from allergies while she's on a hypoallergenic diet, you may need to feed a *micronutrient diet*. Micronutrient diets have all the nutrients predigested into components that are too small to act as allergens. Although these diets are very expensive, they can be useful in quieting your dog's allergic symptoms while you try to determine exactly what allergen she is hypersensitive to. After your dog's symptoms have subsided, you can begin to add regular food components back to her diet one at a time, waiting six to eight weeks after each addition to see if the symptoms return. If they do, then you know what food component(s) your dog is allergic to. The ultimate goal is to find or prepare a food that doesn't contain any of the allergens to which your dog is sensitive.

Just remember that the vast majority of allergies in dogs are due to inhaled allergens. If that's the cause of your dog's allergies, changing her food isn't going to make any difference to her symptoms.

Battling Cancer

Veterinarians and scientists don't know how to prevent cancer, but we do know of several ways we can help dogs who suffer from this disease to feel better and perhaps even live longer.

Although humans with cancer frequently become thin, extreme weight loss usually is not seen in dogs. Dogs with cancer may or may not lose weight, but they frequently do lose muscle. They may weigh the same or even more, but this usually is because there is a shift in body proportions — they lose muscle but gain more fat. Plus, people naturally pamper dogs who suffer from cancer, which can also increase body fat.

If your dog has cancer, feed her a diet that is relatively low in simple carbohydrates and contains a moderate amount of highly digestible protein and a moderate amount of fat. The fat should contain omega-3 fatty acids, which may help suppress cancer cells and prevent them from spreading. To accomplish this, you may feed a diet consisting of 50 percent fish or chicken and 50 percent mixed vegetables. Then supplement this diet with an animal fat (such as fish oil) or olive oil, plus a vitamin/mineral supplement with an appropriate amount of calcium.

Although this homemade diet can help provide the nutrients your dog needs to maintain her energy and attitude during a bout with cancer, it isn't complete and balanced, so don't feed it to your dog for more than six to nine months.

Helping Your Dog with Heart Disease

Dogs with heart failure produce high levels of hormones that cause muscle loss, a condition called *cardiac cachexia*. These hormones also cause a loss of appetite and an increase in the dog's energy requirements. Fatty acids found in fish oil can decrease these hormones. So adding omega-3 fatty acids to the diet of a dog with heart disease can help improve the dog's quality of life, although it won't cure the disease. Ask your veterinarian for specific recommendations on changing the fatty acid composition of your dog's food.

Be sure to control your dog's weight if she has heart disease — this will reduce the stress on her heart. Because every pound of fat contains a mile of blood capillaries, the heart has to pump harder in dogs with extra fat.

Dogs with heart disease should eat a low-salt diet as well, to decrease the volume of blood, and thus the work that the heart has to do to pump the blood. Doggie treats frequently are high in salt, so be sure to check the sodium levels of your dog's treats if she has heart problems. If the sodium levels are not listed on the label, call and request information from the manufacturer.

Getting Gastrointestinal Disease under Control

Digestive upsets are very common in dogs. Sometimes it seems that not a week goes by when I don't have to clean a doggie mess off the floor. Because bouts of diarrhea or vomiting are so common in dogs, and because these usually aren't the result of a serious medical condition, here is a simple protocol to get your dog through those digestively hard times:

- ✔ **Start by withholding food from your dog for 24 hours.** (If the dog is less than 6 months old, withhold food for only 12 hours.) Don't worry — your canine companion can easily go 24 hours without eating. This period of fasting will give her intestinal tract a chance to settle down without having additional foodstuffs to deal with.

- ✔ **Give your dog free access to water as long as she doesn't vomit after drinking.** If she *is* vomiting after drinking water, you can just give her some ice cubes to lick every few hours so she will stay hydrated.

- ✔ **After her fast, give your dog a low-fat diet consisting of easily digestible proteins and carbohydrates.** Two parts of boiled chicken breast to one part cooked white rice is a good choice. Feed this diet for two to three days while her intestine recovers.

- ✔ **Give your dog probiotics.** *Probiotics* are live, beneficial bacteria that will repopulate your canine friend's gut and reestablish her digestive activities (see Chapter 14 for more information on probiotics).

Take your furry friend to the veterinarian if she vomits or has diarrhea for more than 24 hours.

Pleasing your picky pooch

Dogs who are sick are usually picky eaters. Nonetheless, as long as the dog doesn't have a gastrointestinal upset, encourage her to eat so that she can benefit from a continuing supply of nutrients. To encourage your dog to eat, try giving her warm canned food, put a little garlic on the food, and feed several small meals. Many ill dogs will eat if they're hand-fed with lots of tender loving care.

Helping Your Dog Live with Kidney Problems

Kidney disease is very common in dogs, especially in older dogs. Dogs who suffer from chronic kidney disease frequently lose protein in their urine because their damaged kidneys have lost the ability to retain and recycle the protein in the blood that they filter. The result is that these dogs frequently become thin and may develop *ascites* (fluid retention in the abdominal cavity) due to the low protein in the blood). Dogs suffering from chronic renal disease often require a low-protein diet. In a recent study, dogs with kidney failure that were fed a diet with 14 percent protein on a dry matter basis lived 50 percent longer than dogs fed 23 percent protein.

Dogs with renal failure also develop imbalances of calcium and phosphorus that can result in mineral deposits in many different tissues and loss of bone strength. To counterbalance this, they should be fed a diet that is low in phosphorus and they should be supplemented with calcium. As with most medical conditions, there are no hard and fast rules and each dog must be evaluated and assessed for her specific needs. Dogs with renal disease need to be monitored regularly by a veterinarian.

Part III
Recognizing and Treating Common Maladies

The 5th Wave   By Rich Tennant

VETERINARY CLINIC

"Buster and the vet have a special relationship. That's why we always try to coordinate his birthday with a worming."

In this part . . .

If you're like most dog owners, the thought of your dog getting sick is one you hate. But part of being there for your dog is knowing how to help him if he feels a little under the weather, and in the chapters in this part, I tell you what you need to know. I start by giving you a quick tour of your dog's body, so that you're familiar with how your buddy is put together and can understand your vet when she talks to you. I also let you know about some health problems dogs commonly run into, so you're prepared ahead of time and know what you can do to help. And I give you some great tips on acting quickly in the case of an emergency. Finally, I wrap up the part by discussing different kinds of treatment you may want to consider for your dog — everything from traditional drug therapies to alternative approaches.

Chapter 9

Innerspace: How Your Dog's Body Works

*J*ust as it helps to know the fan belt from the fuel pump when talking to your mechanic, gaining a basic understanding of your dog's body parts and how they work together to create a living, breathing animal will help you communicate more effectively with your vet. Your dog's body is like a fascinating machine, only better. It functions surprisingly like the human body, as you'll see in this chapter, which takes you on a short tour of your canine companion's body, inside and out.

The Hipbone's Connected to the Thighbone

Looking at your furry friend, you may have no idea how to tell his pelvis from his patella or his carpus from his clavicle. Dogs have most of the same body parts that we humans have; the main differences are that dogs walk on all four legs and they stand on their toes and fingers. Just like humans, they have shoulder blades and funny bones, kneecaps and shins. Most dogs have something we don't, however: tails, those talking appendages that express all kinds of canine emotions.

The bones are the scaffolding that supports all the other parts of the dog's body (see Figure 9-1). The *spine* is the central scaffold to which all the other supports are attached. It consists of a row of *vertebrae* that surround and protect the spinal cord. The *spinal cord* contains the nerves that transmit messages from the brain to the limbs, telling them to jump the fence or chase after that squirrel. The vertebral bones are wrapped in crisscrossing muscles and, as with all bones, are connected to each other by ligaments. The five parts of the spine are the *cervical* (neck), *thoracic* (chest), *lumbar* (lower back), *sacral* (pelvic), and *coccygeal* (tail) sections.

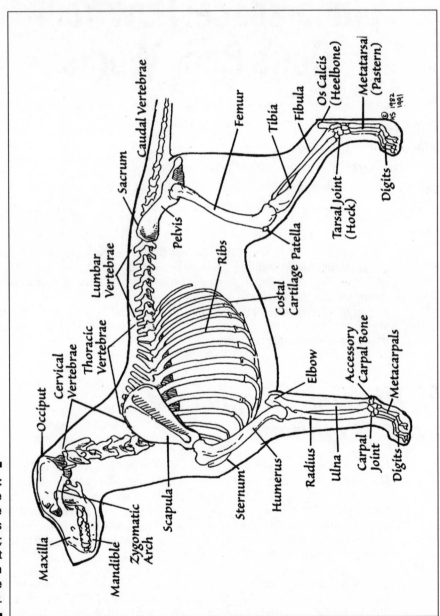

Figure 9-1:
Dogs have all the same bones as humans; they're just shaped a little differently.

TECHNICAL STUFF

Growing pains

Bones are made up of soft tissue with minerals added to harden the tissue. Although it may seem that tissue as solid as bone wouldn't change in shape and size, bones actually change all the time in response to the stresses put on them. So the bones of heavyset dogs are denser than those of lighter dogs, because their bones have responded to the greater weight they are required to support.

There are two kinds of bones: *flat bones* (like the bones of the skull) and *long bones* (like the bones of the legs). The flat bones grow larger in many directions at once; the long bones have a specific area at one or both ends called the *growth plate.* This is where the cells replicate and add to the length of the bone. The growth plate continues to increase bone length until

puberty, when it becomes calcified, like the rest of the bone. Because the growth plates at the ends of the bones are soft, they can easily be injured. If a dog injures a growth plate, the bone may grow abnormally and result in a deformity. That's why you need to be sure to play gently with puppies.

Large dogs mature more slowly than small dogs, so their growth plates close later. The growth plates of the tibia close at 10 months in a Chihuahua, for example, but not until 14 months in a Great Dane. The growth plates are soft areas in the bone that are susceptible to injury. So make sure your dog is at least 14 months of age before he participates in sustained vigorous physical activity or very rough play, to prevent injuring the growth plates.

Your dog's spine has to be strong enough to support his legs and internal organs, yet it must be flexible enough to coordinate movements between the front and back legs whether he is walking, trotting, or galloping to the kitchen for his dinner.

The chest contains the heart and lungs. These two organs are so vital that they are completely surrounded and protected by the bones of the *ribcage.* Many of the fastest breeds, such as the Greyhound, have very deep, narrow chests. This permits expansion of the lungs without increasing wind resistance. The ribcages of most other breeds are more barrel-shaped. Dogs with deep chests have an increased risk of gastric torsion (commonly referred to as *bloat*). For more information about this gastric emergency, see Chapter 10.

The front legs are made up of a *scapula,* a *humerus,* and a paired *radius* and *ulna,* just like human arms. The radius and ulna end at the *carpal joint,* which is similar to the human wrist. Five metacarpal bones extend from the carpal joint to form the *pastern,* which ends at the foot. Your dog's foot is really the equivalent of your four fingers, except that, in your dog, the toes are bent to help reduce impact on the bones. The toes all meet at a central large pad.

The rear legs are joined to the body at the *pelvis,* a large, H-shaped bone attached to the *sacral spine.* Each rear leg consists of a *femur* and a paired *tibia* and *fibula,* just like human legs. The tibia and fibula end at the tarsal joint (or *hock*), which is analogous to the human heel. Below the hock joint extend the five *metatarsal bones,* which then join with the bones of the toes. The area between the hock and the foot is called the *rear pastern.*

The bones meet each other at the *joints* (see Figure 9-2), which are surrounded and held together by the *joint capsule* and by *ligaments* (bands of parallel fibers that join bone to bone). Joints are complex structures designed to permit bones to move against each other with as little friction as possible, while keeping them close to each other. Friction-free movement is achieved with the help of the cartilage covering the ends of the bone and by the fluid that bathes it. This fluid is called *synovial fluid,* and it has properties similar to an engine's oil, which lets the pistons pump up and down in the cylinders billions of times without wearing out. Some joints, such as the knee joint, also have crescent-shaped pieces of cartilage called *menisci* that provide a cushion for opposing bones to rub against.

Every bone in your dog's body has at least one muscle attached to it. Muscles only move in one direction — they contract, which pulls the attached bones closer together. Paired muscles on opposite sides of the bone contract alternately, resulting in movement. Because the muscles and the bones always work together, they often are referred to as the *musculoskeletal system.* The musculoskeletal system is like a crane. The bones are the arm of the crane and the muscles, tendons, and ligaments are the complex system of metal cables, pulleys, and winches that move the crane's arm.

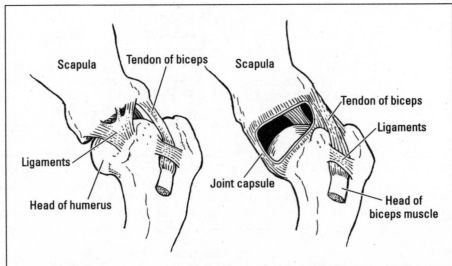

Figure 9-2:
The structure of a joint.

Muscles are bundles of long cells that stretch between two bones and attach to them by tendons. The muscle cells contain bars of proteins called *actin* and *myosin*. When the muscle contracts, adjacent bars grab each other and slide in opposite directions. This causes the cells to shorten in length. As a dog becomes stronger, each muscle cell creates more actin and myosin to increase its ability to contract. Muscle contraction takes a great deal of energy, and muscle tissue is one of the greatest energy-eaters in the body.

Nerves run alongside the muscles of the limbs. A nerve is like electrical wiring that transmits information from the brain to the musculoskeletal system. The brain is like the crane operator who sits in the cab and pushes the pedals and levers to direct the crane's work.

Playing Footsie

Dogs have four weight-bearing toes on each foot. These toes are like the fingers of the human hand. Many dogs also have a dewclaw (which is kind of like the human thumb) on the inner side of the foot between the pads and the pastern. Dewclaws normally are present on a dog's front legs at birth. Most breeds do not have dewclaws on the rear legs. The Great Pyrenees, the Briard, and the Beauceron, however, have double dewclaws on the rear legs, making a total of six toes on each of their rear feet.

In some breeds, the front dewclaws are surgically removed at 3 days of age, usually to prevent the dewclaws from getting snagged on vegetation or crusted ice as the dogs get older. Dewclaw removal is not necessary for health reasons, so if your dog still has his dewclaws, don't worry. The dewclaws will probably help your dog grip the ground when he runs and turns. ***Remember:*** If your dog has dewclaws, don't forget to trim those nails along with his other nails.

The bottom of your dog's foot has five pads — one under each toe and a large one at the center of the foot. The skin of the pads is the thickest skin on the dog's body. The pads provide protection against sharp objects and function as shock absorbers. They also provide traction on slippery surfaces.

An additional pad, called the *accessory carpal pad,* is located at the back of the front leg behind the carpal (wrist) joint. This pad cushions the wrist joint and acts as a braking device during fast running and turning.

About Faces

Just like you and me, dogs have many different facial expressions. They have the wide grin and bright eyes that say, "Let's play!" They also have the upturned eyes and droopy ears that say, "Oops! I didn't mean to." The many different shapes and sizes of dogs' heads contribute to their unique facial expressions.

Experts classify dogs' heads into three types:

- **Dolichocephalic heads** are long and narrow, like those of the Whippet, the Borzoi, and the Collie (see Figure 9-3).

- **Mesocephalic heads** are more moderate in proportion, with the back skull broader than the muzzle. Dogs with mesocephalic skulls include the Dalmatian, the Norwegian Elkhound, and the Chesapeake Bay Retriever (see Figure 9-4).

- **Brachycephalic heads** have wide skulls and shortened muzzles. These dogs frequently have wrinkled skin over the muzzle and face, somewhat protruding eyes, and an undershot jaw. Dogs with brachycephalic heads include the Bulldog, the Pekingese, and the Pug (see Figure 9-5). Sometimes dogs with brachycephalic heads need to undergo surgery to widen their nostrils and open their breathing passages. Despite these potential problems, these dogs appeal to many people. (Psychologists hypothesize that this is because their rounded foreheads and big eyes resemble human babies. Luckily, dogs are not offended by this comparison.)

If your dog has a brachycephalic head, don't exercise him vigorously in hot weather. His shorter nose makes it difficult for him to cool himself by panting. (You'll probably also find that you've got yourself a champion snorer!)

Dogs' nostrils are comma-shaped to encourage scents to swirl around inside the nasal passages. The nose has muscles to allow the dog to flare his nostrils at will to pick up more scent.

Figure 9-3:
Collies have dolichocephalic heads, which are long and narrow.

Figure 9-4:
Chesapeake
Bay
Retrievers
have meso-
cephalic
heads, with
a back skull
that is
broader
than the
muzzle.

Figure 9-5:
Pugs have
brachy-
cephalic
heads,
with wide
skulls and
shortened
muzzles.

Although you may have figured that the purpose of a dog's cold nose was to goose the back of your bare leg in the summer, the moisture on the nose actually encourages scent molecules to waft toward the nostrils. Scent tests have shown that dogs are capable of discriminating a single molecule of one scent in the midst of three trillion others.

Dogs have gladly contributed their superior sense of smell to humankind's well-being. Dogs are used at airports to detect drugs and other types of contraband. They guard monuments and buildings and sniff visitors to detect explosives. Search-and-rescue dogs are used to locate lost people and victims of natural disasters such as earthquakes and avalanches.

The whiskers on a dog's face are not at all like a human male's whiskers, which generally serve little purpose except as a fashion statement or for warmth in the winter. Dogs' whiskers are touch sensors. Just as humans have sensitive fingers, dogs have sensitive whiskers. The whiskers are scattered around dogs' muzzles, over their eyes, on the sides of their cheeks, and underneath their chins.

The whiskers sit anchored under the skin in a small pool of blood surrounded by many nerve endings. When the whisker is moved, waves are created in the pool of blood. This stimulates the nerve endings, sending messages to the dog's brain. When the whiskers around the eyes are touched, a reflex causes the eyes to shut. This helps the dog avoid objects that may injure his eyes. Whiskers are especially important for dogs working in heavy vegetation, and they can be critical for search-and-rescue dogs and for avalanche dogs who work in areas with uncertain footing. Slight alterations in whisker position also are probably used in canine communication.

The Pearly Whites

Most breeds of dogs have 42 teeth (see Figure 9-6). There are six *incisor* teeth on each of the top and bottom jaws, across the front of the mouth. The function of the incisors is to nip and pull at objects. These are the teeth that an Australian Cattle Dog uses on the heels of a cow to get it moving. On either side of the upper and lower incisors is a long *canine* tooth used for gripping and shredding. Behind each canine tooth on the upper jaw are four *premolar* teeth and two *molar* teeth. On the lower jaw, there are four premolars and three molars as well. The premolars and molars, including the *carnassial* teeth, have many points and are used for shearing and grinding.

Each dog has two sets of teeth during his lifetime. The baby teeth begin to appear at about 2 weeks of age. Between the ages of 2 and 6 months, these teeth are pushed out by the erupting adult teeth. The smaller the breed of dog, the later the eruption of his permanent teeth.

Most of the Sporting and Working dogs are expected to have a *scissors bite,* in which the upper incisors overlap the lower incisors. Other dogs, particularly some Herding breeds, have a level bite in which the incisors meet without overlapping. Many brachycephalic dogs have an *undershot jaw,* in which the lower incisors project forward beyond the upper incisors. In contrast, an *overshot jaw* is one in which the upper incisors protrude well out in front of the lower incisors. An undershot jaw or an overshot jaw can be a liability for dogs. It can affect the dog's ability to pick up and carry objects and, if severe, may even affect his ability to eat.

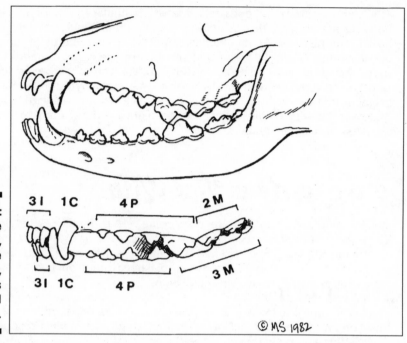

Figure 9-6: Dogs have incisors (I), canine teeth (C), premolars (P), and molars (M).

Because hunters didn't want game birds to be shredded when their dogs retrieved them, most of the Sporting breeds have what is termed a soft mouth. This means that they exert only minimal pressure on the objects they carry.

The Eyes Have It

Canine eyes are similar in shape to those of humans, except that most of the *sclera* (the white part of the eye) is hidden by the eyelids. Dogs can have any shade of brown eyes (from almost yellow to very dark brown), blue eyes, or one of each color. In most breeds, the eyelids should fit snugly to the eyeball. If the eyelids are too tight or if the eyes are set deep in the skull, the eyelids will roll inward. In this condition, called *entropion,* the eyelashes rub on the cornea and eventually can cause blindness if not surgically corrected. If the eyelids are too loose, they will droop outward (a condition called *ectropion*), collecting grass seeds and dirt that can damage the cornea and irritate the eyelid. This condition also may be surgically corrected. Dogs who have undergone surgical correction of ectropion or entropion should be neutered to prevent passing these characteristics on to offspring.

Studies have shown that dogs' visual acuity is similar to that of humans. Dogs, however, are better at detecting motion, have a much wider visual field, and have better night vision than humans. Contrary to popular belief, dogs do see in color, but they are red-green colorblind. They see various shades of blue and purple just as humans do. Green, yellow, orange, and red, however, all appear as yellow to your dog. This is why your furry friend may run right past the bright orange ball you throw for him to retrieve in your backyard. To you the orange ball is very visible against the green grass, but to your dog, the ball and the grass both appear yellow.

The Better to Hear You With

Specialists in variety as they are, dogs come with many different styles of ears. The outer ears may be erect, folded in various ways, or dropped. Dropped ears are common in many Sporting and Working dogs, who have been bred for swimming, because they help prevent splashed water from getting in the dogs' ears. Dropped ears give a dog a kindly look.

Erect ears appeal to many people who like the alert, on-guard look of these sentinels on top of the head. In North America, some breeds have cropped ears, such as the Doberman Pinscher, the Boxer, and the Schnauzer. Their ears are surgically altered at 8 to 12 weeks of age to make them stand erect. Shetland Sheepdogs and Collies have erect ears but with the tops tipped forward.

Breeds such as the Irish Terrier and the Pug are bred to have ears folded forward. This gives a pleasant expression to the face. The Whippet, the Irish Wolfhound, and the Borzoi have folded ears that are laid back along the sides of the neck when the dog is relaxed. These are sometimes called *rosebud ears.*

Dogs use their ears in communication. In a dog showing dominance, the ears are pricked up and pointing forward. A submissive dog will lay his ears flat against his neck. Dogs use many other ear positions to express happiness, playfulness, curiosity, lust, and a variety of other emotions.

Ears may also contribute to a dog's function. The long ears of a Bloodhound or a Basset Hound sway from side to side, wafting scent toward the nose. The Bulldog, which a century ago was used for bull-baiting, has small ears that are laid back flat against the head and out of harm's way.

Dogs have much more sensitive hearing than humans. Dogs can hear sounds at wavelengths up to 50,000 cycles per second (Hz), whereas man has an upper range of 20,000 Hz. In addition, dogs' ears are very mobile; most dogs can turn their ears at least 180 degrees in either direction. They also can point their two ears in different directions. This mobility allows the dog to rotate his ears to face the direction from which a sound originates.

In addition to hearing, the dog's ear is essential for balance. Chronic ear infections can damage the ear and cause loss of balance. A dog with a severe infection of the inner ear may carry his head tilted because of an upset equilibrium.

A Tale of Tails

Dogs' tails come in many lengths from the long, plume-like tail of the Borzoi to the small, bobbed tail of the Rottweiler. Some dogs with bobbed tails are born that way. More often, however, they have their tails surgically docked a few days after birth. *Docking* refers to removal of part or all of a dog's tail. This usually is done at 1 to 3 days of age for cosmetic purposes, to retain the look that is characteristic of that breed. Occasionally, a dog must have his tail docked because of repeated injury.

Some dogs' tails are straight, such as the otter-like tail of the Labrador Retriever. Others, such as the tail of the Siberian Husky, are loosely curved except when the dog is alert or excited, when the tail curls up and over the dog's back. Still other tails are curled in a tight coil like that of the Basenji.

The tail helps the dog maintain his balance, especially when jumping, turning at fast speeds, accelerating, and braking. The tail also is used as a rudder during swimming. The heavy tail of a Retriever can also help balance the weight of the game carried in his mouth.

Dogs use their tails in communication, both with other dogs and with humans, and the tail speaks volumes. A gently wagging tail expresses contentment and is a dog's equivalent of smiles and laughter. A stiffly wagging tail that swishes back and forth deliberately can indicate a threat. A tail held high can indicate confidence or aggression, and a tail held low or tucked between the legs signifies submission or anxiety. (Wouldn't it be great to have a tail to emphasize your point in a heated discussion?)

Got It Covered

Dogs come in hundreds of different colors and color combinations. Their coats probably have been changed more by selective breeding than any other physical characteristic. Dogs have many genes that determine coat color that easily can be reassorted and recombined.

Coat color often is related to a dog's original function. The Nova Scotia Duck Tolling Retriever (a popular Canadian Sporting dog) is a small red dog with white on the tip of the nose, the top of the head, the tip of the tail, and the feet. Tollers play with each other by the side of a pond and attract the attention of ducks overhead. This activity is called *tolling*. Ever curious, the unsuspecting ducks fly in to investigate the moving red-and-white objects, and the ducks are then shot by hunters. The dogs complete their duties by retrieving the ducks.

Another example of functional coat color and texture can be seen in the Komondor, a large dog with a long, white, corded coat. The Komondor's corded coat makes these dogs resemble sheep. They mingle with the sheep, in essence becoming a member of the flock — a dog in sheep's clothing. When the flock is threatened by a predator, the Komondor emerges from the flock to defend his charges. The thick, corded coat then serves as armor against the enemy's teeth. This is a fascinating example of selective breeding in which the adaptable dog has been bred to protect instead of harm what was once his prey.

Some of the original reasons for breeding dogs of specific colors have been lost, and one can only speculate as to why such a variety of unique coat colors were developed. Does the Border Collie have a white collar and feet on a black body so it can be seen readily by the shepherd a long distance away on the Scottish hills? Certainly the coat color of many breeds today is related more to whim or fancy than anything else. What else would account for the coloring of the Dalmatian or the Harlequin Great Dane?

Beware of an unusual coat color such as blue or gray in a dog who is most commonly found in black. Coat color can be associated with debilitating or even fatal diseases in dogs, so investigate carefully if the dog you want to adopt is of an odd color. Some dogs with certain coat colors or types are more likely to have certain diseases. All-white Shetland Sheepdogs and Boxers, for example, frequently are congenitally deaf. A gray coat color in Collies is associated with a condition called *cyclic neutropenia,* in which the dogs suffer frequent bacterial infections. Fawn and blue Doberman Pinschers may have a condition called *color mutant alopecia,* which causes large patches of irreversible hair loss.

Dogs can be either double-coated or single-coated. Examples of double-coated breeds include the Golden Retriever, the Shetland Sheepdog, and the German Shepherd Dog. A double coat is made up of outer coarse guard hairs with densely packed, finer hairs underneath. There is a ratio of approximately one guard hair for every ten undercoat hairs. Air becomes trapped within the dense double coat, and its natural oiliness creates water resistance. The double coat allows dogs to swim in cold water or to work in the rain while still maintaining their body temperature. One good shake usually removes most of the water from the skin surface. Most double coats are of medium length, and all double-coated dogs shed their hair.

In dogs with single coats, all the hairs are of equal thickness and texture. Single coats can be of any length, from the long, flowing coats of the Lhasa Apso and the Yorkshire Terrier to the short coats of the Dalmatian and the Pharaoh Hound. Single-coated dogs generally do not weather the cold as well as the double-coated breeds.

Some single-coated breeds, such as the Poodle and the Kerry Blue Terrier, do not shed. This makes these breeds quite desirable to the many people who prefer not to spend their free time cleaning house. Most of the non-shedding breeds, however, require regular trips to the groomer for a bath and trim.

Most of the terrier breeds have coarse coats that shed minimally. These dogs' coats can be trimmed with clippers, but they will only retain their characteristic coarse texture if they are hand stripped. *Hand stripping* is a process in which a dog's hairs are grasped between the thumb and a tooth-edged stripping knife and pulled out. Because only a few hairs are removed with each pull, hand-stripping is a time-consuming and exacting procedure best done by professional groomers.

For details on how to keep your dog's coat clean and shiny, turn to Chapter 15.

An Inside Look

The organs at work inside your dog are as miraculous as your own are. In the following sections, I give you an insider's look at what goes on inside that ball of fur you love.

See Figure 9-7 for an illustration of the interior of your dog's body, and refer back to it as you read the following sections.

Figure 9-7: The internal organs of dogs are much the same as those of humans, just organized a little differently.

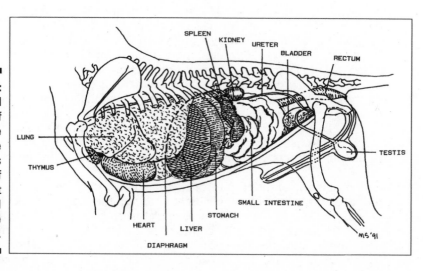

The heart of the matter

Lub dub. Lub dub. This is the sound of your dog's pounding heart as he plans a sneak attack on the kitchen garbage can. His cardiovascular system responds instantly as he jumps up and tries to pry open the lid. His heart rate further increases as you arrive, catching him in the act.

The heart is the center of the *cardiovascular system,* a network of branching blood vessels that course through every millimeter of his body to provide oxygen and nutrients necessary for life. The heart is a muscular pump that first sends blood to the lungs to be oxygenated and then redirects the oxygenated blood and nutrients to every corner of the body.

Defects of the heart are among the most common congenital abnormalities in puppies. Some of these congenital defects delay development and maturation. Others can result in serious illness and death.

If you plan to get a purebred puppy, do some investigative work to determine whether congenital heart problems are prevalent in your chosen breed. If they are, make sure your puppy's parents have been checked and demonstrated to be free of the condition.

Take a deep breath

Dogs normally breathe from 15 to 30 times a minute. When dogs pant to cool themselves, they take very shallow breaths so they don't hyperventilate. The main function of the respiratory system is to extract oxygen from inhaled air (which consists of only 20 percent oxygen) and transfer it to the red blood cells for transport to all parts of the body. Contraction of the diaphragm and expansion of the ribcage cause the lungs to expand. Air is drawn in through the nose, past the larynx, down the *trachea* (windpipe), and finally through multiple branching airways and into the *alveoli* (air sacs) within the deepest lung tissue. The alveoli have thin walls, which allow oxygen to diffuse across and attach to red blood cells in the adjacent capillaries. After this exchange occurs, the diaphragm contracts, pushing the deoxygenated air out of the lungs.

Another function of the respiratory system is vocalization. Barking in dogs is produced by the forceful expulsion of air out of the lungs and past the vocal cords in the larynx. The vocal cords vibrate, producing the noise with which dog owners are so familiar. By contracting the muscles that surround the larynx and by adjusting the strength and timing of the contraction of the diaphragmatic muscles, a dog can growl, howl, yip, yodel, and make many other interesting (and occasionally aggravating) sounds.

Down the hatch

Unlike their feline cousins, dogs rarely are picky eaters. For some dogs, eating seems to be their reason for living. Whether they're nibbling on dog food, delicacies from the garbage can or kitty litter box, or long, luscious stalks of grass next to a fence post, most dogs are keen eaters. The dog's gastrointestinal tract is a wonderful digesting machine. It is designed to grind up whatever enters, to digest and absorb any nutrients found, and to expel the waste.

Nutrients from the gastrointestinal tract pass through the liver before they enter the blood to be distributed throughout the body. The liver screens the nutrients for toxins and attempts to detoxify them if they are present. It also metabolizes fats, carbohydrates, and proteins, storing some of them and turning others into forms more readily utilized by the body.

The canine waste treatment plant

The kidney is a complex physical and biochemical mechanism that filters blood and removes the waste products continually produced by every cell in the body. The waste products (in the form of urine) then enter the bladder where they are stored temporarily and released periodically, hopefully outdoors.

Kidney disease is very common in older dogs. If your canine senior citizen seems to be drinking and urinating more than usual, ask your veterinarian to test for kidney problems.

The puppy works

Remember sex education classes in school? The teacher described the details of male and female anatomy while you wished she would provide you with some different details, like how to ask someone out or how to kiss. What you learned in school will come in handy now, because the reproductive anatomy of male and female dogs, with a few differences in size and shape, is the same as it is in humans.

What are the main differences? The male dog has a bone in his penis, and the female's uterus is long and V-shaped, to accommodate a whole litter of puppies. Female dogs also have six to eight functioning mammary glands — a spigot for each puppy or two. Other than that, the birds and the bees is pretty much the same for dogs and humans.

The Body's Chemicals

The pituitary, thyroid, parathyroid, and adrenal glands as well as the pancreas, ovaries, and testes all are part of the endocrine system. These organs secrete *hormones,* which are biochemical messengers that transmit messages between tissues. The master endocrine organ is the *pituitary,* which is located at the base of the brain. The pituitary secretes regulatory hormones that direct hormone production by the other endocrine organs. In addition, the pituitary secretes its own hormones such as *somatotropic* (growth) hormone, which regulates a dog's growth. Dogs that are deficient in growth hormone may grow to only one-third the size of their littermates. Other pituitary secretions include *prolactin,* which causes the mammary glands to secrete milk, and *melatonin,* which regulates skin color.

Two thyroid glands are located in the neck just below the larynx. *Thyroid hormone* regulates the body's metabolic rate. An excess of thyroid hormone causes the cells to use more nutrients, leading to weight loss and premature aging. A deficiency of thyroid hormone, a relatively common condition in dogs, can result in hair loss and weight gain.

The *parathyroid glands* are two small glands located alongside each thyroid. They regulate the balance of calcium and phosphorus in the body, so they're important for normal bone growth. The *adrenal glands,* located just above each kidney, secrete several hormones. These hormones include *aldosterone,* which regulates thirst, and *estrogen* and *testosterone,* which regulate development of the reproductive organs and reproductive activity. The adrenal glands also secrete *corticosteroids,* the so-called stress hormones that have far-reaching effects on virtually every tissue in the body. Corticosteroids metabolize carbohydrates, fats, and protein and help dogs cope with illness and injury.

The *pancreas,* in addition to helping digest food, secretes *insulin,* a hormone that helps cells absorb sugar from the blood. Because sugar is the main source of energy for cells, a deficiency of insulin (a condition called *diabetes mellitus*) affects the function of every cell in the body.

He's Got Nerve!

Your dog's nervous system is in charge of sending messages throughout his body. The nervous system not only coordinates the functions of all the internal organs, it also controls movement and sensation. Quite an important job!

The voluntary nervous system

The voluntary nervous system consists of both sensory and motor nerves. The sensory part of the nervous system sends information to the brain about your dog's environment, such as the temperature, moisture, and other sensations on the skin. In the brain, the messages are decoded, and he becomes conscious of the sensation.

Motor nerves relay signals for the muscles to contract and move each part of the body. Most of the motor nerves begin in the brain and run down the spinal cord. From there, they go to either the right or the left side of the body, where they branch many times. Each branch provides messages to a different muscle or part of a muscle. The coordinated efforts of motor nerves result in complex movements. They allow your dog to chase his tail or to scratch exactly the right spot on his ear. The motor component of the nervous system is connected to the sensory component because the dog has to know where his limbs are (through sense) before he can use the motor system in movement.

The autonomic nervous system

Most of the time, the body's functions are on autopilot. Your dog doesn't have to think about whether he'd like food to pass from his stomach to his small intestine — it just happens. This is because the autonomic nervous system is in control. The nerves of the autonomic nervous system are of two types: sympathetic or parasympathetic. These two types of nerves have opposite effects on the organs they serve.

Fright, fight, or flight: The sympathetic nervous system

The *sympathetic nervous system* often is referred to as the fright, fight, or flight system. These nerves are stimulated by adrenaline from the adrenal glands in response to something perceived as a possible danger. Adrenaline causes the sympathetic nervous system to shut down functions that are not critical for immediate survival, such as digestion. It also steps up functions such as mental awareness, heart rate, and muscular activity that can help the animal handle the dangerous stimulus. Adrenaline is what allowed Lassie to swim through raging floodwaters to save Timmy. It also is the reason we humans don't feel like eating right before giving a speech.

Day in, day out: The parasympathetic nervous system

The *parasympathetic nervous system* regulates body functions under normal conditions, day in and day out. It causes the digestive system to contract and secrete digestive enzymes, permits reproductive activity, slows the heart rate, and allows blood to be distributed to the skin and the digestive and reproductive organs. The parasympathetic nervous system tells a dog's bladder to empty when it becomes full. When puppies reach about 4½ months of age, their voluntary nervous systems have developed enough that they are able to consciously overrule this action and hold the urine to save your carpeting from damage. Achieving this voluntary control is what housetraining is all about.

Chapter 10

Tackling Common Ailments

At some time in your dog's life, she will probably get sick. It may even just be a minor tummy ache or a little soreness after some extra hard play. But if you're like many people, you may have trouble knowing if your furry friend is just temporarily under the weather or if you should rush her to the vet.

In this chapter, I describe some of the most common illnesses in dogs — conditions that affect the skin; the stomach and intestines; the muscles, bones and nerves; and the kidney and bladder. Throughout the chapter, I give you specific criteria to help you decide whether a trip to the vet is in order. I also provide you with some of the most important background information on what causes these illnesses and how they affect your dog. This way, you'll know some of the most important questions to ask your veterinarian. You find information about how your veterinarian, with your help, can treat these common complaints. And finally, I let you know how you can be your dog's best friend during times of illness — as well as an informed consumer.

Paying Attention to Your Dog's Skin

The skin is the largest organ of your dog's body, and it takes a lot of beating in its job as the first line of defense against the environment. A dog's skin has to be able to handle the cold temperatures of a trek through Alaska and the heat of an Alabama summer. It gets muddy in the local pond and scraped when your dog chases a bunny through the woods.

A dog's skin and coat are said to mirror her physical and emotional health. A full coat of shiny hair usually means your dog is eating a complete and balanced diet, she's getting enough exercise, and all body systems are go. There's a biochemical reason for this: Hormones released from the adrenal gland during stress can cause hair loss and dry skin, so if your dog is stressed by illness, her coat won't look its best. One good thing about the skin is that, in contrast to the internal organs, you can easily see when something goes wrong with it. In the following sections, I cover some common symptoms of skin problems and let you know what they may mean for your dog.

Take your dog to see the veterinarian if you see the any of the following symptoms:

- ✔ **Persistent scratching, biting, or licking at the skin, especially of the feet or groin.** This can indicate allergies or stubborn fleas.

- ✔ **Hair loss above and beyond routine shedding.** This can be caused by a hormonal imbalance.

- ✔ **Sores, scabs, or weeping areas on the skin.** This is often due to a bacterial infection.

Scratching

Intense scratching is most likely a result of allergies, and your dog will most likely itch on the skin of her feet, face, ears, and belly. Dogs can be allergic to all the same inhaled *allergens* (things in the environment that sometimes trigger an allergic response) as humans, including grasses, tree and flower pollens, molds, and even house dust. Dogs can have *inhalant allergies* (those caused by breathing in allergens) seasonally or throughout the year. Sometimes dogs who are allergic to certain components of dog food also get itchy skin.

Many breeds seem to be susceptible to allergies, but the incidence of inhalant allergies is especially high in West Highland White Terriers, Cairn Terriers, Scottish Terriers, and other harsh-coated Terriers, as well as Dalmatians, Shetland Sheepdogs, Golden Retrievers, and Labrador Retrievers.

Intense scratching can result in raw, bleeding skin and makes the skin susceptible to secondary bacterial infection. Experiments have shown that dogs are more likely to scratch during times of stress, at night, when it's warm, and when their skin is dry. When a dog starts scratching, an itch-scratch cycle is set up because damage to the skin from scratching makes the skin more itchy, which only makes the dog want to scratch even more.

The best way to determine whether your dog has allergies — and if so, to what — is for a veterinary dermatologist to perform skin tests, just like the ones performed on people. A dog can be tested for 60 or more different allergens. The veterinarian will shave an area of skin and inject a tiny amount of the test substance. The vet then observes the area to see whether a bump forms, indicating that a local allergic reaction has taken place. A diagnosis of allergies can also be made on the basis of blood tests. Blood tests are an acceptable first test for allergies, but they aren't nearly as sensitive as skin tests are.

After performing skin tests, a veterinary dermatologist will tell you the specific proteins to which your dog is allergic. Identifying the offending allergen is important so that, if possible, you can limit your dog's exposure to that allergen. In addition, you will need to identify your dog's allergies if you want to desensitize your dog by giving her allergy shots. Allergy shots involve injections of gradually increasing amounts of the allergen in an effort to reduce your dog's sensitivity to the allergen. Up to 16 allergens can be included in each shot, and the dog is given shots once or twice a week over a period of months.

Treating allergies in dogs is often a frustrating endeavor. Even if your vet identifies the allergen through skin testing, you may have a very hard time preventing your dog from being exposed to that allergen. Many dogs are allergic to common, everyday substances such as dust or grass. Allergy shots help about 75 percent of dogs with inhalant allergies.

If these treatments fail and the itching is bad enough, your veterinarian may prescribe antihistamines or maybe even a short course (one week) of *corticosteroids* (drugs that suppress immune responses) to stop the itch-scratch cycle. If the symptoms persist and continue to be severe, your dog may have to be on steroids for a longer period of time. In this case, the steroids should be given every other day as prescribed by your veterinarian to reduce the considerable side effects that accompany their use.

Because of the side effects, long-term use of steroids for treatment of allergies should be considered *only* when all other alternatives have failed.

Hot spots

No, I'm not talking about Arizona in the summertime or the new nightclub downtown. *Hot spots* are small to large areas of skin that are red and ooze *serum* (fluid that seeps from the blood). They occur most often in dogs with allergies and commonly appear on the face, neck, flank, and around the tail. Hot spots can pop up very quickly and can spread to involve an area several inches in diameter.

No one really knows how a hot spot gets started, but it probably starts with a break in the skin, either from scratching or from moisture. Bacteria that live peacefully on intact skin enter and reproduce, causing irritation and inflammation.

> # We want you!: Helping your dog do battle against her own immune system
>
> When your dog's immune system gets a little overzealous and starts to attack her body, the skin often is the battleground. Autoimmune disorders that affect the skin have a variety of exotic names such as *pemphigus foliaceus* and *systemic lupus erythematosis,* but they share many common features. They often involve the skin around the eyes, the mouth, and sometimes the feet. And they can cause loss of pigment, blisters, and scabs in these locations. If you see any problems on your dog's eyelids or lips, take a trip to your friendly neighborhood vet to discuss the problem.

To heal, a hot spot needs to be kept as dry and clean as possible. You can treat a small hot spot by soaking it with an astringent, such as tannic acid (just place a wet tea bag on the hot spot). This will help to form a scab over the affected area. If a large area of skin is affected, visit the vet. He will shave the hair over the affected area to promote air circulation and then treat the affected skin with an astringent and an antibiotic.

Discharge or odor in ears

Ear infections are very common in dogs, especially dogs with allergies. About 80 percent of ear infections occur in dogs with dropped ears, such as Cocker Spaniels and Poodles. High humidity or moisture in the ears from swimming can soak the skin of the ear canal, reducing its ability to protect itself from infection.

Initially, the infection may involve only the outer ear, but if left untreated, it can move to the middle and inner ear, interfering with your dog's hearing and balance. A routine weekly check of your dog's ears for abnormal discharge or smell is an important preventive measure against ear infections.

If your dog gets frequent ear infections, keep the hair around her ear opening trimmed (to increase air circulation) and shake a little bit of athlete's foot powder in her ears once a week.

Licking

If your dog incessantly licks herself, she probably has a good reason for it. If she licks and bites her feet, she may have allergies. If she is licking her footpads, she may have a cut there. If she is always licking her rear end, have your veterinarian check her anal glands; they may be plugged or infected. The bottom line: Any time you see your dog licking repeatedly at one spot, take a look. If she's licking a cut or an area of infection, you can give your dog some relief by treating it.

Dogs sometimes have the tendency to lick their front legs, especially in the area of their wrists, often for no apparent reason. They sometimes lick and chew their front legs until the areas develop thick, scarred lumps with raw skin above them. These sores are called *acral lick granulomas,* and veterinarians really don't know why some dogs mutilate themselves this way. Sometimes a dog with allergies will get into the habit of licking her legs until it becomes a vicious cycle of irritation and injury. Other times a dog will lick her front leg after an injury to the leg, continuing even after the injury has healed. Some people believe that this behavior is a mild form of obsessive-compulsive disorder. Talk to your veterinarian about this problem and potential treatment options.

Sometimes dogs lick their front legs, because they have been chewing a rawhide bone and have gotten some juicy pieces of bone and saliva on their legs. If your dog tends to lick obsessively, wash her legs after she finishes with a particularly delectable bone.

Bald spots

Most dogs who shed lose a little hair every day. Their shedding is much more intense in spring and fall, however, as they change coats in preparation for the new seasonal temperatures. When your dog is shedding, you can accelerate the process by bathing her in warm water and then brushing her thoroughly after she's dry. This loosens and removes any dead hair.

Some dogs, such as Whippets and Pharaoh Hounds, have very thin coats on their bellies and on the insides of their legs. It is not normal, however, for dogs to have bald spots or areas on their backs and sides with hair that is so thin that you can easily see the skin beneath. Patchy bald spots or a very thin coat may mean your dog has a hormonal imbalance. An excess of adrenal corticosteroid hormones, a deficiency of the thyroid hormone, or an imbalance in the sex hormones (such as estrogen) all can result *alopecia* (the medical term for hair loss). These hormonal abnormalities can only be diagnosed with blood tests. If your dog has abnormal hair loss, talk with your veterinarian to see whether she may have a hormonal imbalance.

Lumps and bumps

During your weekly once-over of your dog (see Chapter 1 for more information), check for lumps within and under the skin. Skin lumps can be caused by anything from infections to insect bites to tumors.

Take cover

Just like humans, dogs can get sunburned, so make sure to protect your dog from the sun, especially during the spring and early summer months when she may not have as much pigment in her skin. Give your outdoor companion a shady spot to rest, and apply some unscented sunscreen to her head, ears, and nose in particular.

By nature, infectious organisms almost always cause inflammation. Inflammation, in turn, almost always involves swelling and heat. If a lump in your dog's skin is warm to the touch, it may be caused by an infection. There also may be serum or pus oozing from the surface of the lump. When these substances dry, they form a scab.

Insect bites also can cause skin lumps and bumps. Bees and wasps are particularly bad actors in this area. Some dogs, like some humans, are allergic to bee stings and can become quite ill if they're stung. Biting flies can nibble on the ear tips of prick-eared dogs, causing significant irritation.

If the dog is bothered enough, she may shake her head until her ears bleed under the skin, forming a *hematoma* (a blister of blood under the skin). Hematomas are a serious complication that require veterinary treatment. The ears are particularly susceptible to hematomas, because they have so many large blood vessels right under the skin. When a hematoma forms, the weight of the blood causes the dog to shake her ears more, causing even more bleeding.

Tumors in or under the skin also appear as lumps. For more information on how to recognize and deal with skin tumors, see Chapter 18.

Plop, Plop, Fizz, Fizz: Dealing with Digestive Dilemmas

Your dog's digestive system is an amazing mechanism that takes in food, grinds it up, and converts it to nutrients that can be absorbed and used by your dog's body. The digestive tract converts food into all the nutritional building blocks your dog needs to grow and develop, to run and to play. It even provides your dog with extra energy to carry your underwear around the house in the morning.

Every now and then, however, something goes awry with this complex system. So in the following sections, I describe some common digestive problems, let you know what you can do about them, and tell you when your dog needs to see a vet.

Bloat

Gastric dilation and torsion (more commonly referred to as *bloat*) is a serious medical emergency that often ends in death. In this condition, the dog's stomach becomes dilated with gas and twists on itself, blocking off blood flow to the stomach and preventing the stomach from emptying. This results in further buildup of gas and initiates a vicious cycle.

The actual cause of the condition is not known, but large dogs with deep, narrow chests (such as Doberman Pinschers, Irish Wolfhounds, and Borzoi) have a higher incidence of gastric torsion than smaller dogs with barrel-shaped chests (such as Beagles and Dachshunds). Another factor that contributes to bloat is eating rapidly. Dogs who are picky, slow eaters seem to have a lower incidence of bloat than dogs who scarf down their food like there's no tomorrow.

Interestingly, researchers have also found an association between stress and bloat. Dogs who bloated were more likely to have experienced a stressful event in the previous few hours. We used to think that exercise right before or after eating increased the chances of a dog bloating, but a recent study did not prove this to be true. However, it did show that dogs given some canned or fresh food every day seemed to have less risk of bloat than dogs fed only dry food.

Bloat is one of the most urgent medical emergencies a dog ever faces. A dog suffering from bloat has a distended abdomen and retches, salivates, and has trouble breathing. She may pace back and forth and appear very uncomfortable. If the dog is not given veterinary treatment within a few hours of developing gastric torsion, she most likely will die. Because bloat is such an acute, life-threatening condition, a dog who develops it when alone usually is found dead by her owner, highlighting the importance of immediate veterinary attention.

If your veterinarian suspects bloat, he will x-ray your dog's abdomen. If he sees that the stomach is twisted, he will immediately perform surgery to return the stomach to its normal position and tack it to the body wall so that it can't twist again in the future. Even after the stomach is decompressed, there still is the risk of death for several days afterward because the damaged stomach releases toxic substances that can cause sudden heart failure.

Dogs who have suffered from bloat should, in the future, be fed multiple, small feedings each day rather than a single large meal.

Bad breath

A detective on television in the 1980s always called perpetrators "dog breath," and it's true that some dogs have disgusting breath worthy of criminals. Rather than being a normal state of affairs, however, bad breath usually is a sign that all is not well in the dog's mouth.

If your furry friend has a bad case of dog breath, it can be the result of poor dental hygiene. Approximately 70 percent of dogs have *gingivitis* (inflammation of the gums). When plaque and calculus build up on the teeth, they give bacteria lots of nooks and crannies in which to grow. And bacteria produce smelly byproducts that result in bad breath.

Check your dog's teeth, especially the *carnassial teeth* (the big molars on the sides). If there is yellow or brown material on the teeth adjacent to the gums, make an appointment with your vet for your dog to have her teeth cleaned. The vet will remove the accumulated plaque, polish the teeth, and check for loose or fractured teeth. Voilà — no more dog breath!

After you get your pup's pearly whites all fixed up, be sure to brush her teeth as often as possible — every day is best. This helps prevent gingivitis and the possibility of your canine friend losing her teeth.

Another cause of dog breath is the nasty habit of eating feces. When your excrement-eating dog runs out to the yard, munches on some manure, and then comes in and licks your face, you have every right to be disgusted. And it figures that dogs who feel compelled to do this often have breath that smells like the poop they've had in their mouths.

So why do some dogs eat feces? No one really knows for sure, although there are a number of theories. Some think that dung-eating dogs are fulfilling a nutritional need. Others believe that Retrievers and other dogs with the carrying instinct may view feces as another object to retrieve. Still others attribute it to boredom or attention-seeking behavior. If the poop-eating pooch is a female, she may be instinctively cleaning up the environment, just as female dogs clean up after their young pups. You can find suggestions for curing poop-eating pooches in Chapter 17.

Drooling

Drooling is another unappetizing canine foible. And breeds with loose-fitting lips are more likely to be droolers. Saliva normally runs down the sides of the mouth and into the cheeks, where it is channeled into the back of the mouth and swallowed. But if a dog's lips are saggy, the saliva just succumbs to gravity and flows down the sides of the lips, ready to be thrown onto an innocent passerby with a mere shake of the head.

4 out of 5 dentists recommend . . .

A dog's teeth eventually wear down with age. Dogs who play with rocks or do a lot of chewing on bones may show tooth wear as early as 2 to 3 years of age. If the wearing occurs slowly, the tooth will repair itself by laying down a new layer of enamel over the pulp. The repaired area appears as a brown spot on the grinding surface of the tooth.

It is relatively common for dogs to have broken teeth. One study found fractured teeth in 27 percent of the dogs examined. Fractures generally occur as a result of catching or chewing on stones or other hard objects. Surprisingly, dogs with cracked or fractured teeth frequently do not seem to be in pain unless the fracture extends deep enough to involve the nerve. A fracture or crack in a tooth, however, provides a niche in which bacteria can flourish. This eventually can result in a painful *abscess,* a deep infection of the tooth. If you suspect your dog has an abscessed tooth, take her to the vet. He will treat the infection with appropriate antibiotics and will repair or extract the tooth.

If you have a loose-lipped canine, wipe his lips with a towel before introducing him to guests.

Even tight-lipped dogs will drool a little at the sight of food, especially if they concentrate on the food and not on licking their chops. Drooling also can be a sign of nausea. A dog who has motion sickness often will hang her head and drool. Drooling also may occur when a dog eats something very unpleasant or when a dog has something stuck in her mouth.

If your normally tight-lipped dog starts to drool, take a peek down the hatch. If you don't see a foreign body and the drooling continues, taking your friend to the vet is a good idea.

Loss of appetite

It's not very common for a dog to refuse to eat. Even a dog with broken teeth or loose teeth due to gingivitis will usually have a healthy appetite. In fact, most dogs don't really chew when they eat — they just gulp.

One common reason for a dog to stop eating is a viral or bacterial infection of the digestive tract. A number of viruses that cause digestive problems, such as coronavirus and parvovirus, circulate continuously in the dog population. Take advantage of the safe, effective vaccines available to prevent these infections.

Dogs who are over-bonded to humans sometimes refuse to eat when their people are away for extended periods of time. These dogs may miss a few meals until hunger gets the better of them. Very rarely, a dog will refuse to eat at all when her owner is away and will need to be force-fed.

Occasionally, a dog will become a picky eater as a way to get attention. At some point in her life, she learned that when she refuses to eat, her person is more attentive and offers her a variety of more delicious alternatives. This inadvertently rewards the canine curmudgeon for refusing to eat and creates a vicious cycle — the dog refuses to eat each new offering, and the owner rewards Her Fussiness with more and more delicious food. The solution is simple but often tough for the owner: Give the dog her regular dog food and 15 minutes to eat it. When time's up, pick up the bowl and throw the food out. Offer food again 12 hours later, again for only 15 minutes. Most dogs figure out this game pretty quickly and dig right in.

If your usually ravenous dog doesn't eat for 24 hours, have her checked by a veterinarian, especially if she's showing other signs of digestive upset such as vomiting or diarrhea.

If you *free-feed* your dog (meaning you keep the bowl full and she eats whenever she wants), you may not be able to tell whether and how much she's eating. This is one of several reasons why most veterinarians don't recommend free-feeding.

Vomiting

Dogs vomit occasionally, for several reasons. If a dog feels a little queasy, she can voluntarily vomit to relieve the irritation. In fact, occasionally a dog will eat a huge meal, vomit it up, and eat it again. Veterinarians don't know why dogs do this — but perhaps this is a cure to deal with the problem of their eyes getting bigger than their stomachs.

Sometimes a dog gets an irritable stomach about 10 to 12 hours after her last meal and regurgitates a little greenish bile. You can relieve this stomach irritation by feeding her less food more frequently — twice or three times a day, for example, instead of once a day.

Another common reason for vomiting is the condition that veterinarians affectionately call *garbage gut.* Most dogs are pretty indiscriminate about what they eat, and they can develop *gastritis* (inflammation of the stomach) from eating garbage, especially if they consume a few indigestible ingredients such as aluminum foil along with the edibles. A dog with garbage gut often vomits several hours after eating, after the stomach has made a good try at digesting the indigestible. After the dog regurgitates the offending material, she's usually fine.

The grass is always greener

There are many theories as to why some dogs graze on grass like cattle do. Some people think it's a sign of an upset stomach, and the grass is soothing. But I think many dogs do it just because they like to have something in their mouths. Retrievers and other dogs who love to carry things in their mouths seem to be particularly fascinated with grass. And it seems that some dogs just like the taste of it. Dogs' stomachs, however, are not always so thrilled with grass. Dogs often vomit up the grass a few minutes after eating it.

The only reason you should try to curb your dog's grass-eating is if the grass is chemically treated (although the ideal would be to just stop treating the grass altogether). If your dog likes to eat grass, add fresh green vegetables to her food. She'll enjoy it, and it's good for her.

If your dog vomits two or three times but doesn't seem seriously ill, give her stomach a rest by withholding her food for 12 to 24 hours. But make sure she has access to fresh water to replenish the fluids lost in the vomit. If your dog is gulping down lots of water, give her a few ice cubes every four hours or so to prevent her from drinking too much water and vomiting it up. After a day of fasting, feed her small amounts of a bland diet consisting of boiled chicken, rice, and cottage cheese for a day or two. Then gradually mix in increasing amounts of her regular food over the next two to three days.

If your dog still is vomiting after a 24-hour fast, if the vomit contains blood, or if your dog has other signs of illness such as fever, diarrhea, or depression, make an appointment to see your veterinarian. She may have ingested a toxin or have an infection.

Diarrhea

Just like their people, most dogs get an occasional bout of loose stools. Diarrhea may just be the body's way of clearing the intestine of something disagreeable.

The best thing you can do for a simple case of the runs — other than giving your dog frequent access to the outdoors — is to fast your dog for a day. Missing a meal or two won't harm your dog, but it will give her gastrointestinal tract a chance to repair itself. Be sure to give her access to water to replace the fluids she's lost in her feces. Follow the fast with a couple days of bland diet, and your diarrheic dog usually will be back to herself in no time.

If your dog continues to have diarrhea after a day of fasting, if there is blood in your dog's stools, or if your dog has other signs of illness such as a fever, take her to your veterinarian. She may need intravenous fluids to replenish fluids lost in the stools and perhaps antibiotics to fight infection. With persistent or severe diarrhea, finding out the cause is important. Several viruses and bacteria passed among dogs can affect intestinal function and cause diarrhea. There are many other causes of diarrhea including impaired pancreatic function, autoimmune diseases, and food allergies. Your veterinarian can perform tests to make a diagnosis so that appropriate treatment can be instituted.

Constipation

A constipated dog spends longer than usual defecating, and the resultant stools are small, round, and hard. You can bet that if your dog is constipated, she's uncomfortable.

One of the main causes of constipation is insufficient water, often coupled with too much time between potty breaks. Always make sure your dog has plenty of fresh water to flush her intestinal tract. If you will be away from home for a long time, arrange for a neighbor or a professional pet sitter to let your dog out to relieve herself.

If you have cut back on your dog's food intake to help her lose weight and regain her svelte figure, you can prevent constipation by adding vegetables to her diet. Many people use green beans or other canned or fresh vegetables as a source of vitamins and fiber for their dieting dogs.

Don't forget that exercise is a great constipation cure. A long walk or a vigorous game of fetch does a great job of kick-starting a sluggish bowel. With a combination of vegetables and exercise, your dog will be as regular as clockwork in no time.

Don't give laxatives to your constipated dog. Over-the-counter laxatives are more likely to do harm than good.

Gas

If your furry friend's flatulence has you thinking about investing in a gas mask, it may be time to think about changing her diet. Diet is the main reason for flatulence. A sudden change in diet after a long period of the same food can produce gas, as can sensitivity to certain dog-food ingredients. Many dogs are sensitive to soy or other grains or meats found in dog foods, for example, so switching diets may be the solution to your dog's gas problem.

If your dog's flatulence is caused by an inability to adequately digest certain types of foods, such as proteins or carbohydrates, try giving him *probiotics* (nutritional supplements that contain beneficial bacteria such as *Lactobacillus acidophilus* that can help with the digestive process). Sprinkling her food with digestive enzymes may also help. These enzymes predigest the food before it reaches the bowel. Check with your veterinarian for the best kind of probiotics or digestive enzymes to buy.

Exercise is a great gas passer. Get your canine companion out for some fun and games every day to help get that gas out of her system.

Scooting

You may notice your dog scooting across the carpet, leaving a little brown trail. Although many people mistakenly believe that worms are the cause of this behavior, the real culprits are the *anal glands,* the little sacs of smelly fluid on either side of your dog's anus. The anal glands are related to the scent glands of the skunk, and they apply small amounts of scent to dogs' stools as a kind of signature. Sometimes these glands get plugged with secretion, however, especially when the stools are not firm enough to stimulate the anal glands to expel their secretion.

If your dog is scooting regularly, have her anal glands *expressed* (emptied) by your veterinarian. If the anal sacs have become infected, your vet will instill an antibiotic into the sacs after they have been emptied. If plugged anal glands are a frequent cause of distress for you and your dog, you may ask your veterinarian to teach you how to express the glands yourself. Invest in a box of latex gloves and some cotton batting to collect the secretion, breathe through your mouth, and you're all set to go.

Occasionally a dog will have chronically impacted anal glands. This can result in chronic inflammation around the anal glands and eventually scarring of the surrounding area, which makes it even more difficult for the anal glands to be emptied and sets up a vicious cycle. If your dog's anal glands are chronically impacted and scarred, you may want to consider having them surgically removed. This requires a serious and painful surgery with the potential for complications, however, so it should not be undertaken lightly.

Walk This Way: Knowing What to Do When Your Dog Has Trouble Putting One Foot in Front of the Other

The chances are very good that, at some point in her life, your dog will become lame, even if only temporarily. She may get banged up while running and playing with another dog, or maybe she's one of the unfortunate dogs with a hereditary disorder such as hip dysplasia that eventually results in arthritis. The following sections describe some of the many contributors to lameness (including size and genetics), what orthopedic problems are often associated with lameness (including hip dysplasia), and helps you figure out whether your dog's lameness is serious enough that your vet should take a look.

The factors that contribute to orthopedic problems

Many factors contribute to orthopedic problems in dogs, and I cover the major ones in the following sections.

Size

One of the delights of dogs is that they come in all sizes and shapes. But selective breeding for specific sizes and shapes — particularly giant and dwarf breeds — sometimes increases a dog's susceptibility to orthopedic problems.

If your dog is a dwarf or a giant, pay special attention to her bone and joint health and to her diet, especially during puppyhood. See Chapter 8 for more information on diet and orthopedic problems.

Giant breeds

The giant breeds, such as the Mastiff (shown in Figure 10-1), grow very rapidly during the first year of life. In fact, no other species of animal multiplies its birth weight so many times in such a short period. For example, an Irish Wolfhound may weigh 1 pound at birth and 170 pounds a year later. That's an increase of 170 times in a single year! In contrast, the tiniest mouse and the largest whale only increase their birth weight 10 to 30 times in the first year.

The giant breeds have more orthopedic problems because of their rapid growth and the effects of increased weight on their bones and joints. Here's a list of the giant breeds of dogs:

- ✔ Anatolian Shepherd
- ✔ Bernese Mountain Dog
- ✔ Borzoi
- ✔ Bouvier Des Flandres
- ✔ Briard
- ✔ Bullmastiff
- ✔ Giant Schnauzer
- ✔ Great Dane
- ✔ Great Pyrenees
- ✔ Irish Wolfhound
- ✔ Mastiff
- ✔ Newfoundland
- ✔ St. Bernard
- ✔ Scottish Deerhound
- ✔ Tibetan Mastiff

Figure 10-1:
Partly because of their rapid growth rate, giant breeds like this Mastiff are more susceptible to bone and joint ailments.

Dwarf breeds

The dwarf breeds also have an increased incidence of some orthopedic problem. Dwarfs come in two different shapes. *Pituitary dwarfs,* such as the Toy Poodle (shown in Figure 10-2), have leg and body lengths that are in proportion but are just smaller than their family-size counterparts. These dogs are small because their pituitary glands produce less growth hormone. *Luxating* patellas (kneecaps that slip to the side when the leg is flexed) are a particularly common problem in pituitary dwarfs. The following are dwarf breeds:

- Affenpinscher
- Brussels Griffon
- Cavalier King Charles Spaniel
- Chihuahua
- Chinese Crested
- English Toy Spaniel
- Italian Greyhound
- Japanese Chin
- Maltese
- Toy Manchester Terrier
- Miniature Pinscher
- Papillon
- Pekingese
- Pomeranian
- Toy Poodle
- Pug
- Shih Tzu
- Silky Terrier
- Yorkshire Terrier

This normal state for the Toy breeds, which are bred to have reduced levels of pituitary hormones, should not be confused with the dwarfism that occasionally affects a large-breed puppy. In that case, a puppy who *should* grow large never reaches her proper size because of a congenital problem with the production or secretion of pituitary hormone.

Figure 10-2:
This Toy Poodle is one of the dwarf breeds that are smaller because of reduced production of the pituitary hormone that normally stimulates and regulates growth.

Chondrodysplastic dwarfs, such as the Cardigan Welsh Corgi (shown in Figure 10-3), have short legs attached to a regular-size body. These dogs are small because they have a genetic mutation that shortens their legs. So they're medium-sized dogs that have short legs. (The same mutation can occur in humans and results in an individual with a normal sized torso and head but shortened arms and legs.) *Intervertebral disc disease* is especially common in the chondrodysplastic dwarfs. These kinds of dwarfed dogs include the following breeds:

- ✔ Basset Hound
- ✔ Cardigan Welsh Corgi
- ✔ Dachshund
- ✔ Dandie Dinmont Terrier
- ✔ Pekingese
- ✔ Pembroke Welsh Corgi
- ✔ Skye Terrier
- ✔ Tibetan Spaniel

Figure 10-3:
This Cardigan Welsh Corgi is an example of a *chondrodys plastic breed,* which has short legs and a regular-sized body.

Nature and nurture

A dog's orthopedic soundness is a function of both her genetics and her environment. Genetics are the responsibility of the breeder; the environmental component is where you can make a difference.

Blame it on DNA

Because genetics are such an important factor in your dog's orthopedic health, getting your puppy from a breeder who is familiar with the orthopedic problems that can occur in your chosen breed and who has a program in place to reduce or eliminate these problems from the dogs she produces is especially important. For example, most breeds of dogs have the potential to develop *hip dysplasia,* a debilitating condition that starts with looseness of the hip joint and that usually results in the development of arthritis. Responsible breeders do not breed *dysplastic dogs* (dogs with hip dysplasia) nor would they breed a male or female who has dysplastic parents or grandparents.

When you search for your next dog, especially if you plan to get a large or giant breed, make sure the puppy's parents have been tested for hip dysplasia. The parents should be registered with one of the organizations that records the names of dogs who have been demonstrated to be free of hip dysplasia. The two main organizations are the Orthopedic Foundation for Animals and PennHipp. For information on how to contact these organizations and on checking for hip dysplasia, see Chapter 1.

If you're getting an adult dog, whether from a breeder or from a shelter, you may want to first get her checked for orthopedic problems by a veterinarian. In fact, every adult large or giant breed dog, whether purebred or mixed bred, should be checked for hip dysplasia. Testing is especially important if you plan to spend any time participating in outdoor activities such as hiking or in any of the canine sporting events such as agility, obedience, retrieving, or herding trials.

Testing for hip dysplasia is not just for purebred dogs or dogs who will be bred. If you have an active mixed breed dog, get her hips checked for dysplasia as well.

If your dog has hip dysplasia, you can reduce the severity of arthritis by providing her with regular, moderate exercise and by keeping her lean.

Raise your pup right

Several scientifically controlled studies have demonstrated that rapid growth increases the incidence of a number of orthopedic problems such as hip and elbow dysplasia. And although genetics plays a role in rapid growth, diet also is an important factor — and one you can control. If you allow your puppy to get fat, the excess weight puts stress on the pup's growing bones, joints, and ligaments. So be sure to manage your puppy's weight (when in doubt, talk with your vet to be sure your pup is on the right track weight-wise).

Large- and giant-breed puppies need diets with appropriate levels of calcium. The recommended level of calcium for large and giant breeds during the first year of life is 1 percent on a dry-matter basis. (Check your dog food label and talk with your vet to determine whether your pup is getting the right amount of calcium.) Never feed your growing pup supplements such as bone meal that contain calcium or phosphorus, because this changes the amount of calcium your pup is getting.

Although you generally shouldn't give a puppy vitamin or mineral supplements, there is some evidence (although not yet proven scientifically) that giving vitamin C to growing puppies can help prevent hip dysplasia and other bone and joint problems associated with rapid growth. A dose of 500 to 1000 milligrams daily is adequate for large and giant breeds. *Remember:* Talk with your vet before giving your dog any kind of supplement.

Before your puppy is 4 months of age, let her exercise herself in puppy play — playtime should be enough exercise at this age. Between the ages of 4 and 12 months, you can take her for walks and play fetch, tug, and other games, but don't let her become exhausted. And don't exercise your dog heavily before she is skeletally mature (10 months for small dogs, 14 months for medium to large dogs, and 18 months for giant breeds). Avoid having her run or hike long distances before the age of two. For more information on exercise for dogs of all ages, see Chapter 16.

The orthopedic problems dogs commonly face

Just as the pistons in a car engine eventually wear out from chugging up and down within the cylinders for years, your dog's joints, which also are moving parts, suffer the effects of wear and tear over time. The wear on a joint greatly increases if there is any abnormality in the fit or the structure of the joint. And some common orthopedic problems occur precisely because of this kind of abnormality in the fit or structure.

Some orthopedic problems are more common than others, but the ones listed in the following sections are the ones your dog is most likely to run into.

Hip dysplasia

Hip dysplasia starts with looseness of the hip joints, which results in abnormal wear of the bones and the eventual development of arthritis. Several surgical treatment options are available, particularly if the condition is diagnosed early. Many dogs with mild hip dysplasia lead very active lives and only develop signs of arthritis in older age.

Elbow dysplasia

In dogs with *elbow dysplasia,* abnormal growth of the bones that form the elbow joint results in looseness and arthritis. Early diagnosis and surgical repair can slow the development of arthritis, however.

Osteochondrosis

In *osteochondrosis,* the cartilage of the joint degenerates, causing an irregularity in the usually smooth surface of the joint. This irregularity causes increased wear on the joint, resulting in arthritis. Early diagnosis and surgical treatment can significantly reduce the development of arthritis.

Patellar luxation

In *patellar luxation,* the dog's kneecap (or *patella*) is loose and slips to one side of the knee joint, causing the knee to lock. Dogs with this condition often hold a rear leg up for a few steps until the patella slides back into place. In mild cases, the dog may get along just fine. Surgical repair should be considered in severe cases, to reduce pain and the development of arthritis.

Legg-Calves Perthes disease

Legg-Calves Perthes disease occurs most often in small breeds. In this condition, the blood supply to the head of the *femur* (the bone that runs between the hip and the knee) is impaired, and the femoral head degenerates and collapses. The eventual result is arthritis. Early diagnosis and surgical removal of the collapsed femoral head is the best chance for preventing pain and lifetime lameness.

Rupture of the anterior cruciate ligament

The *anterior cruciate ligament* is the major ligament that holds the knee joint together. It can rupture suddenly when the leg is *torqued* (twisted) while the dog is putting weight on it, such as when a running dog steps in a groundhog hole. If the ligament is completely ruptured, surgical repair is essential to avoid the development of arthritis.

Intervertebral disc disease

The *intervertebral disc* is a soft cushion between vertebral bones, and in intervertebral disc disease, the disc degenerates. The disc may suddenly push up into the spinal canal, pressing on the spinal cord and causing weakness or paralysis. Usually the dog's lower back is affected and sometimes the neck. Many dogs with intervertebral disc disease get better with rest and nursing care. If there is significant spinal cord damage, the degenerate disc material should be removed surgically.

Spondylosis

Spondylosis (also known as *arthritis of the spine*) is a condition in which adjacent vertebral bones, usually in the lower spine, grow bony extensions. These extensions rub against each other and may cause pain. The treatment for this condition is rest and *analgesics* (painkillers). Many dogs eventually get better when the bony protrusions on one vertebral bone fuse to those of the next.

Panosteitis

Panosteitis is one of the rare bone conditions that does *not* involve a joint. It affects young, rapidly growing dogs. Dogs with panosteitis develop areas of inflammation in the bones of the legs. The condition often starts in one bone and then appears in another, shifting from leg to leg. Panosteitis eventually clears up without treatment, but anti-inflammatory drugs can ease the discomfort in the meantime.

Arthritis

As they age, dogs suffering from other orthopedic problems commonly develop *arthritis,* which is caused by new, irregular bone growth around the joint. There is no cure for arthritis (also called *degenerative joint disease*).

Treatment consists of reducing the amount of continuing damage to the joint while giving the joint time to heal. Maintaining muscle tone and keeping the joints from stiffening up is essential. Swimming is the best exercise for a dog with arthritis, because it exercises the muscles without stressing the joints by putting weight on them. Heat and gentle massage are beneficial in relieving muscle spasm and pain. Another good exercise is walking on-leash. Depending on the severity of the arthritis, your dog can be jogged slowly or allowed to saunter at her own pace. For dogs with severe arthritis, walks should be interspersed with rest. Daily exercise also should include periods of supervised play. The following sections cover some of the treatment options for arthritis.

Massage

Massage is one of the most underused treatments for dogs with arthritis. Here's how to give your arthritic dog a simple massage:

1. **Wrap the affected joint in a moist hand towel heated in a microwave.**

2. **Lay a heating pad over the joint and turn it to medium heat.**

   Put your hand under the pad every now and then to make sure it isn't too hot.

3. **After ten minutes of heat treatment, use the heel of your palm to slowly and gently rub the muscles above and below the joint using a circling motion.**

   By using the heel of your palm, you'll be sure not to apply too much pressure.

4. **Use the balls of your first three fingers to gently massage these same muscles and the joint itself.**

   If your dog seems uncomfortable or pulls her leg away, move to a more comfortable location on the leg.

5. **Then make long strokes with the flat of your hand over the muscles above the joint, continuing over the joint and then over the muscles below the joint.**

6. **Gently flex and extend the joint without forcing it.**

   Always support the leg with one hand while you work with the other.

Never massage your dog against the grain of the hair. This is very irritating to dogs.

Acupuncture

Tremendously helpful in reducing the pain of arthritis, acupuncture is an ancient form of medicine that has been used successfully for millennia in China (Westerners are only now starting to recognize the benefits). When a dog is treated with acupuncture, small needles are inserted at specific points in her body. These stimulate the body's natural defenses and can significantly help to dull pain. Ask your veterinarian for a recommendation for an acupuncturist in your area who works with animals. For more information on acupuncture, see Chapter 14.

Medication

As a general rule, you should only give your dog painkillers when necessary to reduce pain. When administering painkillers, make sure your dog doesn't suddenly celebrate her lack of pain by over-exercising and causing further damage to her joints.

Aspirin is the most commonly used analgesic, and it can be quite effective. It also, however, can cause stomach upset and even ulcers. Enteric-coated or buffered aspirin can help prevent this. Giving your dog aspirin after a meal also can help avoid stomach upset.

Never use ibuprofen or acetaminophen in dogs. And always consult your veterinarian before administering painkillers, even those available over the counter. Never increase the dose or combine painkillers unless prescribed by your veterinarian.

Carprophen (Rimadyl) and Etodolac (Etogesic) are new anti-inflammatory products that alleviate the pain of arthritis in dogs. They are reported to be highly effective and to have minimal side effects in the majority of dogs. There is a small risk of liver toxicity with Rimadyl, however, so make sure to consult with your veterinarian before treating your dog. Your vet will probably want to take a blood sample before starting your dog on long-term treatment and periodically during treatment with these drugs to be sure your dog is healthy and can handle them.

Joint protectants

There's a whole new class of drugs called *nutraceuticals* that are not man-made; instead, they are derived from naturally occurring joint-protective substances, often of animal or plant origin. Nutraceuticals can dramatically reduce the pain of arthritis and may even repair damaged joints, although sometimes it may take six to eight weeks for the oral form to take full effect. Talk with your veterinarian about which one may be right for your dog.

Only buy joint-protective nutraceuticals from a company that has been in business for many years and has a reputation to uphold. Studies have shown that a significant percentage of nutraceuticals do not contain the levels of active ingredients that are listed on the label. There is currently little federal regulation of this industry, so the buyer has to beware.

Detecting whether your dog has a problem

With a little observation, you can become quite good at detecting when your dog has a little hitch in her gitalong. Early detection is important so you can get your dog the appropriate treatment to minimize her discomfort and prevent the problem from becoming more serious.

Lameness is caused by pain in the bones, muscles, tendons, ligaments, or nerves or by a mechanical problem affecting function. Initially, you may just observe that your dog seems to be moving awkwardly. Here are some clues that your dog may have musculoskeletal pain:

- She prefers to lie down rather than stand or sit.

- She frequently shifts her weight when standing.

- She is reluctant to climb stairs or jump into the car or onto the sofa.

- When she walks or trots, her head bobs up and down irregularly, as if she is trying to take the weight off one leg.

- She pulls her leg away or yips when you handle it.

If your dog has repeated episodes of lameness or if she is lame for more than 24 hours, take her to the vet. Your veterinarian should perform a complete examination and a thorough lameness evaluation. The evaluation also may include x-rays and perhaps a neurological examination. Your veterinarian also may want to test your dog's blood and urine. If your vet can't make a definitive diagnosis of the cause of the lameness and it persists for more than a week, ask to be referred to a veterinary orthopedic specialist. Getting a diagnosis is important.

Remember: A dog who seems to be lazy may be avoiding exercise because she feels pain or instability when moving. Always get your dog checked by a veterinarian if she seems to have lost her get up and go.

Handling Problems with the Plumbing

If your usually good-as-gold dog starts peeing in the house, think *dysfunction* not *disobedience.* A healthy dog who is thoroughly housetrained will hold her urine until she is in agony rather than go in the house. If your dog is having accidents or is always hounding you to let her out, she could have a problem with her plumbing. The following sections let you know what to look for and when to see the vet.

Excessive thirst and urination

If you notice your dog urinating more frequently than normal, pay attention to how much she's drinking. Odds are, she's urinating more because she's drinking more water. Increased thirst may be caused by a hormonal imbalance called *hyperadrenocorticism*. (What a mouthful!) Dogs with hyperadrenocorticism often have other symptoms such as hair loss and weight gain. Any time your dog is drinking excessively, get her checked by your vet — and look out for other symptoms as well.

Another hormone-based problem that causes excessive drinking and urination is diabetes. Just as in humans, in diabetic dogs the pancreas does not secrete enough *insulin,* the hormone that signals sugar in the blood to enter the cells. The result is high blood sugar, which causes thirst. The thirsty dog drinks water and urinates more. The treatment for this condition is to strictly control food intake and provide insulin, usually by injection. Long-term effects of untreated diabetes in dogs include blindness, non-healing wounds, and coma, so be sure to talk with your vet if you recognize increased thirst.

Incontinence

Incontinence is the inability to hold urine until it's the right time to urinate. Neurological, hormonal, and behavioral problems all can result in incontinence. Occasionally, a spayed or castrated dog will begin to have accidents in the house. In this situation, the dog typically gets up after a rest and leaves a small spot of urine behind. This condition is caused by a loss of control over the *urethral sphincter,* the muscle that controls the expulsion of urine. It is more common in spayed females, but it also can affect castrated males as well. The good news is that the leaking of urine can be controlled by hormone replacement therapy or by drugs that strengthen the sphincter muscle.

Damage to the spinal cord can cause serious incontinence as well. Nerves that run down the spinal cord and exit in the area of the lower back control emptying of the bladder. These nerves can be damaged if a dog is struck by a car or if an *intervertebral disk* (the cushion between adjacent vertebral bones) breaks down and protrudes into the spinal canal. In these cases, weakness or paralysis of the rear legs usually accompanies the incontinence. As the damaged nerves heal, the dog usually recovers her control over urination; however, this can take weeks or months.

Sometimes a very submissive dog will urinate when greeting her person or another dog. This urination is a deeply instinctive behavior and is impossible for the dog to control. If you get annoyed or try to discipline the submissive dog for staining your carpet, the problem will only get worse. The solution to this dilemma is to ignore the spills and elevate your dog's self-esteem. Although most dogs grow out of this insecurity, you can accelerate the process with a little judicious handling. Make your homecomings low-key by ignoring your dog (as hard as it may be) for the first five minutes after you get home. When you greet your furry friend, avoid reaching over her body from above. Instead, crouch down to her level and calmly rub under her chin or on her chest. If your voice usually is loud or gruff, speak quietly.

TIP

Dealing with a dog who has to go more often

Sometimes a healthy dog just can't make it through a full workday. But several options can make life more comfortable for both you and your dog:

✔ **Install a doggie door that leads to an enclosed dog run or a securely fenced yard.** This way, your dog can go out whenever she needs to.

✔ **Hire a pet sitter to offer your dog relief in the middle of the day.** A responsible neighborhood kid may be able to stop over on his way home from school to let your dog out and maybe even take her for a walk.

✔ **Consider paper training (or actually "pad" training) your dog.** You can purchase disposable pee pads that have an absorbent layer on one side and plastic on the other. These pads can be found at a pharmacy or through a pet-supply catalog. To teach the dog to urinate on the pad, initially restrict the dog to a small room completely covered with pee pads, absorbent side up. (The pads slip around a bit on the floor, so it helps to tape them down.) Put your dog in the room when she needs to urinate. When she goes, praise her and give her a treat. After she has the idea of peeing on the pads, you can leave her in the room unsupervised. Remove the pads one at a time, praising your dog each time she aims successfully. Eventually, there will be only one pad left. Each day when you arrive home, you can just pick up the pad and — voilà! — your floor is clean. **Warning:** This strategy only works with dogs who don't lift their legs to pee.

✔ **Use a doggie litter box.** This option is especially helpful for small dogs. Be sure to use litter made from sawdust or recycled newspaper; scoopable kitty litter can obstruct the bowel if your dog ingests it. If you have a male dog who lifts his leg, get a box with a lid.

✔ **Modify your dog's pee patterns a bit by restricting her access to water during the day and by monitoring her water intake at other times.** Leave just a little water in the bowl when you depart for work, for example, so your dog doesn't consume a large amount of water while you're away and spend the afternoon pacing uncomfortably by the door. **Warning:** Never restrict the water supply of a dog with kidney or bladder problems; talk to your vet about what's best.

Some dogs, especially Sporting dogs and dogs who like to play in water, develop the bizarre habit of abstaining all day (even when water is available) and then drinking to excess as soon as you come home from work. Of course, about 30 minutes later, the dog urgently needs to go outside — and 30 minutes after that, and 30 minutes after that . . . all night long. The best way to control this behavior is to teach your dog the command "That's enough!" and to monitor her behavior at the water bowl when you're home.

Bladder infections

A dog with a bladder infection feels like she has to urinate even when there is little or no urine in her bladder. Bladder infections usually are caused by bacteria that work their way up the urinary tract from the surface of the body or from the environment.

If your dog suddenly needs to go outside more frequently, go out with her and watch her urinate. If she just produces a few drops of urine each time or if she is straining or looking uncomfortable — particularly if the urine has blood in it — she may have a bladder infection.

Before you pack your canine companion into the car for a visit to the vet, collect a urine sample. This makes it much easier for the vet to make a diagnosis. Collect the urine sample first thing in the morning. This morning sample provides the information your vet needs. (See the nearby sidebar for tips on collecting a urine sample from your dog).

If your veterinarian suspects a bladder infection, he will prescribe an antibiotic and perhaps a drug to acidify the urine (because most bacteria dislike acid environments). You should notice an improvement in your dog's frequency of urination within 24 hours of starting the antibiotic, but certainly within 48 hours. If your dog does not experience significant relief, be sure to call your veterinarian. He may want to change the medication or perform further tests.

Be sure to administer your dog's medications exactly as prescribed. Even though your dog may seem completely fine in three or four days, continue the antibiotics for the complete dosing period, to ensure that your dog has fully recovered.

If your dog suffers repeated bladder infections, your vet should try to figure out why. As a general rule, if your dog has three bladder infections within a year, your vet should look for another contributing factor. The dog may have bladder stones or a tumor.

Old age incontinence

Seeing our furry family members age faster than we do is always difficult. Their faces get gray, and their gaits stiffen a little. Then one day your canine senior citizen gets up from a deep sleep and leaves a little puddle behind. Incontinence is one of the signs of old age in dogs. Obesity can increase the chances of old-age incontinence because it increases the pressure on your dog's bladder. Lack of exercise may be another predisposing factor.

If your older dog starts to have problems with incontinence, have her examined by a veterinarian. The vet will check her for kidney disease, bladder infections, and other causes of increased urination. If a diagnosis of senile incontinence is made, ask your vet about new medications that improve mental functions in older dogs. This can increase your aged friend's awareness of her bladder functions.

I have to do what?

Here's how to collect a urine sample that will be of most use to your veterinarian:

1. **Using soapy water and a washcloth, wash your dog's penis or vulva thoroughly, rinse it, and towel it dry.** Washing is important so the urine doesn't collect bacteria, hair, and other debris from your dog's genital area on its way out.

2. **Clean and dry a large, flat plastic or glass container (such as a shallow casserole dish) to use as your collecting vessel.** If you use a large container, you stand a greater chance of catching the urine, especially if your dog is a little shy and steps aside when you are trying to collect. A flat container

works best for females so you can get it under them as they crouch to urinate.

3. **Let your dog urinate for a second or two to flush out any bacteria or dead cells in the urethra before collecting.**

4. **Place the container into the path of the urine stream.**

5. **Transfer the collected urine to a smaller container with a lid and take it to the veterinarian as soon as possible.** Using a urine sample cup, which is sterile and has a secure lid, is best, (you can get one from your vet or local pharmacy) but most covered containers will do.

Kidney failure

As dogs get older, certain organs start to function less efficiently, including the kidneys. The kidneys filter the blood and expel waste products. In fact, they filter the dog's entire volume of blood several times a day. These are two very busy organs!

Chronic infections, toxins in the environment, and autoimmune disease can damage the kidney and can cause it to permanently malfunction. Kidney failure may occur suddenly or gradually over the course of months and years. When the kidneys fail, they expel too much fluid in the urine along with the waste products. As the dog loses body fluid, she becomes thirsty. The result is a vicious cycle of drinking and urinating.

Kidney failure is a common malady in older dogs. Unfortunately, we frequently don't recognize the signs until the damage is advanced. So it's a good idea to bring a morning urine sample to your dog's annual checkups when your dog reaches 7 or 8 years of age. If kidney failure is detected early and your dog is given proper care, she may be able to live for many comfortable years.

A dog in kidney failure usually needs a special diet with lower levels of high-quality protein and constant access to water. Your veterinarian also may recommend specific medications, depending on the cause of the kidney failure.

Chapter 11

Fighting Off the Bugs That Want Your Dog

We know of millions of species of viruses, bacteria, fungi, and parasites — and we discover new ones every day. Although this chapter discusses bugs that become problematic to our dogs, most infectious organisms don't cause disease at all. They live in the soil and infect plants, animals, and even humans, but we don't even know they're there unless we look. In fact, they are an important part of the circle of life. Without bacteria and fungi to decompose organic matter, humans would long ago have been buried in debris. Without the bacteria that digest plant material in the stomachs of cows, we would have no milk or beef. Without the bacteria that inhabit our bodies, we would soon die of infection. Yes, ironically, beneficial bacteria even protect us from infection by their nasty relatives. The bugs discussed in this chapter are the rare ones that infect dogs and cause *systemic diseases* (ones that affect the entire body).

Vaccinating against Viruses

Viruses are the smallest bugs we know of. You can fit 25 million viruses on the period at the end of this sentence. Viruses must grow inside a host cell; they can't replicate on their own. Although this may seem like it would be a disadvantage to a virus, it's exactly what makes viral infections so hard to fight. After all, how do you kill a virus that's living in a cell without killing the cell itself? Because of this very problem, we have very few drugs that effectively treat viral infections, and many of the antiviral drugs we do have are quite toxic.

The key to fighting a viral infection, therefore, is to make sure your dog never gets infected, and the best way to accomplish this is to vaccinate him. Most of the vaccines we give our dogs are designed to prevent viral infections: rabies, distemper, parvovirus, and kennel cough, but there are some vaccines against bacteria, too (see Chapter 2). The following sections provide a little bit of information about the worst of the bad bugs. When you know what they can do to your furry friend, you'll never want to get behind on his vaccinations.

Rabies

This viral infection is the most important infectious agent that you should vaccinate your dog against. Rabies vaccinations are so important, in fact, that in North America it is illegal to have a dog who is not vaccinated for rabies. In most states, a dog who has bitten a person and is not vaccinated for rabies can be impounded and perhaps destroyed. Why does the government care whether your dog gets rabies? It's simple: Rabies can be transmitted to humans by the saliva of an infected dog, either through a bite wound or a cut. When a person becomes ill with rabies, it is *always* fatal.

If you want to see the incredible (and justified) fear people had of rabid dogs in the days before the rabies vaccine was developed, watch the film *To Kill a Mockingbird*. In that movie, a rabid dog stumbles down a residential street while people hide in their homes, watching it and hoping that someone will have the courage to confront the dog and shoot it. The reason for such fear is that rabies is transmitted by dog bites and is fatal to humans.

Rabies usually infects an animal (or human) through a wound such as a bite. When the virus enters the body, it moves to a nerve and then travels up the nerve to the spinal cord and brain, where the virus replicates and kills brain cells. The victim then begins to act in bizarre ways: Dogs may become very hyperactive and aggressive, or they may become weak and nonresponsive. Death occurs in just a few days.

Luckily, vaccination of dogs against rabies is virtually 100 percent effective, and we can share home and hearth with our canine companions without concern. Today, it is rare for anyone in a developed country to contract rabies. In less developed countries like India, however, 50,000 people, mainly children, still die every year from rabies.

Puppies should be vaccinated against rabies for the first time after 12 weeks of age and then again at 1 year of age. After that, they should be vaccinated yearly or every three years, depending on state laws. When your dog is vaccinated, you will receive a vaccination certificate and a rabies tag. Always make sure your dog wears his rabies tag, and keep the rabies vaccination certificate in a safe place where you can easily find it. If, by chance, your dog escapes and bites someone, his rabies tag (and your vaccination certificate if you're able to be found) will provide proof to animal control officers, veterinarians, and physicians that the dog was vaccinated. This will prevent the person from having to undergo *post-exposure prophylaxis,* a series of rabies shots designed to stop the virus in its path through the body to the brain.

Many species of wild animals throughout North America can be infected with rabies. The most common species are foxes, raccoons, skunks, and bats, but other animals can be infected too. In many species, including skunks and raccoons, the virus can be present at high levels in the saliva and blood without even causing the animal to become ill. This is why it is never a good idea, and in some states and provinces it is illegal, to keep these wild animals as pets. The risk of exposing humans to rabies is just too high.

Never touch a dog, cat, or any wild animal who is staggering, acting aggressively, or otherwise behaving bizarrely. If such an animal bites you — or if *any* animal you don't know bites you — get medical attention immediately. Never touch a wild animal that approaches you. Wild animals should have a natural fear of humans. If they don't, it can be because they are suffering from rabies.

Canine parvovirus

Canine parvovirus enteritis was first identified in the late 1970s, when it swept through dog populations worldwide, killing thousands. The veterinary community worked tirelessly to determine the most effective ways to treat the condition and to identify the virus and produce a vaccine. An effective vaccine was developed and put into use within three years, quickly reducing the number of deaths.

Parvovirus attacks and kills the cells that line the small intestine. As a result, the dog cannot absorb the fluids in the intestine and the dog develops diarrhea, often with blood. Dogs with parvovirus often vomit because of the upset in their digestion. Some people say that they can actually smell a particular odor in parvovirus-infected puppies. Mildly affected dogs may recover in a few days, but severely affected dogs become depressed, dehydrated, and can die within a day or two. The severity of the parvovirus infection depends on the dog's immunity to the virus. Dogs with inadequate immunity, especially puppies, still continue to die of parvovirus enteritis despite treatment. If your dog has diarrhea for more than 24 hours or if he has diarrhea with blood in the stools, seek veterinary attention.

Unfortunately, parvovirus is here to stay. It continues to kill puppies who have not been vaccinated. In addition, vaccinated puppies may still contract parvovirus if they are vaccinated while they still have antibodies that they obtained from their mother's milk. Although every puppy gets antibodies in milk, and these antibodies are important to protect the puppy from infectious disease while the pup is very young, these maternal antibodies can also interfere with vaccination by neutralizing the viral proteins that are inoculated during the vaccination. Because puppies lose their maternal antibodies at different rates, it is difficult to know whether, when you first vaccinate a young puppy, he still retains maternal antibodies. For this reason, vaccinating puppies against parvovirus several times during puppyhood is critical. The hope is that, if the first vaccine was neutralized by maternal antibodies, the next vaccination will have the desired effect of stimulating the puppy to make his own antibodies.

Puppies should receive their first vaccinations against parvovirus at 5 to 7 weeks of age. They then should receive booster shots every 3 to 4 weeks until they have had three shots. Your veterinarian will provide you with a schedule for your puppy's vaccinations. Stick to the schedule as closely as possible. The virus is very stable in the environment and can survive for months on inanimate objects such as clothing and floors. This makes it even more important that you vaccinate your dog against this virus.

Kennel cough

Kennel cough got its moniker for obvious reasons: Dogs commonly contract it from other dogs in kennels, and it causes coughing.

Kennel cough, also called *infectious tracheobronchitis,* can be caused by a single virus or a combination of viruses, particularly canine adenovirus-2 and canine parainfluenza virus. A bacterium called *Bordatella bronchiseptica* also can cause kennel cough alone or in combination with one or more of the viruses. Sometimes the viral infection impairs the normal defense systems of the lung, allowing bacteria to enter the lung, replicate, and cause pneumonia.

Dogs infected with kennel cough have a dry, hacking cough that often has a honking sound. At the end of a series of coughs, the dog may gag or retch so severely that it seems as if the dog will vomit. Indeed, sometimes the dog brings up a little frothy material at the end of the cough. The coughing worsens if the dog is exercised or becomes excited. Dogs may also have a watery discharge from the nose or eyes. Kennel cough itself lasts from seven to ten days, and dogs recover without treatment. If a dog contracts a secondary bacterial pneumonia, however, the results can be much more serious and, without treatment, can result in death.

The infection is highly transmissible between dogs and can spread like wildfire through dogs in a kennel or at a dog show. Dogs are infectious before they show signs of coughing, and sometimes even after they have recovered, so it is hard to prevent transmission.

The best prevention for kennel cough is vaccination. Because several agents can cause this infection, vaccination is not foolproof, but vaccinated dogs who do become infected usually have milder symptoms. The most effective vaccination protects against parainfluenza virus and Bordatella and is instilled into the nose of the dog. This vaccine consists of a live virus that has been modified so that it cannot cause severe disease. It can, however, cause a mild cough for a few days after vaccination, and can even be transmitted to other dogs during that time. Because of these side effects, however mild, most veterinarians suggest vaccination only for dogs who are at high risk for infection. This would include dogs who regularly go to dog shows, are boarded at kennels, attend doggie daycare, or commonly have contact with other dogs.

If your dog has a persistent hacking cough for more than 24 hours, call your veterinarian instead of visiting her. She then can decide over the telephone whether you should come to the clinic and risk transmitting this highly contagious infection to other dogs in the waiting room or hospital. If she decides it is a simple case of kennel cough, she may prescribe some cough suppressants and advise you to have your coughing canine rest for seven to ten days until he is better. If your dog is not eating or is lethargic, he may have a secondary bacterial infection. Your veterinarian will want to examine him and will probably prescribe antibiotics and other supportive care.

There is some evidence that Bordatella can be transmitted from dogs to immunosuppressed individuals, such as people who are taking immunosuppressive drugs after transplants or to fight cancer, or those suffering from AIDS. Keeping coughing dogs away from these individuals is probably best.

Distemper

Distemper is a vaccination success story. Once the scourge of the pooch population, most people have never heard of a dog actually having this infection, because vaccination programs have been highly successful in reducing the incidence of the disease.

The canine distemper virus is particularly wily. The first thing it does after entering the body is spread in the blood to all the lymph nodes and kill the lymphocytes that reside there. *Lymphocytes* are the major cells for antiviral defense, so the infected dog becomes severely immunosuppressed (and at risk for many other illnesses). This allows the virus to replicate in the lungs (and cause pneumonia), in the gastrointestinal tract (and cause diarrhea and dehydration), and even to enter the brain (and cause encephalitis, paralysis, and seizures). In addition, because the virus causes immunosuppression, infected dogs frequently contract secondary bacterial and parasitic infections that can also be life-threatening.

The first signs of distemper may be a discharge from the eyes accompanied by a fever. There may also be coughing, weight loss, diarrhea, and a lack of interest in food. The signs of distemper are so varied that any young puppy who is sick should be taken to the veterinarian for a definitive diagnosis. About 50 percent of adult dogs and 80 percent of puppies who contract distemper die, and dogs who do recover often retain lifelong debilitations such as seizures, blindness, or lameness.

As with most viral infections, treatment for distemper is limited. With supportive care, some dogs can pull through, but the key to beating this disease is to prevent infection by vaccination. Inoculating puppies when they are still very young is very important.

Battling Bacteria

Bacteria are veritable giants in comparison to viruses. You can only fit 25,000 bacteria (as compared to 25 million viruses) onto the period at the end of this sentence. Bacteria differ from viruses in that they can live on their own and don't need a host cell in which to replicate.

Bacteria live in the soil, in plants, and in animals — humans included. Although most species of bacteria are beneficial or at least cause no harm, the following sections discuss a couple of problems caused by some nasty bacteria.

Lyme disease

Lyme disease is a tick-borne bacterial disease that was first recognized in humans in Lyme, Connecticut, in 1975 and in dogs in 1984. The Lyme disease bacterium is transmitted to your dog by the tiny deer tick (shown in Figure 11-1) and probably, although less commonly, by other species of ticks, too. Deer ticks live on white-tailed deer and white-footed mice in the wild. They are very small — no larger than the head of a pin — making them very hard to see, especially in a dog's thick coat. A dog's greatest chance of becoming infected is from May to September, when the ticks are most active, but transmission can also occur at other times. Up to 40 percent of the deer ticks in the northeast, mid-Atlantic, north-central and Pacific coast of the United States contain the bacterium that causes Lyme disease.

Although many dogs get infected with the Lyme bacterium, only a few develop Lyme disease. Typical acute infection results in swollen joints, lameness, and muscle pain. However, the bacterium can also cause vague symptoms such as fever, loss of appetite, and lethargy, which can make infection difficult to diagnose in a timely fashion.

If your dog is suddenly lame without evidence of trauma, has a hot, swollen joint, or has a fever, especially if you know he was recently bitten by a tick, take him to the veterinarian. She will perform a complete physical examination and will take blood to be tested for antibodies to the Lyme bacterium.

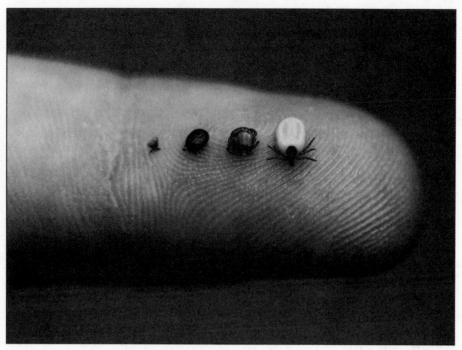

Figure 11-1:
From right to left: An engorged adult deer tick, an adult before attaching to the skin, an engorged nymph (young tick), a nymph before it has attached. Both adults and nymphs can transmit Lyme disease.

Photograph courtesy of Fred Dubbs

If Lyme disease is undiagnosed or left untreated, permanent damage to the joints can occur, and the bacterium also can spread to the heart and kidneys. Infected dogs should be treated with appropriate antibiotics as soon as possible.

Prevention of Lyme disease requires a two-pronged attack. Vaccines are available to protect your dog from infection. The vaccine is unique because it actually kills the bacterium inside the tick before it ever gets a chance to enter your dog. However, as with all vaccinations, there may be side effects, so discuss the pros and cons of vaccination with your veterinarian. Vaccination probably is a good idea for dogs who live in areas where Lyme disease is more common and for dogs who are frequently outdoors, like the one shown in Figure 11-2.

Figure 11-2:
Dogs who
work or play
outdoors
are exposed
to ticks and
are at higher
risk for
contracting
tick-borne
infections
such as
Lyme
disease. If
your dog is
in this
category,
talk with
your vet
about
vaccination.

The second part of your Lyme disease prevention plan is to try to ensure that your dog doesn't become exposed to the Lyme bacillus. Apply a product that repels ticks before your dog goes out for an adventure in the wild outdoors. Use a product recommended by your veterinarian — repellents purchased at pet stores and grocery stores frequently are not as effective. Examine your dog daily for ticks during the spring and summer months and remove them gently (see Chapter 2).

Leptospirosis

Leptospirosis is another disease that, like distemper, used to be a major dog-killer but has been very uncommon during the past three decades. We can thank effective vaccines for that. In the last three years, some unusual strains of leptospirosis were diagnosed in an increasing number of dogs. Veterinary scientists went to work and have now designed new vaccines to be effective against these canine killers.

Leptospirosis is caused by any one of about 200 different but related strains of bacteria. The bacteria infect many different species of wild and domesticated animals, including raccoons, skunks, opossums, and cattle. The infected animal sheds large numbers of bacteria in urine. Leptospira bacteria are specialists in water survival, so if the urine drains into standing water, these bugs can survive for a long time, just waiting for your dog to come along and have a drink. The bacterium then enters the blood stream and travels throughout the body to many tissues, where it replicates and causes damage. Leptospira particularly like to grow in the kidney and can cause severe renal failure in dogs. Of course, by replicating in the kidney, the bacteria has easy access to the urine so that it can be expelled to the environment and infect another unsuspecting animal.

The signs of disease in dogs include a sudden onset of fever and chills, lethargy, nausea, jaundice, vomiting, and diarrhea. If the dog is not quickly treated with antibiotics, he may stop producing urine and hemorrhage into the lung and intestine. Luckily, with antibiotics and supportive care, most dogs recover, but complete recovery may take several weeks.

Leptospirosis also infects humans. Most people, just like dogs, get infected by exposure to urine from wildlife or farm animals. However, the potential for dogs to transmit the infection to their people does occur. In areas where leptospirosis outbreaks are occurring, keep pets away from children's play areas, including sandboxes and wading pools.

Fighting the Fungus among Us

Fungi inhabit the soils in various locations throughout the United States and Canada. Some inhabit the soil of the Mississippi Valley, the mid-Atlantic states, and southern Canada; others grow in soil contaminated with bird or bat excrement; and still others call the dry southwestern soils home. Active dogs who spend a lot of time running outdoors (like the hunting dog in Figure 11-3), especially those who love to dig, risk becoming infected with fungal organisms that live in the soil. Usually a strong immune system will

---

Rickettsia: What a racket!

Rickettsia are poorly understood organisms that are intermediate in size between viruses and bacteria. They live inside cells like viruses do, but they are susceptible to some of the antibiotics that kill bacteria. The two main rickettsial diseases of dogs are Ehrlichiosis and Rocky Mountain spotted fever. Both are carried by those diabolical disease-delivery units — ticks.

Ehrlichiosis and Rocky Mountain spotted fever are both characterized by fever, rashes, anemia, hemorrhages, and joint and muscle pain in dogs. If your dog is ill for more than 24 hours, particularly if you know a tick has bitten him, it's a good idea to have a veterinarian give him the once-over. Only a vet can differentiate between these two diseases, which can appear quite similar clinically. Blood tests are required to make a definitive diagnosis, and even they aren't foolproof. Treatment of rickettsial infections requires antibiotic treatment for six to eight weeks.

keep these bad bugs at bay. But if the dog is weakened by another infection or has a weak immune system, these organisms can get a foothold in the dog's body and cause serious disease.

Figure 11-3:
Hunting dogs like Flyer are exposed to fungal organisms in the soil.

These fungal agents cause arthritis, pneumonia, infections in bones, and signs of systemic infection such as fever, loss of appetite, and malaise. No vaccines are available for these organisms. If you live in an area where fungi are present, the best thing you can do to prevent infection is to keep your dog from digging, especially around the holes of burrowing animals where the fungi are especially abundant. Also, keep your dog away from areas frequented by large numbers of bats or birds.

Preventing Parasites

Parasites are the ultimate opportunists, living on the skin, in the intestine and just about anywhere they can gain a foothold. Luckily, with the excellent veterinary preventive medicine programs we have today, our dogs don't have to suffer parasitic infections any more.

Fleas

Fleas are the bane of a dog's existence. They make him itch, itch, itch. And the more a dog scratches, the itchier he seems to get. These irritating insects can cause itching in two different ways. First, they bite on a big chunk of skin and start sucking blood. They stay at one spot until they are full, or hop around, drinking at many different sites. Worse, they often bite in thin-skinned, sensitive areas such as near the ears, at the base of the tail, and in the groin area. Flea bites are irritating enough, but many dogs actually develop an allergic reaction to the saliva of the fleas, and they become extremely itchy all over, even with the bite of only one flea. Sometimes the allergy is so severe that a dog will chew at himself until he loses big patches of hair, bleeds, and ultimately develops thick, crusty skin, especially on his feet, at the base of his tail, and around his back legs.

If you see your dog scratching vigorously or biting aggressively at himself, it's time for a bug check. Start by looking around your dog's ears, at the base of his tail, and on his tummy. Part the hair and look for brown, flat, oval bugs about ⅛ inch long. Keep your eyes peeled because a startled flea can jump quickly into the air and land several inches away. Frequently you won't actually see a flea, but you can see flea dirt stuck in the dog's hairs. This is flea excrement, a crumbly black material that consists mainly of digested blood. You can identify flea dirt by placing a drop of water over the dirt, letting it soak up the water for a minute or two, and then smearing the dirt on a piece of white paper towel. A reddish smear confirms that it is, in fact, flea dirt.

If you identify a flea or flea dirt, leap into action. The only thing that will give your dog relief is ridding his body and your house of those pesky pests. See Chapter 2 for complete instructions on how to ban these bugs from your dog's body and keep them away. With the many safe anti-flea products that are available today, there is no longer any reason for your dog to suffer.

Fleas are especially fond of cats, so if you share your digs with an animal of the feline persuasion, be sure to include her in your flea prevention and treatment protocol.

Ticks

Ticks are major pests not only because they can bite your dog and cause local skin irritation, but because they carry a host of other pesky germs that can make both you and your dog sick. Ticks live on long grasses and shrubs, and they have a sticky substance on their bodies that enables them to easily cling to the fur of passing animals such as your dog. They then crawl down the hair to the skin and latch on, taking a big bite. They suck blood for hours and even days until they are full to bursting. During this time, they can transmit whatever infectious organisms they happen to be carrying.

If you live in an area where ticks are prevalent (most of the U.S. except the Southwest and Alaska), it is important that you check your dog for ticks every day, at least during tick season (which is during the spring and summer months). Carefully remove every tick you find. For tips on removing ticks, turn to Chapter 2.

If your dog enjoys the outdoors (and most dogs do), apply a product that prevents ticks from attaching to the skin. Be sure to get advice from your veterinarian on which product is best, because new products enter the market all the time. Also, continue to check your dog from head to toe every time he comes in from outside. The places you're most likely to find ticks are around your dog's face, eyes, and ears, although they really can be anywhere. Be sure to look inside the ears, too!

Worms

Dozens of kinds of worms can set up shop in your dog's body, often in the intestine. Puppies are especially susceptible to infections with worms, because some species of worms are transmitted from the mother before the puppy is even born. This is why deworming puppies is so important (see Chapter 2).

The general level of care for our dogs these days is so high, however, that adult dogs rarely have problems with worms. Nonetheless, it is a good idea to bring a fecal sample to your annual veterinary visit for the first few years of your dog's life, just to be sure.

If you adopt a dog from a shelter or find a stray, be sure to have him checked for worms, because you won't know whether he has had adequate veterinary care from puppyhood.

Being Aware of Which Bugs Infect Humans

Just as we share our lives with dogs, we sometimes share our infections, too. Being aware of the potential for transmission of organisms from dogs to humans, called *zoonosis,* so you can take preventive measures is important. The most important zoonotic disease in dogs is rabies, but there are many other infectious organisms that dogs can unwittingly share with us on occasion, including leptospirosis, roundworm, and even ticks and fleas.

Humans also can be infected by the canine roundworm, _Toxocara canis_. If a human accidentally ingests Toxocara eggs, the eggs will hatch and larvae will migrate through the body causing fever, rash, and cough. This condition is called _visceral larval migrans_. If the worm larvae migrate to the eye, they can cause blindness. These infections usually occur in children who live in conditions of poor sanitation. Toxocara eggs must mature in the environment for one to three weeks before they are infectious, so humans don't become infected by handling dogs directly. They must contact eggs in the environment. Toxocara eggs are very hardy, however, and can survive in the environment for weeks or months.

Here are some tips to prevent human infection with Toxocara:

- ✔ Deworm all puppies, regardless of whether Toxocara eggs are detected in fecal samples, twice (21 days apart) during their initial vaccination period.
- ✔ Do not allow children to play where dogs defecate.
- ✔ Always clean up after your dog in public places.

Several other infectious organisms can be transmitted from dogs to humans, but these only infect immunosuppressed humans, such as those undergoing cancer treatment or organ transplantation and individuals with AIDS. If you are immunosuppressed and want to have a dog, your best bet is to get a clinically normal adult dog from a private family. If this is not possible, the prospective four-legged family member should be given a thorough physical examination by a veterinarian including fecal and blood tests.

Chapter 12

Canine First Aid

In This Chapter
▶ Keeping a first-aid kit at the ready in your car and in your home
▶ Knowing how to administer CPR to your dog
▶ Using basic first-aid techniques to deal with common injuries

Accidents happen to all of us, including our dogs. Although you can take some safety precautions to help your dog avoid these pitfalls, you can't guarantee that she'll never run into trouble. And that's where knowing first aid comes in handy.

In this chapter, I tell you everything you need to know to care for your dog when she's injured or ill — from bites to breaks and everything in between. Read this chapter now, while your pooch is sleeping by your side. Don't wait until you need it.

Being Prepared

One of the best things you can do to help your dog in the event of an emergency is to be prepared before the emergency strikes. Administering first aid is very difficult — if not impossible — without a few essential supplies. And you can do a lot beforehand to get to know your dog, so that when you're faced with an emergency, you're ready to do what's required. I cover these important topics in the following sections.

Assembling a canine first-aid kit

Before you're faced with an emergency, assemble two first-aid kits for your dog — one for your car and one for home. Always keep the kits in the same place so you can get your hands on one right away in an emergency.

Your first-aid kit doesn't need to be big or expensive to be useful.

Getting the container ready

Find a water-resistant container that's large enough to carry everything without being cumbersome. Fishing tackle boxes work well because they have trays with dividers to keep things organized.

Put a large red cross and the words *first aid kit* on each side of the container. Someone may need to locate and use it in an emergency, and labeling the kit clearly can be a big help.

To the inside of the lid, tape a piece of paper with the following information in clear letters:

- **Your name, address, and telephone number.** You may also want to include additional methods by which you can be reached, such as a pager number or an e-mail address.

- **The breed, name, and date of birth of your dog.** If you have more than one dog, provide this information for each dog.

- **Any medical conditions your dog has and any medication she takes regularly.** Again, be sure to provide this information for each animal.

- **The names, addresses, and telephone numbers of emergency contact people in case you are incapacitated.**

- **The name, address, and telephone number of your veterinarian.** Be sure to provide the contact information for your after-hours emergency clinic if that number is different from your vet's regular information.

- **Contact information for the National Animal Poison Control Center.** You can reach them at 888-426-4435 24 hours a day, 365 days a year to inquire about the toxic potential of various household products and plants your dog may have found tasty. You also can get advice about emergency care for a dog who has gotten into a toxin. The cost per case is $45, which includes follow-up (including contacting your veterinarian if you request) and is charged to a major credit card. To have the fee charged to your telephone bill (and avoid having to track down your credit card number in an emergency), dial 900-680-0000. If you want to find information on the service in a non-emergency situation, you can visit their Web site at www.napcc.aspca.org.

- **A list of the contents of your first-aid kit.** For each of the drugs in the kit, you should also have a note indicating the appropriate dose for each of your dogs. That way you won't have to do any calculations in your head in a time of crisis. When preparing the kit, be sure to check the doses with your veterinarian.

The information in this list can be useful at home as well as on the road. I keep this information posted on my refrigerator so it is easily accessible in an emergency.

In addition to taping this list on the inside lid of your first-aid kit, for the kit that you keep in your car, place the following:

- **Your dog's rabies certificate.** Some states require that you have a rabies certificate at all times if you are traveling with a dog.

- **A photograph of each dog with her name, tattoo, and microchip number.** This information will help a rescuer identify each of your dogs individually if you are incapacitated.

Keep these materials in a resealable plastic bag, so that they're all together and won't get lost.

Knowing what to put in the first-aid kit

Following is a list of the components of an all-purpose first-aid kit and a brief description of what each item is used for. You can find most of these items at your local pharmacy; the rest you can purchase from your veterinarian or from a dog supply catalog.

With time and experience, you may identify other items you want to include in the kit, particularly because you may find yourself using the kit for yourself and other humans in need. You may also find that you don't need some of the items listed. Eventually, your first-aid kit will reflect you, your dogs, and your individual needs. But the following supplies are a good place to start:

- **ACE brand elastic bandage.** You can use this bandage to hold an ice pack to a dog's leg, to wrap a sprain temporarily until you can get veterinary assistance, or to secure an injured dog to a makeshift stretcher.

- **Adhesive tape.** Use tape to secure bandages and splints. Make sure that you have a large roll, and replace it when it gets close to running out.

- **Alcohol swabs.** Look for individually packaged swabs, which you can use to sterilize instruments or small areas of skin.

- **Aspirin (enteric coated).** Give 5 milligrams per pound every 12 hours to temporarily relieve pain. Many dogs vomit after taking regular aspirin, so be sure to get the enteric-coated variety.

  Never substitute ibuprofen or acetaminophen for aspirin. Both of these substances can be very toxic to dogs.

- **Athlete's foot powder.** Shake a little powder into an infected ear after cleaning it. If your dog is susceptible to ear infections, you can also shake a little powder into her ears once a week and after swimming, to prevent infection.

- ✓ **Bacitracin or Neosporin.** Apply this or another antibiotic ointment to wounds that may be dirty and are likely to become infected.

  Never use these ointments in the eye. Special antibacterial formulations are used for the eyes, and these should be used only with your veterinarian's recommendation.

- ✓ **Benadryl.** You can use Benadryl for insect bites or stings. Give your dog 1 to 2 milligrams per pound, every 8 hours.

- ✓ **Cohesive bandage.** Use this stretchy wrap to cover and secure gauze bandages. It clings to itself so you don't need adhesive tape.

- ✓ **Cold pack.** Use a cold pack to prevent or reduce swelling after a sprain or strain or to treat burns. Buy the kind that becomes cold when you fold the pack in half.

- ✓ **Cotton squares.** You can use these to clean and protect wounds. They're better for cleaning wounds than cotton balls because they don't shed fibers when you wipe them over sticky areas such as where blood is drying.

- ✓ **Cotton swabs.** Use these to clean your dog's ears.

- ✓ **First-aid instructions.** Photocopy the pages of this chapter that discuss first-aid treatments and store it in your first-aid kit. That way you will have written instructions always available in an emergency. When you're trying to take care of a sick or injured dog, remembering all the details can be difficult.

- ✓ **Gauze bandage roll.** You can use these to bandage wounds and to hold splints in place. Cut off a length of bandage and fold it up to cover a wound, or wrap the bandage around the leg to keep a cold pack in place or to secure a splint to the leg.

- ✓ **Gloves (latex).** Any time you need to keep your hands protected or clean, wear a pair of latex gloves. I use them when cleaning up after a dog who is vomiting or has diarrhea and when I need to remove a tick with my fingers.

- ✓ **Green Soap or Hibitane.** You can use any gentle liquid antibacterial soap used for cleaning skin and wounds.

- ✓ **Hydrogen peroxide.** Give your dog 1 to 3 teaspoons of hydrogen peroxide every 10 minutes to induce vomiting. Don't give more than three doses 10 minutes apart. Do not use it to clean wounds.

- ✓ **Imodium A-D.** Give your dog 1 milligram per 15 pounds once or twice a day to relieve diarrhea.

- ✓ **Lubricating jelly.** Use this to lubricate a thermometer or to prevent gauze bandages from sticking to a wound. You can buy it in individually wrapped packets.

- ✔ **Muzzle.** You can use a length of gauze bandage, a belt, or a soft rope to make an emergency muzzle for your dog. Even if your dog has never showed signs of aggression before, if she is in pain or frightened, she may snap at you, so be sure to muzzle her — for your safety and hers.

- ✔ **Needle and thread.** You can use a needle and thread to stitch wounds when you know you won't be able to get veterinary help within six hours.

- ✔ **NuSkin liquid bandage.** Use this instead of sutures to close a small, clean, recent wound.

- ✔ **Penlight flashlight.** Use a flashlight to look down your dog's ears or throat — anywhere you need extra light. You can also use it to check whether a dog's eyes respond to light in case of an injury to the head.

- ✔ **Pepto-Bismol liquid.** Give 1 teaspoon per 25 pounds every 6 hours to relive diarrhea and vomiting. The liquid form is faster-acting than the tablet form.

- ✔ **Plastic bags (resealable).** These are handy for temporarily packaging items that are leaking, protecting open packages from drying, or collecting specimens such as fecal samples.

- ✔ **Razor blade (retractable) or blunt-ended scissors.** Use these for cutting bandages and tape and for trimming the hair around a wound.

- ✔ **Safety pins.** You can use safety pins to fasten bandages together if you don't have tape.

- ✔ **Sterile saline solution.** Use this to rinse out the eyes or to clean wounds.

- ✔ **Stockinet or bootie.** Put one of these on your dog to protect a bandage on a leg or foot.

- ✔ **Styptic powder.** Use this to stop small areas of bleeding, such as when you accidentally clip your dog's nails too close.

- ✔ **Sun block.** Apply this lotion to your dog's nose or any areas of light skin if your dog has a thin coat.

- ✔ **Syringe.** Use a syringe to flush your dog's eye with saline or to administer peroxide to induce vomiting.

- ✔ **Thermometer (rectal).** Use a thermometer made for dogs. A dog's normal body temperature is between 100.5 and 102.8 degrees.

- ✔ **Tweezers (flat-ended).** You can use these to remove foreign objects, such as ticks, thorns, and foxtails, from your dog's skin.

Be sure to keep a blanket in your car when you travel as well. You can use it to warm a dog suffering from frostbite, to wrap a dog who is in shock, or as an emergency stretcher.

Label each item in your first-aid kit with its name and expiration date.

Go through your kit every year, replacing medications that have expired or for which the labels have become hard to read, and replenishing supplies. Be sure to do this before you take a trip with your dogs, too.

Getting familiar with your dog before emergency strikes

Before an emergency happens, find out as much as you can about your dog's anatomy and her inner workings (see Chapter 9 for more information), so that you will be prepared to examine her and make decisions quickly when necessary.

In the following sections, I cover a few techniques you should become familiar with now, before emergency strikes.

Taking your dog's temperature

Know how to take your dog's temperature quickly and without causing her any undue stress. You'll need a rectal thermometer, some lubricating jelly, and a clean cloth. Here's how to do it:

1. **Gripping the thermometer tightly, shake it down until it registers below 98 degrees.**

2. **Dab some lubricating jelly onto the end of the thermometer.**

3. **With your dog standing or lying down on her side, gently raise your dog's tail and insert the thermometer into the rectum, using a slow twisting motion.**

   Talk to your dog and praise him for remaining still. The first few times you do this, you may want to have someone give her a treat while you are inserting the thermometer, to keep her mind on her taste buds and not the other end of her body.

4. **After one minute, remove the thermometer slowly, wipe it with a clean cloth, and read the temperature.**

   A dog's normal temperature ranges from 100.5 to 102.8 degrees. The temperature can rise significantly after exercise, but it should return to normal within 20 minutes.

There are new electronic thermometers on the market that allow you to take a person's temperature by placing a plastic probe just inside the ear canal. Before you use one of these thermometers on your dog, ask your veterinarian whether your model will work on dogs.

Counting your dog's breathing rate

Become familiar with your dog's breathing. Count how many times a minute she breathes while she's resting and compare it to her breathing rate after she exercises. Most dogs have a resting breathing rate of 15 to 30 breaths per minute. The breathing rate may rise when a dog is in pain or has a fever.

Checking your dog's pulse

When you check your dog's pulse, locate the *femoral artery,* which lies just below the skin on the inside of the leg, between two large muscles where the leg joins the body. With your dog standing, reach around in front of the rear leg where it joins her body, and slide your fingers into the groin area. You will feel the artery pumping each time the heart contracts and sends blood down the aorta to the femoral artery, which supplies blood to the leg. When you have found the artery with your dog standing, try it with your dog lying on her side. Count how many pulses you feel in 15 seconds and multiply by 4 to get the number of beats per minute.

Become familiar with your dog's pulse rate and how her pulse feels when she is relaxed as well as after exercise. Dogs normally have a pulse between 70 and 120 beats per minute. In puppies, the pulse ranges from 120 to 160 beats per minute.

Examining your dog's gums

Look at your dog's gums while she is at rest. Lift your dog's lip up and look at the color of the gums above an upper canine tooth — the gums should be pink. Press on the gums with your finger. When you remove your finger, the gums should briefly be white but should return to their pink color within two seconds. This is the capillary refill test.

The appearance of the gums is very informative. If the gums are blue, the dog lacks oxygen. If they are white, the dog has lost blood, either internally or externally. If the gums are purple or gray and there is a slow capillary refill, the dog is probably in shock. If they are bright red, she may be fighting a systemic infection or may have been exposed to a toxin.

Sometimes normal dogs have black-pigmented gums, which can make assessment more difficult. For these dogs, you need to examine the pink tissue on the inside of the lower eyelid by gently pulling the eyelid down. In this case, you can only observe the color of the tissue — you can't perform the capillary refill test — but any of the colors in the preceding paragraph apply to the eyelid tissue as well as to the gums.

Knowing What to Do in an Emergency

Just as you need to have a first-aid kit assembled and know how to check your dog's vital signs, you also need to be aware of what you should do in the case of an emergency. In the following sections, I cover how to help an injured dog, how to give CPR, and how to treat common injuries and problems.

Approaching an accident scene

When you come upon an accident scene in which a dog has been injured, always be sure that *you* are safe before you try to help the dog. Every year people are killed on roads and highways because they put their own lives at risk to assist injured dogs or other animals. If the dog is in an unsafe area, secure the area and move the dog to a safe place *before* assessing her. If the dog is already in a safe area, you can begin to assess her medical condition immediately.

If other people are nearby, try to organize them to be a help rather than a hindrance:

- ✔ Ask a few people to keep passersby away from the dog.
- ✔ Ask one person to call a local veterinary clinic.
- ✔ Have another person arrange to transport the dog.
- ✔ You may also have someone assist you in performing CPR and have another person apply pressure to any wounds.

Handling an injured dog

Whenever you approach an injured dog, always start by protecting yourself from being bitten. If your dog is in severe pain and is afraid, even your best friend may bite the hand that feeds her. You can make a temporary muzzle out of a length of bandage, a belt, a shoelace, or some pantyhose. If it turns out the muzzle was not necessary because your dog responded to your examination and treatment well, your dog will forgive you for having used one. If it was necessary, you'll be glad you had the foresight to protect yourself.

To apply a muzzle, follow these steps:

1. **Approach the dog slowly, using a soothing tone of voice.**

2. **Bring the bandage (or other material) up under the dog's chin about halfway between the leather of the nose and her eyes.**

3. **Tie the two ends in one loop on top of the dog's nose.**

4. **Bring the bandage back under the dog's chin and tie another single knot under the chin.**

5. **Bring the two ends of the bandage to the back of your dog's neck behind her ears and tie them in a bow.**

6. **Tie the loops of the bow into another single knot to keep the muzzle securely fastened.**

The muzzle should be fairly tight, enough that your dog cannot open her mouth, but not so tight that it impedes breathing.

Examining an injured dog

When your dog is injured or ill, your primary job is to remain calm and be deliberate in your actions. Try to keep your voice from revealing the fear you may feel inside. Use the A-B-C checklist outlined in the following sections whenever you come upon a scene in which a dog is seriously injured and appears to be unconscious or in shock. Even if the dog has a bleeding wound, carry out this preliminary assessment first. Respiratory and circulatory problems usually are more life-threatening than wounds. When you are certain the dog is breathing and is not in circulatory collapse, you can deal with the wound.

Airway

If the dog is unconscious and there are no apparent neck or back injuries (excluding bleeding wounds), tilt her head back slightly, open her mouth, and look inside for any objects that may be impeding airflow. Gently pull her tongue forward (holding the tongue is easier if you grab it with gauze or cloth), and check for objects that may be deeper down the throat. Pulling the tongue forward also opens the airway, making breathing easier.

Breathing

Check for the rise and fall of the chest that indicates that the dog is breathing. If the dog is not breathing and the airways are clear, begin rescue breathing immediately:

1. **Cup your hands around the muzzle and seal your lips around the edge of the leather of the dog's nose.**

2. **Breathe into the dog's nostrils for two seconds.**

3. **Watch for the dog's chest to rise, indicating that air is entering the lungs.**

4. **If the chest doesn't rise, check the airway again.**

   Repeat for a total of three breaths.

Give *gentle* puffs of breath (the amount will depend on the dog's size). Don't blow as though you're trying to inflate a balloon.

Circulation

Assess the dog's circulation by checking the pulse at the femoral artery. If you've practiced on your dog before, this should be no problem; if you haven't, check out the section called "Checking your dog's pulse," earlier in this chapter for tips.

A healthy dog's pulse is approximately 10 to 14 beats per 10 seconds and feels strong. (Smaller dogs have a more rapid pulse.) If the pulse is there but feels weak, the dog is probably in shock.

If you have trouble feeling the pulse in the groin, place your thumb and fingers on either side of the chest wall just behind the elbows to see if the heart is beating. If you detect no pulse or heartbeat, begin CPR immediately (for instructions see the following section).

Examine the dog's gums to check circulation, too. If the gums are blue, the dog may not be getting enough oxygen. Be sure that you've checked the airway and cleared it of any foreign objects. If the dog has a weak or rapid pulse, shallow breathing, gray, purple, or pale gums, glazed eyes, weakness, or collapse, she is in shock and you should make arrangements to get her to a veterinarian *as soon as possible.* In the meantime, keep her quiet, cover her with a blanket, and keep her head as low as the rest of his body. If the dog is not breathing or if you cannot feel a pulse, begin CPR.

Administering CPR

If your dog is not breathing or doesn't have a pulse, follow these instructions to administer cardiopulmonary resuscitation (CPR):

1. **Position the dog on her side.**

2. **Clear the dog's mouth of any foreign matter (see Figure 12-1).**

3. **Hold the muzzle closed with your hands and give mouth-to-nose respiration at a rate of 12 to 15 breaths per minute (see Figure 12-2).**

   Watch for the chest to rise to be sure the air is getting into the lungs. If the chest doesn't rise, check again for anything that may be obstructing airflow.

Figure 12-1:
Before administering CPR, clear the dog's mouth of any foreign matter.

Photograph courtesy of Angela Koeller

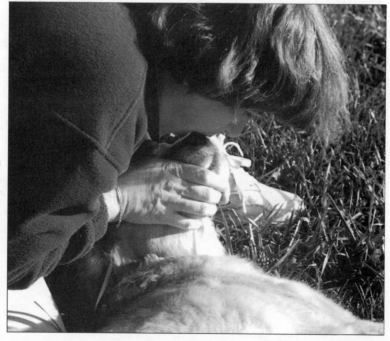

Figure 12-2:
Hold your dog's muzzle closed with your hands and breathe into the nose 12 to 15 times a minute.

Photograph courtesy of Angela Koeller

4. **Begin chest compressions.**

   With a large dog, kneel at the dog's back. Push the dog's uppermost front leg forward out of the way. Lay one hand over the other and compress the chest wall over the heart (right about where the dog's elbow would be with the leg at rest) with the heel of your hand (see Figure 12-3). Push gently, and then let go immediately. For a very small dog (one weighing less than 30 pounds), lay the dog on her right side, place your thumb and fingers on either side of the chest and compress from both sides.

   Regardless of the size of the dog, do 60 to 80 compressions per minute (approximately one compression a second), and don't compress the chest for more than a split second or the heart won't have room to beat.

   If you're alone, give one breath and then five chest compressions. If you have help, one person can perform mouth-to-nose respiration while the other compresses the heart. In that case, give one breath for every 3 to 4 chest compressions.

Figure 12-3:
Place your hands over the heart and compress the chest 60 to 80 times per minute.

Photograph courtesy of Angela Koeller

Giving first aid treatment

When you're sure that an injured dog is breathing and has a pulse, you can start attending to her injuries. In the following sections, I cover some common injuries and problems requiring first aid.

Knowing these first aid techniques should help you in an emergency. But remember, this is first aid — basic techniques to help you aid your dog *before you can get veterinary assistance*. First aid is *not* a substitute for the care and expertise of a veterinarian.

Allergic reactions

In addition to normal allergic reactions (like itching and sneezing), some dogs may experience more severe symptoms, including the following:

- **Hives or swelling of the muzzle.** Some dogs respond to an allergen with swelling of the face or bumps that appear over a large part of the trunk. You may also see the dog biting or licking at herself or she may have red, weeping eyes. Apply a cold pack to the swollen area if it is small. If the swelling continues or there is swelling over a large area, administer Benadryl (at 1 to 2 milligrams per pound) and contact your veterinarian. Check your dog's respiration periodically, because there may also be swelling of the throat, which can impair her breathing.

- **Shock.** Signs of shock include weak or rapid pulse, shallow breathing, gray, purple, or pale gums, glazed eyes, weakness, or collapse. Lay the dog on her side and cover her with a blanket. Administer CPR if necessary. Transport the dog to a veterinarian as soon as possible.

Bleeding

Blood from an artery is bright red and sprays from the vessel in time with each beat of the heart. A dog can lose a great deal of blood quickly if an artery is cut. Blood from a vein or from small vessels under the skin is burgundy-colored and pours slowly or seeps from the wound.

To stop bleeding, apply pressure to the wound with a piece of gauze or cloth for several minutes. Even if the gauze is soaked with blood, don't lift it to see if the bleeding has stopped, because the gauze actually helps clot the blood. Just add extra layers of gauze. Depending on the area of the body and the size of the wound, it may take 10 to 15 minutes for bleeding to stop.

If ice is available, place it around the area of the wound to slow blood flow. Once the bleeding has stopped, you can bandage the wound (see the "Wounds" section later in this chapter) and arrange to get the dog to a veterinarian for assessment.

Never use a tourniquet to stop bleeding because it can cut off necessary circulation to the area.

Broken bones

When your dog has a fracture, the goal is to stabilize the dog until she can be examined and treated by a veterinarian. A broken bone will be very painful in the area of the break. Fractures are sometimes obvious, such as when the leg is lying in an abnormal position or when a piece of bone is poking through the skin. But sometimes a fracture may be present when the leg looks only swollen. If you try to move the bones, you may feel a grinding under your fingers caused by the two broken ends of the bone rubbing against each other.

If veterinary care is available, do not apply a splint. Carefully place the dog on a firm, level surface and take her to the clinic. If you are far from veterinary help, the leg should carefully be splinted before your dog is moved. The best splint is something rigid but padded such as a board wrapped in a towel. The splint should be placed against the dog's limb, avoiding movement of the bones as much as possible. The leg and joints above and below the break should be taped or wrapped to the splint. (Do not bandage fractured ribs, spine, or pelvis.) Transport the dog to a veterinary clinic as soon as possible.

A *fracture* is a partial or complete break in a bone. Fractures are classified by severity, and the same classifications are used for both dogs and people:

- **Greenstick fracture:** The least serious type of fracture is the *greenstick fracture,* in which one side of the bone is broken but the other side is just bent. The two ends of the bone are not moved from their original positions. This type of partial fracture is seen more often in young, growing dogs because their bones are less brittle than those of adult dogs. A dog can walk (although gingerly) on a leg with a greenstick fracture; this kind of fracture can only be diagnosed by x-ray.

- **Complete fracture:** A *complete fracture* is one in which the bone is broken through its width. Generally, the two ends of bone are moved from where they should be, because contractions of the muscle move the broken pieces of bone away from their original location. A complete fracture is more serious than a greenstick fracture; the damage to the bone is greater, and the surrounding muscles and maybe even ligaments and tendons are usually damaged. Complete fractures can be

  - Simple, in which there are just two pieces of bone, or

  - Comminuted, in which there are many pieces of bone.

  - Compound, in which pieces of bone have punctured through the skin.

No matter what kind of fracture, all the pieces of bone have to be replaced to their original location by a veterinarian before healing can begin.

Burns

Dogs are most often burned when hot or *caustic* (strong acids or cleaning solutions such as lye) liquids are spilled on them. Burns may also be caused when a dog gets too close to a candle, a stove, or a fire. Some dogs can even get a blistering sunburn, especially on the first sunny day after the winter.

Burns are classified by degrees, depending on their severity:

- **First degree:** In a first-degree burn, the hair is singed and the skin may be reddened.
- **Second degree:** In a second-degree burn the hair is burned off and the skin is red and blistered.
- **Third degree:** In a third degree burn, the skin is black, brown, or white. If the third-degree burn is extensive, the dog may go into shock.

If the burn was caused by a caustic liquid, wipe or rinse it off before treating it. For all burns, here are treatment suggestions:

- **Minor burns (first and second degree):** If the burn occurred within the last hour, apply a cold pack for 20 to 30 minutes and then treat the burn as a superficial wound (see "Wounds" later in this chapter).
- **Severe burns (third degree):** If your dog permits, apply a cold pack or a cold, wet cloth to the area, cover gently with gauze, and take her to the veterinarian as soon as possible.

Never apply ointments or butter to severe burns, and never touch the skin or rub anything on it.

Choking

Dogs are ever curious — and second only to their noses, they use their mouths to investigate new and interesting things. Dogs can choke on just about anything that is the size of the opening to the trachea, but the most common offenders are small balls such as golf and squash balls, rawhide and real bones, cellophane, and plastic children's toys.

A dog who is choking will make retching motions and will look panicked, often pacing back and forth and pawing at her mouth. Her chest may be heaving but she isn't making any airway noises.

If you suspect your dog is choking, first examine her mouth. Pull the tongue forward and remove the foreign object if possible. If you can't see the foreign object, use the canine Heimlich maneuver to try to dislodge the object:

- **For large dogs:** Stand behind your dog and place your arms around her body. Make a fist with one hand, and place the thumb of the hand with the fist against your dog's abdomen just where the sternum ends. With the other hand, grasp your fist and push upward and forward (toward the dog's shoulders), suddenly and forcefully (see Figure 12-4). Do this thrusting motion four or five times. Check the dog's airway again and clear any debris from the mouth. Repeat the chest thrusts if necessary. If the dog is unconscious, clear the airway and perform rescue breathing.

- ✔ **For small dogs:** Hold the dog with her head up so that her spine is against your chest. Make a fist with one hand, and place it against your dog's abdomen just where the sternum ends (see Figure 12-5). Grasp the fist with your other hand, and give four or five rapid thrusts inward and upward. Check the dog's airway again and clear any debris from the mouth. Repeat the chest thrusts if necessary. If the dog is unconscious, clear the airway and perform rescue breathing.

Cold exposure

Hypothermia is a lowering of the dog's body temperature caused by cold exposure. Dogs don't suffer from hypothermia very often because they carry their fur coats with them everywhere they go. However, if a dog is wet or if she has a very thin coat, she may get cold quite easily. The first response that a dog has when she's cold is to shiver. Later, the dog may act lethargic and become unresponsive.

If you recognize that your dog has hypothermia, follow these suggestions:

- ✔ Move the dog to a warm environment and cover her with a blanket.

- ✔ Rub her body (not her legs) gently to increase circulation.

- ✔ If she's wet, dry her with towels or a blow dryer on medium heat.

- ✔ Take your dog's temperature to monitor her recovery.

- ✔ Offer warm sugar water if the dog is conscious.

Do not apply sources of heat, such as heating pads or hot water bottles, directly to your dog's skin.

If the dog begins to lick her paws or appears uncomfortable, she may have frostbite. Restrain the dog and place warm compresses on the affected area.

Diarrhea

If you have a dog long enough, you'll have to deal with diarrhea eventually. Diarrhea can be caused by a dog's propensity to eat garbage or rotten animals, by a viral or bacterial infection, or sometimes just by stress.

Figure 12-4:
To treat choking in a large dog, place your hands under your dog where the chest joins the abdomen and grasp your fist. Thrust upward and forward.

Photograph courtesy of Angela Koeller

Figure 12-5:
To treat choking in a small dog, hold the dog against your chest and compress the lower ribcage with your fist several times.

If your dog has diarrhea, withhold food for 24 hours in adults or 12 hours in puppies (under 6 months). Instead of water, offer the dog ice cubes, so that she takes in the water slowly. Administer Imodium A-D (1 milligram per 15 pounds once or twice a day) and/or Pepto-Bismol (1 teaspoon per 25 pounds every six hours) to help calm an upset stomach and stop diarrhea. For the next 72 hours, feed the dog a bland diet (75 percent rice, 25 percent low-fat protein such as skinless chicken) in small but gradually increasing amounts. Then shift to the dog's regular diet over the next two days.

If your dog has bloody diarrhea, is depressed and dull, or continues to have diarrhea for 24 hours while you are withholding food, she should be examined by a veterinarian.

Drowning

Most dogs are excellent swimmers. Occasionally, however, a dog will drown because she gets caught in something underwater or gets overwhelmed by an undertow. Sometimes a dog who is an experienced swimmer drowns inexplicably. Some breeds have trouble swimming and may drown in shallow, safe water. Bulldogs, Pugs, and Pekingeses all have bodies that can make swimming difficult.

The first thing to do when you have brought the dog ashore is to empty the lungs of water. If the dog is small, you can elevate the rear end of the dog and water will drain out of the dog's mouth. If necessary, you can hold the dog upside down and swing her gently until the water is expelled. Pumping the chest and opening the mouth periodically may be helpful as well. If the dog is large, try to sling her over your shoulder so that the head, front legs, and chest hang down in front of you and the rear legs hand down your back.

When the water is expelled, start rescue breathing. When the dog is breathing on her own, wrap her in a blanket and transport her to a veterinarian immediately.

Ear infections

Chronic ear infections are extremely uncomfortable to dogs and can ultimately affect hearing and balance. If your dog has ever had an ear infection, check her ears weekly and keep them clean — this is the best way to prevent infections and to recognize them quickly when they do occur.

To clean the ears, moisten a cotton swab with alcohol or hydrogen peroxide and clean the outer ear, making sure to clean around all the bumps inside the ear and down into the ear canal. Don't go farther into the canal than you can see — you don't want to risk breaking the eardrum. Shake athlete's foot powder into the ear — it has drying properties and acts as an antifungal. If your dog has hair inside her ear canal, pluck it regularly to help with air circulation.

Electric shock

Occasionally a dog, usually a puppy, will bite down on an electric cord and suffer electrical shock, often accompanied by burns. The dog may be unconscious and have burns around her mouth and on her tongue.

If you find your dog unconscious near an electrical cord, turn off the power to the socket *before* touching your dog. Then examine the dog using the A-B-C protocol described earlier in this chapter. Administer CPR if the dog is in shock or is unconscious. When the dog is conscious, give first aid for burns and get her to your veterinarian immediately.

Eyes

The eyes are very delicate and easily injured, especially in dogs who love to play in the great outdoors.

Dogs who run through fields may get dust or grasses in their eyes. The best solution is to wash the eye with sterile saline. Hold your dog's eye open and gently pour the saline over the surface of the eye. Using a penlight flashlight, examine the insides of the lids to be sure you removed the offending particles. If repeated flushing doesn't help, get your dog to a veterinarian.

If a foreign body is penetrating the eye or the skin near the eye, do *not* touch it. Stop the dog from pawing at the eye by taping her hind legs together or by having her wear an Elizabethan collar (a wide plastic or cardboard cone-shaped collar that prevents the dog from being able to scratch her head). You can make a temporary Elizabethan collar by cutting a head-sized hole into the bottom of a bucket and placing the bucket over the dog's head, fastening the bucket to the dog's collar. Then get your dog to a veterinarian immediately.

Fishhooks

Every now and then, a dog playing near a fishing pond will get stuck with a fishhook left by a careless fisherman. As you can imagine, a fishhook can be very painful, particularly if the hook is in the foot and the dog has come running to you or tried to remove it with her mouth.

Start by calming the dog down with gentle words and quiet motions. Getting your veterinarian to remove the hook is best, but if you have no access to a veterinarian, you can push the hook through the skin until the tip and barb come back out. Then cut the hook and barb off and back the rest of the hook out the way it came. Treat the hole as a wound (see "Wounds" later in this chapter).

If your dog swallows a fishhook, cut most of the remaining fishing line off, leaving approximately 12 inches dangling. *Do not* attempt to dislodge the fishhook by pulling on the line. Take your dog to a veterinarian immediately. Do not allow your dog to eat in the meantime.

Foxtails

Foxtail plants grow by roadsides and in fields throughout much of the United States. Dogs sometimes inhale or swallow their seeds in their exuberance outdoors. The foxtail seeds have a long, barbed appendage so that they can stick in the hair and even penetrate unbroken skin. When the seed is in your dog's body, it travels from place to place, damaging tissues and causing infections. If you live in an area where there are foxtails, always examine your dog's susceptible parts (nose, throat, armpits, and between the toes) thoroughly after she has been outdoors. Use tweezers to gently remove any foxtails you find.

Heatstroke

The temperature doesn't have to be very high for a dog to suffer heatstroke. Working sled dogs in Alaska begin to suffer from the heat at 20 degrees because of their level of physical activity. Dogs are descended from wolves, animals that live in northern climes and thus have not developed natural mechanisms to fight the heat. As a result they, like their wolf ancestors, don't have very good heat-control mechanisms. Breeds with flat faces, such as Bulldogs and Pugs, can suffer heatstroke even on mild days. Puppies also are more susceptible to heatstroke.

More dogs die of heatstroke in cars than any other way. Even on a mild day, the temperature in a car in the sun can rise to over 100 degrees in a matter of minutes. Every year, thousands of dogs die of heatstroke after being left in cars for "just a minute."

Never leave your dog in the car in the summer, even with the windows down. And never leave your dog in a yard without shade in the summer.

A dog suffering from heatstroke will pant heavily and salivate excessively. Her eyes may be glazed and she will stagger or act listless. The dog's pulse will be rapid and weak.

If you suspect your dog is suffering from heatstroke, you must act quickly. Move the dog to a cool area indoors or at least to the shade. Submerge her in cool water (not ice water), and apply cold compresses to her head. Take her temperature to monitor her body's cooling. Keep her wet until her temperature reaches 103 degrees, and then remove her from the water and dry her off. Encourage but do not force her to drink water. Get her to the veterinarian as soon as possible.

Hot spots

Hot spots are localized areas of skin infection that are usually round, red, and warm to the touch. They can start very quickly and can grow to several inches in diameter in a matter of a day or two. The infection is exacerbated by the dog's scratching or chewing.

The first thing to do if you identify a hot spot is to clip the hair away from the area, if possible. This is the best way to prevent the infection from spreading. Once or twice a day, wash the area thoroughly with liquid soap and apply an astringent. The best astringent is tea (green or black). Wet a tea bag and apply it to the area. Keep applying the astringent several times a day until the area is dry and covered with a scab — usually 24 to 36 hours. After the area is scabbed, let it heal, but watch it carefully in case the infection begins to spread again. Keep the dog from scratching or biting at the area while it is healing; you may need to use an Elizabethan collar (see the "Eyes" section earlier in this chapter for more information). If you cannot get the hot spot under control in 36 hours, see your veterinarian, who may prescribe oral antibiotics and/or anti-inflammatory agents to treat it.

Insect bites

Many insects bite or sting, so becoming familiar with the ones that live in your area is a good idea. That way, you can try to prevent your dog from exposure to these bugs if at all possible.

Usually an insect bite will appear as an area of swelling. If the bite is from a bee or a wasp, remove the stinger. If it is from a tick that is still attached, use tweezers to grasp the tick as close to the skin as possible and pull gently until it lets go (see Chapter 2 for more information on removing ticks). Apply a cold pack if the swelling is severe.

Poisoning

We have many poisons in our houses, in our yards, and in the environment, and their treatments can differ greatly. See Chapter 24 for more information on common household poisons.

If you suspect that your dog has been poisoned, contact your veterinarian immediately for instructions. If you cannot reach your veterinarian, call the National Animal Poison Control Center at 888-426-4435 for help.

If you know your dog ingested the poison within the last hour, induce vomiting by pouring 1 to 3 teaspoons of hydrogen peroxide into her mouth between the cheek and the back teeth. If the dog hasn't vomited within ten minutes, repeat. Do not use hydrogen peroxide more than three times at ten-minute intervals apart.

Do *not* induce vomiting if the poison is unknown, corrosive, or a petroleum product or if the animal is not completely conscious.

Wash the skin if the toxin can be absorbed through the skin.

Porcupine quills

Porcupines roam around the woods on sunny days in the winter — and some curious canines just can't mind their own business. The result is usually a face full of painful porcupine quills. If you find your dog in this kind of a fix, here's what to do: Calm the dog down as best you can (porcupine quills are very painful, and dogs tend to scratch and paw at their faces) and transport her to your veterinarian as soon as possible. The vet will anesthetize your dog and remove the quills while she is in dreamland. If veterinary assistance is not available, muzzle the dog and have someone hold her while you pull the quills quickly straight out, not at an angle. Feel the skin for deeply embedded quills and look in the mouth for quills, too — these should be removed by a veterinarian.

Never remove quills from the eye. If your dog has a quill in her eye, calm her down (it is very painful) and tie her legs together to prevent her from pawing at the eye. Protect the eye until you can get her to a veterinarian.

Seizures

Seizures in dogs can be caused by many things, from trauma to tumors to poisoning. In some dogs, seizures occur periodically for unknown reasons (in a condition called *idiopathic epilepsy*). Here's what to do when a seizure occurs.

- ✔ Sit with your dog during the seizure, talking soothingly to her.
- ✔ Only restrain her if necessary to prevent her from hurting herself. During the seizure, she will have uncontrollable movements and may defecate or urinate.
- ✔ Keep your dog quiet for 30 minutes after the seizure.
- ✔ If the seizure lasts longer than five minutes or recurs within two hours, take your dog to a veterinarian.

Do not attempt to pull the dog's tongue out or in any way get near the mouth because severe bites can occur.

If your dog has a seizure, take her to a veterinary neurologist for evaluation.

Snake bites

The most common poisonous snakes in North America are the rattlesnake, the cottonmouth, the coral snake and the water moccasin. If poisonous snakes live near you, learn to identify them and stay away from them. Consider taking your dog to a snake-proofing session, where she will be taught to stay away from snakes. You can obtain information from your local dog club.

If your dog is bitten by a poisonous snake, here is what to do:

1. **Restrain and calm your dog to slow uptake of the venom.**

   Arrange for the dog to get to a veterinarian immediately.

2. **Allow the snake bite to bleed freely for 30 to 60 seconds and then cleanse and disinfect the area.**

3. **Place gauze over the wound and apply pressure.**

   If the wound is on a leg, leave gauze over the wound and wrap the leg with cohesive bandage tightly, but not tight enough to cut off circulation.

4. **Take the dog to a veterinarian immediately.**

Do not cut into the wound caused by a snakebite. Do not apply suction to the wound. And do not apply a tourniquet.

If you and your dog hike frequently in snake-infested areas, talk to your veterinarian about whether you should carry an antivenin with you.

Spinal injury

If you suspect that your dog has suffered a spinal or neck injury, be very cautious about moving her or you can further damage the spinal cord and cause permanent paralysis or even death.

Muzzle your dog and slide her gradually onto a flat surface such as a board or a piece of heavy cardboard. Secure the dog to the makeshift stretcher with wide strips of tape or an ACE brand bandage and transport her to the veterinarian immediately.

Sprains and strains

A *sprain* is a torn ligament and a *strain* is torn tendon, but the results of both injuries are the same — swelling and inflammation in the area of damage. The key to treating these injuries is to get ice onto the affected area immediately. Apply the ice for 20 minutes, then remove the ice for 20 minutes, and then apply ice again for 20 minutes. The ice will help to reduce the swelling and keep further damage to a minimum.

Try bandaging the ice onto the affected area if your dog doesn't want to let you hold the ice on her body for that long.

Take your dog to a veterinarian if you suspect a fracture or if your dog doesn't bear some weight on the leg within an hour or two. The dog should rest for at least 48 hours after the injury — no running or playing, just short walks on a leash to go potty. If the dog is still limping after 48 hours, she should be seen by a veterinarian.

Wounds

In their inimitable love of life, dogs can get themselves into some pretty fixes. They may run into tree branches or rub against sharp objects. They may even get in an occasional fight and end up a little worse for the wear. So knowing what to do for your walking wounded canine is important.

Wounds fall into two main categories: shallow and deep. Shallow wounds involve just the skin; deep wounds penetrate to the muscles and other tissues below the skin.

Shallow wounds

To treat a shallow wound:

1. **Wash your hands thoroughly.**
2. **Use cotton pads and mild antibacterial liquid soap to clean the wound thoroughly.**
3. **Rinse the wound with sterile saline solution.**
4. **Apply antibacterial ointment to the wound.**
5. **Cover the wound with gauze, wrap it with a bandage, and cover it with cohesive bandage (but not so tight that you cut off circulation).**

   You can slip a stockinet or bootie over a foot and secure it with tape for extra protection.
6. **Periodically feel your dog's toes.**

   If they become swollen or cool to the touch, remove the bandage and reapply it after the swelling has diminished.

If the wound is small and clean, you can use NuSkin to glue the ends of the wound together. It works just like sutures.

Cuts that may require sutures should be examined by a veterinarian immediately. If a cut is more than about six hours old, it should not be sutured closed because it almost certainly is contaminated with bacteria from the environment. Suturing the wound closed would just trap the bacteria within the wound, resulting in infection and increased scarring. An older cut should be thoroughly cleaned and allowed to heal gradually as an open wound. If the wound is large, it may be partially sutured and a drain left in to help the infection escape.

Deep wounds

To treat a deep wound:

1. Stop the bleeding by applying pressure.

2. When the bleeding has stopped, bandage the wound and seek immediate veterinary treatment.

Chapter 13

Drug Therapy for Dogs

• •

In This Chapter

▶ Knowing how drugs get into your dog's body and what they do after they get there

▶ Recognizing the different types of drugs your dog may need

▶ Administering medication to your dog

▶ Being aware of problems with toxicity and knowing the symptoms to watch out for

• •

*W*hen you have a headache, you reach for aspirin. When you have an infection, your physician prescribes antibiotics. Drugs are so much a part of our lives today that we sometimes take them for granted. But it's important to remember that drugs have saved millions of lives and are used to treat everything from anxiety to zoonosis. Just 50 years ago scientists hadn't even discovered antibiotics yet; in those days, if you developed a severe infection, death was almost inevitable.

Our canine companions have benefited from drugs, too. Not only are most of the drugs that were designed for humans available for dogs, there is also a booming veterinary pharmaceutical industry that designs drugs for the special needs of our furry friends. We have vaccines to prevent viral diseases, drugs that prevent heartworm infection, chemotherapy to battle cancer, and an array of anesthetics that will put your dog gently to sleep and wake him up within minutes. In addition, we have drugs that work on specific organs of the body to care and cure your dog. There are drugs to treat diarrhea, potions to improve pulmonary function, and sedatives to soothe seizures.

The ironic side to these helpful chemicals, however, is that they also can be harmful to our dogs. If drugs are administered incorrectly or if the dose is miscalculated, the results can range from minor mishap to major misfortune. In this chapter, I describe the main classes of drugs and discuss the conditions they treat. I also provide pointers to help you ensure that the drugs you give your dog heal rather than harm.

How Drugs Enter Your Dog's Body

For a drug to do its job, it has to first enter your dog's body and then be delivered to its *target site* (the part of your dog's body that needs help). Your dog can get the drugs he needs in one of three main ways: orally (by swallowing a pill or a liquid medication), by injection, or topically (through the skin):

- ✔ **Oral drugs:** If the drug is given to your dog orally, it is absorbed into his body through the lining of the stomach or the small intestine.

- ✔ **Injected drugs:** If the drug is given by injection, it can be done in four ways:

  - • Under the skin, where the drug slowly enters the bloodstream

  - • Into a muscle, where the drug quickly enters blood vessels

  - • Into a vein, for immediate effect

  - • Directly into the target tissue (for example, a joint)

- ✔ **Topical drugs:** These drugs can be absorbed directly through the skin.

Oral drugs

Oral drugs come in a variety of forms including tablets and capsules, powders, syrups, liquids, and pastes. These drugs are absorbed through the lining of the stomach and small intestine and pass through the liver before they enter the bloodstream to be distributed throughout the body. Oral drugs that may cause stomach ulcers, such as aspirin, can be coated so that they don't dissolve until they have passed from the stomach into the small intestine. Oral drugs may also be designed to dissolve slowly over a period of several hours — so-called *timed-release* drugs — so that the effect of the drug is maintained for a longer period of time.

Oral drugs are convenient and relatively safe. Drugs taken by mouth tend to be maintained at effective levels in the body for a longer period of time than injected drugs. However, oral drugs take longer to reach effective levels because they must first dissolve before they can be absorbed into the bloodstream. Plus, if your dog is vomiting or suffering from diarrhea, this may keep the oral drugs from being absorbed.

Injected drugs

Drugs that are administered *intravenously* (into the vein) reach effective levels immediately, but the levels are not maintained as long because the drug is more rapidly removed from the blood by the liver and kidneys. Drugs administered *subcutaneously* (under the skin) or *intramuscularly* (into the muscle) reach the bloodstream in 10 to 30 minutes and exit the body somewhat more slowly than intravenously injected drugs.

Topical drugs

Some drugs are most effective when they are applied to the skin. These are commonly used to treat skin disorders such as inflammation or burns. There are some preparations, however, that can carry a drug right through unbroken skin, where the drug is absorbed into the bloodstream. One such class of drugs you may have heard of are the pour-on formulations of antiparasitic drugs that are used to prevent flea and tick infestations. These drugs are poured onto the skin at the back of the dog's neck, where they are absorbed through the skin and into the bloodstream and then redistributed to the skin of the whole body.

Where Drugs Go When They Get In

When a drug has entered the bloodstream, it is distributed to all the organs in your dog's body. When the drug reaches the liver it begins to undergo a process called *biotransformation,* in which the drug is chemically altered to an inactive form so that the body can excrete it. Liver cells contain a wide variety of enzymes that break the drug molecules down into smaller, nontoxic components (called *metabolites*) and release the soluble metabolites to the bloodstream, where they travel to the kidneys and are eliminated. (Excretion of these metabolites by the kidneys is the reason samples of urine are taken for drug testing in humans.) Because of these important functions, the liver and kidneys frequently suffer toxic effects when a drug overdose occurs.

When the liver is diseased, its ability to metabolize drugs is often impaired. So drugs administered to dogs with hepatitis (which is a disease affecting the liver) may have a prolonged effect or may even be toxic because of the inability of the dog's liver to metabolize them.

Different drugs remain in your dog's body for varying lengths of time (depending on how quickly they're absorbed and how fast they're metabolized). When your veterinarian prescribed drugs for your dog, she takes into consideration how long the drugs remain in your dog's body so doses can be administered at appropriate intervals. That's why giving your dog the drugs on a regular schedule determined by your vet is so important.

Well-nourished animals normally metabolize and eliminate drugs with little difficulty. But a number of circumstances can alter a drug's effectiveness in individual animals:

- ✔ **Body weight:** In obese dogs, fat-soluble drugs may be stored in the fat and released gradually over time, thus slowing the elimination of the drug from the dog's body.

- ✔ **Diet and nutritional factors:** Dogs suffering from malnutrition may be less able to absorb, distribute, metabolize, and/or excrete drugs.

- ✔ **Kidney or liver disease:** When the function of one or both of these organs is impaired, drug metabolism and excretion may also be impaired.

- ✔ **Temperament:** Excitable or hyperactive dogs may have a reduced response to drugs that act on the central nervous system.

- ✔ **Ambient temperatures:** Absorption, metabolism, and excretion of drugs may be slowed in very cold temperatures and increased when the dog has a fever.

- ✔ **Other drugs:** Some drugs, such as the anti-seizure drug phenobarbital, may increase the rate at which the liver metabolizes other drugs.

Side effects occur when a drug affects tissues other than the target tissue. People suffering from allergies, for example, commonly use antihistamines to decrease nasal secretions. But cells in the brain also have receptors for antihistamines, and the effect on the brain is drowsiness. Side effects are somewhat like weeds in a garden. They may be doing the right thing, but it's in the wrong place!

How drugs work

Drugs don't usually cause completely new reactions in the cell. Instead, they enhance or modify the existing cellular functions. In some cases, a drug will stimulate chemical reactions in cells. This is the case with digitalis, a drug used to treat congestive heart failure. Digitalis causes the cardiac muscle to contract more strongly, thus increasing the amount of blood pumped by the heart. Drugs may also inhibit cellular functions, such as when anticancer chemotherapy drugs stop the production of DNA, thus preventing cancer cells from multiplying. The key to making drugs work effectively without causing toxicity is to design drugs that work at the desired site and to administer a dose that will cause the desired response over a certain period of time without causing an undesirable response.

Some formulations of drugs contain mixtures of two or more drugs that complement each other's activity. For example, a drug that is best absorbed in the upper small intestine may be formulated with a compound that slows intestinal contractions, thus allowing more of the drug to be absorbed. When your dentist gives you an injection of novocaine to numb the nerves to your teeth, epinephrine (which constricts blood vessels) may also be included in the shot to prolong the duration of effect.

Always be careful when using drugs in pregnant or nursing dogs. Many drugs pass from the mother across the placenta and into the fetuses. Depending on how many months pregnant the dog is, the drug may cause fetal death or deformities. In addition, some drugs may cause premature birth. Because the potential of many drugs to cross the placenta or to pass into the milk is unknown, avoid giving drugs to pregnant and nursing females if at all possible. As always, talk with your vet about her recommendations.

The Kinds of Drugs Your Dog May Need

Drugs can be divided into two broad categories. *Chemotherapeutics* are drugs that destroy disease-causing organisms or kill tumor cells. *Systemic therapeutics,* on the other hand, are drugs that act to treat diseases of various body systems such as *bronchodilators,* which improve respiratory function, or *antidiarrheals,* which affect digestion. In the following sections, I describe chemotherapeutics in some detail, because you or your veterinarian are most likely to administer these drugs to your dog sometime in his life. I also touch briefly on the less common systemic therapeutics as well.

Chemotherapeutics

The goal of treatment with a chemotherapeutic drug is to kill the offending foreign organism without harming the dog. Sometimes this goal is one we can reach, as in the case of antibiotics that selectively kill certain species of bacteria. But treatment usually involves achieving a balance where we neutralize the foreign organism while only causing an acceptable level of harm to the dog. For this reason, the dose of the drug may be critical, which is why you need to be sure that you don't vary from the dose and treatment schedule prescribed by your vet.

In addition to the effects of the drugs themselves, the body defense systems are hard at work battling the foreign invader. Supportive care, reduction of stress, and good nutrition are major contributors to a successful chemotherapeutic program.

Antibacterial agents

Antibiotics are drugs that kill infectious organisms such as bacteria, viruses, and fungi. The key to an effective antibiotic is that it must kill the infectious organism but not harm the dog. To avoid harming the dog's cells, antibiotics are designed to attack very specific parts of the infectious agent.

Antibacterial drugs are antibiotics that act against bacteria. Because many antibacterial drugs act only on certain species or classes of bacteria, you'll have a higher chance of successful treatment if your veterinarian specifically identifies the bacteria that are causing the infection and determines which antibiotics will destroy it. Unfortunately, this isn't always possible. Sometimes the veterinarian must make an educated guess as to which bacteria may be causing the infection and then treat the dog accordingly. Your vet will then observe your dog to determine whether the antibiotic is effective. If there is no change in the infection within three to four days, your vet may need to change the antibiotic she has prescribed.

If your dog develops an infection, never give your dog an antibiotic without consulting your veterinarian. Even if the infection seems to be the same one that was treated with a certain antibiotic last time, get a professional opinion first. Your veterinarian may recognize that the infection has changed or may decide that a different antibiotic is required for effective treatment.

Using a combination of antibacterial drugs may be beneficial in certain cases. This strategy works particularly well when an infection is caused by several different species of bacteria or when there is a strong chance that drug-resistant bacteria will emerge. Such mixtures should be prescribed only by a veterinarian, however, because certain combinations of antibiotics may be completely ineffective and others may be toxic.

Unfortunately, bacteria are very wily. They mutate very quickly and commonly develop resistance to antibiotics. They can even transfer the genes for antibiotic resistance to other bacteria. For years, there has been an ongoing battle between medicine and microorganisms. The pharmaceutical companies continually scramble to produce new and different antibiotics, and the bacteria just as quickly develop resistance to those antibiotics. Some strains of bacteria are resistant to so many different antibiotics that a dog (or a person) who becomes infected with one of those strains is likely to die.

Bacteria are more likely to become resistant to antibiotics if the antibiotics are given in insufficient doses, if they aren't given for a long enough period of time, or if they are used indiscriminately. Here are some guidelines to help minimize the emergence of resistant strains of bacteria:

✔ **Whenever possible, your veterinarian should culture the area of infection to identify the exact strain of bacteria that is causing the infection and to determine the specific antibiotics to which the strain is susceptible.** This way you and your vet can be more certain that the right antibiotic treatment has been selected for your dog.

✔ **Always follow your veterinarian's recommendations for antibiotic treatment to the letter.** Even if your dog appears to be healed, continue to administer the antibiotics for the full recommended treatment period.

✔ **Never give your dog an antibiotic that was prescribed for another dog or for a different infection.** Discard any antibiotics that remain after treatment of an infection is finished.

Antiviral agents

Because all viruses live and multiply within cells, antiviral agents have to enter the cells in order to kill the viruses — so they tend to be quite toxic. Because of their toxicity and because of the difficulty of identifying the specific virus that is causing a disease, antiviral agents aren't routinely used in veterinary medicine. Plus, many viral diseases in dogs (such as coronavirus infection and kennel cough) are short-term and self-limiting.

In general, we rely on vaccines to prevent the more severe viral diseases such as rabies and distemper. So be sure your dog has been properly vaccinated.

Antiparasitic agents

Parasites come in all shapes and kinds. Some live in the intestine, some live on the skin, and some even travel around in the blood. Antiparasitic agents have to be just as versatile. They have to get to the location where the parasite is and kill the creature without killing any of the dog's cells. Because they have to be so targeted, antiparasitic agents often are administered locally at the site where the parasite lives.

The battle against bacteria

Antibiotics are not a cure-all in bacterial infections — they're just one component of a whole-dog approach to fighting infection. Treatment of bacterial infections may fail for many reasons. Here are the most common ones:

✔ The bacteria are resistant to the antibiotic.

✔ The bacteria live inside cells and, thus, are not exposed to the antibiotic.

✔ The antibiotic couldn't penetrate to the center of the infected area.

✔ An inappropriate dose or route of administration was prescribed.

✔ The prescribed dosage regimen was not reliably followed.

✔ The animal's own defense mechanisms were compromised by malnutrition, disease, or concurrent treatment by immunosuppressive drugs such as corticosteroids.

✔ The antibiotic had to be withdrawn due to adverse side effects.

✔ Supportive therapy, nutrition, or nursing care was inadequate.

Systemic therapeutics

An almost endless variety of pharmaceuticals act on specific organ systems. But the systemic therapeutics that you will most commonly use are those that affect the gastrointestinal tract. Because of dogs' propensity to eat discarded, disgusting, decaying matter, they suffer frequent digestive upsets. Plus, a number of viral and bacterial infections attack the intestinal tract. The result is that dogs suffer frequently from vomiting and diarrhea.

The best approach for intestinal upset is to be prepared. Ask your veterinarian for her recom-

mendations on how to treat your dog for digestive upsets, and stock your cabinets. Because dogs will be dogs, you'll certainly get a chance to use your supplies.

The other commonly used systemic therapeutics are those that affect the central nervous system, particularly sedatives and anesthetics. Sedatives produce drowsiness and hypnosis. They are often used prior to anesthesia, to smooth the transition as a dog becomes anesthetized and to make the recovery from anesthesia easier.

To design effective antiparasitic agents, scientists first have to learn as much as they can about the lifestyle of these creatures. Some worms, for example, use their muscles to attach to the inside of the intestine. So scientists designed drugs that paralyze the worms' muscles so that the parasite ends up being flushed out in the stool.

The most common antiparasitic agents that you will deal with are those that kill fleas and ticks and those that neutralize the heartworms that are transmitted by the mosquito. Newer anti-flea and anti-tick preparations, such as Frontline and Advantage, contain insect growth regulators that prevent these crawling creatures from multiplying and spreading. Ivermectin and milbemycin oxime, the most commonly used and most effective monthly heartworm preventatives, inhibit the cellular functions necessary for the survival of the heartworm larvae that have been transmitted by the mosquito. These products are quite safe and have revolutionized control of these disease-carrying parasites.

Many antiparasitics are extremely toxic if taken at a higher dose than recommended. Be sure to follow your veterinarian's instructions for treatment.

Anti-inflammatory agents

Inflammation is the body's response to injury. The purpose of inflammation is to remove the injurious agent and to heal the damaged tissues. So if your dog steps in a gopher hole and sprains his wrist, the joint will become swollen, warm, and painful. These are all signs of inflammation — the body is trying to repair itself. If your puppy has little pimples on his tummy that are raised and red around the edges, this is the body's inflammatory response to a common bacterial infection.

Sometimes the inflammatory response is a bit too much, however, and the result is damage rather than repair. Anti-inflammatory agents can dampen some of the inflammatory responses and stop the vicious cycle of inflammation and scarring. They reduce swelling, lower the temperature in dogs with fever, and relieve pain.

Steroids are an excellent example of anti-inflammatory agents — not *anabolic steroids* (which bodybuilders and other athletes sometimes take), but *corticosteroids* like the kind you may apply to a bad case of poison ivy. Unfortunately, corticosteroids injected or taken orally affect so many tissues in the body that they have many side effects in addition to the desired anti-inflammatory effect. When taken over a long period of time, they can cause weight gain and increased thirst and urination. High doses of steroids may impair healing, and they can be *immunosuppressive,* which means that if the inflammation being treated is caused by an infection, the steroids may impair the body's natural defense mechanisms enough to make the disease even worse.

Because of the problems corticosteroids sometimes bring with them, scientists have developed *nonsteroidal anti-inflammatory agents* (NSAIDs), which have more focused activity. They cool the inflammatory response without the broad effects of steroids. Many NSAIDs are available for dogs; the most commonly used are aspirin, carprofen (Rimadyl), and etodolac (Etogesic).

Several common non-steroidal anti-inflammatory agents used in humans are not recommended for use in dogs. These include ibuprofen and acetaminophen and other related drugs.

NSAIDs are not totally without side effects. Prolonged administration of aspirin, for example, can cause gastric upsets and even stomach ulcers. Use of enteric-coated or buffered aspirin can help decrease the risk of gastric ulceration, however. Administering the analgesic on a full stomach also can help to prevent stomach upset. Carprofen has been associated with serious liver problems in a small percentage of dogs. Because of these potential side effects, you should never administer NSAIDs to your dog without first consulting a veterinarian.

Always check with your veterinarian before medicating your dog with any drug, whether prescription or over-the-counter.

Just a Spoonful of Sugar: How to Give Your Dog Medicine

At some point, you'll need to give medications to your ailing canine. Knowing how to medicate your dog is important because, if you don't, you won't be able to get him the medicine he needs when he needs it. The following sections discuss a few tricks of the trade that make medicating a snap.

Getting your dog to swallow a pill

The best way to give your dog a pill is to put it on or in a treat. You can prepare a cracker with cheese or peanut butter (or both) and embed the pill in the topping. Most dogs are glad to down the drug if they can have the goodie that is grabbing it.

If your dog has no appetite, however, you may need to pop the pill down his throat yourself. With your hand over your dog's muzzle, place your thumb on one side of the upper jaw and your fingers on the other side and gently pry your dog's mouth open (see Figure 13-1). Holding the pill between the thumb and index finger of the other hand, quickly place the pill as far back on the tongue as possible. Hold the dog's mouth closed for a few seconds and rub his throat until you see him swallow.

Making sure your dog gets all the liquid medication he needs

Oral liquids are a little harder to administer than pills because they easily dribble from the dog's mouth, making it hard to determine exactly how much of the drug the dog consumed. In addition, if the fluid is squirted way back in the mouth, the dog may choke and get some of the fluid in his lungs.

If the oral medication is dissolved in a tasty children's medicine preparation, your dog may be quite happy to lick the medication from the end of a dropper or syringe (see Figure 13-2).

If the bitterness of the medicine cannot be disguised, you may need to administer the oral medication in such a way that your dog has no choice but to swallow it. With the fluid in a syringe or dropper, tilt the dog's nose upward, sliding the syringe through the corner of the lips and into the space between the cheek and the molar teeth (see Figure 13-3). Inject the fluids slowly while holding the dog's head still. When the dog feels the fluids draining into his throat, he will swallow. Make sure you have a really tasty and flavorful treat ready to reward your patient — and to cover the bad taste of the medicine.

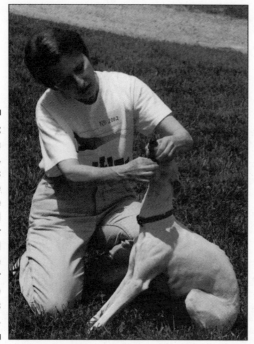

Figure 13-1:
To give a dog a pill, open his mouth wide with one hand and use your other hand to place the pill as far back on the tongue as possible.

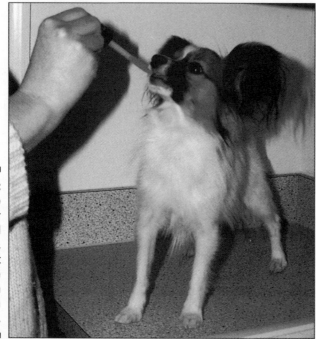

Figure 13-2:
To administer tasty oral liquids, slowly squirt it into the dog's mouth with a dropper.

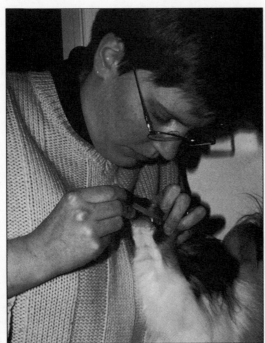

Figure 13-3:
To administer oral medicine that is bitter or distasteful, you can squirt the liquid slowly between your dog's lips and his side teeth with a syringe.

Giving eye medication to your dog

There are two main forms of eye medication: drops and ointment. Administer eye drops to your dog just as you would for yourself. Tilt your dog's nose upward with one hand, and put the drops onto the eye with the other. Hold your dog's head up while he blinks several times to be sure the drops are distributed over the surface of the eye.

When administering eye ointment, your goal is to dispense the medication underneath the lower eyelid so it will be distributed over the eye rather than squeezed out by blinking. To administer eye ointment without any help, you'll need a cooperative dog who will sit still while you work on his eyes. If your canine is not feeling very cooperative, find an extra set of hands and have a tasty treat ready for a reward. With one finger, pull on the skin just below the lower eyelid. This pulls the eyelid away from the eye. With your other hand, squeeze a line of ointment into the pocket between the lid and the eye. Then release the eyelid, trapping the medication.

Administering ear medication

Administering a liquid into the ear is much like administering eye drops. The goal is to make sure the medication stays in the ear for at least a few seconds while it coats the skin of the ear.

With your dog sitting, position the ear so that the opening is facing upwards. (This is easy in a prick-eared dog, but it may take a little manipulating in a dog with dropped ears.) Use one hand to hold the ear open and the other to put the liquid in. Then squeeze the sides of the ear opening together and rub the base of the ear gently. This distributes the medication throughout the ear so that as little as possible flies out when your dog shakes his head, which he inevitably will do.

Getting comfortable with giving injections

Your dog may be diabetic and need daily injections of insulin, or he may suffer from kidney failure and need fluids to be administered under the skin.

The easiest way to inject fluid under the skin is to make a tent of skin with the thumb and index finger of one hand and then insert the needle through the skin at the base of the tent. After the needle is in, you can let the skin tent go and start injecting while you hold the needle still. The injected fluid usually will appear as a little bulge under the skin. Have a delicious treat ready to give your brave pooch.

Make sure you don't stick your needle through the skin and out the other side again.

Toxicity: Too Much of a Good Thing

The suggested doses for drugs are just that: *suggested* doses. These doses have been arrived at by testing a limited number of dogs. But they aren't always right for every dog. Just as in humans, dogs have individual resistances and sensitivities to drugs. A dog may be more or less sensitive to a drug if he is very old or very young, if he is obese, or if he has liver or kidney failure, for example. Some breeds are particularly sensitive to certain drugs as well.

Very young puppies are very susceptible to drug toxicity. At this age, the barrier that prevents drugs from entering the brain of adult dogs is not fully formed, and this can allow drugs that are toxic to the brain to enter and cause harm. In addition, the young puppy's liver is not fully functional, so it can't quickly metabolize drugs to prepare them for excretion by the kidney. Never administer drugs to a puppy less than 4 weeks old without first consulting your veterinarian.

Drug doses are usually determined in relation to body weight. A very obese dog, however, may weigh twice his lean body weight, which means the extra weight consists almost entirely of fat. If the drug to be administered is not soluble in fat, the nonfat portion of that dog's body may be exposed to twice the amount of drug that it would if the drug was administered on the basis of lean body weight. If, on the other hand, the drug is absorbed by fat, it may be difficult to achieve and maintain effective levels of the drug in the obese dog, because the excess fat absorbs the drug.

Individual animals vary in their capability to absorb and utilize drugs, so drug dosages always should be considered on an individual basis. Never use a drug recommended for one dog on another dog without first consulting your veterinarian.

Very young and very old dogs are more likely to have adverse drug reactions. The tissues of dogs less than 1 month old may not have all the biochemical components needed to metabolize a drug. Older dogs may have developed hypersensitivity to a drug or may have organ dysfunction such as liver failure, which can reduce the amount of drug metabolized by the body and increase the likelihood of toxic effects. Interestingly, dogs with inhalant allergies seem to be more susceptible to adverse drug reactions than those without allergies.

If your dog has had an adverse reaction to any drug, even just once, be sure to remind your veterinarian before she prescribes drugs or treats your dog. (The veterinarian should have the information in her records, but remind her anyway, just to be safe.) During the first visit to a new veterinarian or to a specialist, be sure to explain the nature of your dog's drug sensitivity and request that she make note of the problem in her records.

Drug interactions also can increase or decrease the effects of another drug in a given tissue. For example, several drugs can alter the level of administered thyroid hormone in the body. The incidence of adverse drug reactions increases exponentially when more than one drug is administered because of the greater potential for drug interactions.

Some antibacterial or antifungal agents can have toxic side effects as well. Tetracyclines, for example, can discolor puppies' teeth and slow bone development. For these reasons, their use is not recommended in either pregnant dogs or puppies. Gentamicin, a broad-spectrum antibiotic, can cause kidney damage. Dogs taking this antibiotic on a long-term basis should be monitored for signs of early renal damage. If this occurs, the drug can be discontinued and the kidney given time to repair itself.

The most life-threatening adverse drug reaction is *anaphylaxis,* which is an acute systemic allergic reaction that can lead to shock, or cardiovascular collapse. A dog suffering from anaphylactic shock may pace and usually will pant heavily. He may vomit and/or have diarrhea. His gums will appear purple or dark, muddy red. Anaphylactic shock requires immediate emergency veterinary treatment.

Despite the possibility of side effects and adverse reactions, drugs continue to cure our canine companions ills and prolong their lives. When used with understanding, pharmaceuticals have the potential to make a huge difference in the quality of our dogs' lives.

Chapter 14

Complementary and Alternative Therapies

In This Chapter

▶ Discovering what vets know about complementary and alternative therapies

▶ Taking advantage of these therapies to help your dog feel her best

Many things in life are mysteries to us. Most people believe in a higher power — yet we don't have scientific proof that one exists. Many people have had experiences in which they had a sense that something was going to happen — and it did. In the mid-18th century, William Withering, an English physician and botanist, found that he could treat heart failure with minute amounts of the leaf of the foxglove plant — but more than 200 years passed before scientists discovered the biochemical explanation for this observation. Just because scientists didn't know exactly why *digitalis* (the chemical derived from the foxglove leaf) was effective doesn't mean it didn't save many people's lives. Yet today, many people (including some veterinarians) disregard alternative and complementary veterinary therapies simply because they don't understand how they work.

In this chapter, I delve into the origins and explanations of the most common of the complementary and alternative therapies, covering them in alphabetical order so you can find what you're looking for easily. Keep in mind that this is only a small introduction to a very large subject. Many of these therapies are in the realm of the unproven and unconventional — and many also are accessible, effective, and there for you to use if you have an open mind.

For more information on complementary and alternative therapies, you can also turn to *Four Paws Five Directions: A Guide to Chinese Medicine for Cats and Dogs* by Cheryl Schwartz.

Complementary and Alternative Medicine 101

Before you start thinking about using complementary and alternative medicines for your dog, you need to get familiar with the terms themselves, what they mean, and the science behind them. In the following sections, I define these terms for you and let you know the difference between theories that have been disproved and those that just haven't been proven yet.

Knowing what complementary and alternative therapies are

Complementary therapy is therapy that is used in addition to traditional therapies. An example of a complementary therapy would be massage treatment for a chronic injury. *Alternative therapy* includes a number of nontraditional healing methods, such as the use of acupuncture instead of drugs to treat pain. *Complementary* and *alternative medicine* are all-encompassing terms that describes a diverse group of what *we may consider* to be nontraditional medical therapies. (I put the emphasis on "we may consider," because many complementary and alternative therapies have been in existence much longer than the modern medicine we're familiar with today.) Complementary and alternative therapies include acupuncture, chiropractic, massage and physical therapy, magnetic therapy, botanical medicine, nutritional therapy and nutraceutical therapy, homeopathy, aromatherapy, and Bach flower therapy, among others.

Many people use the term *holistic medicine* to refer to these therapies as a group, but the term really refers to medicine that examines and attempts to treat the entire animal and her environment rather than just the symptoms of a disease. The word *holistic* is derived from the word *whole,* because the whole animal is considered. At its best, holistic medicine incorporates complementary and alternative therapies in addition to conventional medicine.

Today, complementary and alternative forms of therapy are experiencing an incredible surge in interest. Westerners are rediscovering the healing arts that many Asian, African, and South American cultures have known for centuries and even millennia. The various forms of complementary and alternative medicine often derive from Eastern thought, so they start with a different concept of the body in sickness and in health. In Western medicine, people talk about "waging war on disease," and their emphasis is on curing disease through the use of drugs and surgery. In Eastern medicine, however, the emphasis is on helping the body heal itself by restoring the body's physical and emotional balance and maintaining that balance to prevent illness. Each of these viewpoints has value, and each complements the other.

Relying on a sixth sense

Recently, I was at work when I suddenly had the feeling that my dog Bannor was dying. I ignored the thought and dismissed it as morbid thinking — Bannor was 14 years old, and I wasn't going to have his smiling face and wagging tail beside me forever. But when I got home that evening, Bannor was indeed very ill and was saved only by emergency surgery. Later, as I related this story to a friend, she reminded me that, years ago, I had told her about a dream I had that my 10-year-old dog Cajun had died. That afternoon Cajun did die, very suddenly and unexpectedly.

Is this magic? Do I have a special ability to foresee the future? I don't think so. Most people have submerged sensitivities that haven't been developed. This *sixth sense* frequently surfaces when they're dealing with family members (in my case, my dogs) with whom they have a strong connection. Many of the complementary and alternative therapies described in this chapter were first discovered by ancient peoples thousands of years ago. Without machines or computers, these people relied on and honed *their* sixth senses — their ability to understand nature and the relationship between the earth and the people living on it.

In many ancient cultures, medical practitioners treated animals as well as humans. Today's division between veterinary medicine and human medicine did not exist — it was all considered part of the healing art. Ancient drawings show acupuncture points on dogs, horses, and humans. In addition, the *meridians,* or lines that joint acupuncture points, have the same names, regardless of species. This information has been of great benefit to veterinary medicine, because many of these modes of treatment did not have to be rediscovered for animals.

Recognizing that many theories haven't yet been proven

To begin to understand and use complementary and alternative therapies, you need to understand the difference between therapies that have been proven incorrect or ineffective and those for which scientifically controlled studies have not yet been carried out. The fact that a phenomenon has not yet been explained by scientific study doesn't mean that the phenomenon isn't real.

Science says that we should base our decisions about diagnosis, therapy, and prevention on *quantitative evidence* — that is, we should understand how the disease develops and have evidence that our interventions will do more good than harm. The ideal test of the effectiveness of a specific therapy is the *randomized clinical trial,* in which dogs with exactly the same disease process are divided into groups of treated and untreated animals. After the treatment period, strict statistical analysis is used to determine whether the treated animals had a better outcome than the untreated ones. Although randomized clinical trials are ideal, in reality, if veterinarians waited for therapies to be proven effective in randomized clinical trials, few therapies would be used and many animals would die.

So how do vets proceed in the absence of strong evidence of the effectiveness of certain therapies? They use their individual experience, listen to the experience of others, and ask questions of veterinary specialists. Good vets encourage and contribute to studies that work to determine the effectiveness of therapies. They also take personal responsibility for their treatment decisions and are open and honest about the strength or weaknesses of the evidence they do have.

Understanding Which Complementary and Alternative Therapies May Help Your Dog

Many different alternative and complementary therapies are out there, and making sense of them can sometimes be an overwhelming prospect, especially if your dog is sick and you're trying to get her help sooner rather than later. In the following sections, I outline the most common complementary and alternative therapies and let you know what they may be able to do for your dog. *Remember:* Talk with your veterinarian about any therapies that you're interested in — whether they're "traditional" or not.

Avoiding quacks

Whether your veterinarian uses only conventional medical therapies or also practices complementary and alternative medicine, be a good consumer. During the process of diagnosis and treatment of your dog's ailment, ask yourself whether, if you were dealing with your *own* physician, you would be satisfied with the care you are receiving. If the answer is yes, you can feel pretty confident that you're getting excellent care for your canine companion.

If your veterinarian practices only conventional medicine and you're interested in alternative therapies, ask for a referral for a second opinion to a vet who understands the potential of alternative therapies and how to use them appropriately. But beware of vets who practice *only* alternative and complementary forms of therapy and don't take advantage of the tremendous advancements in veterinary medicine that modern scientific research has provided. **Remember:** The complementary and alternative therapies I describe in this chapter are best used along with traditional therapies in a whole-animal approach.

Acupuncture

Acupuncture is an ancient healing art in which specific areas of the body are stimulated, usually by inserting needles, in order to elicit a tissue response. Acupuncture has existed as a healing art in India for more than 7,000 years and has been practiced in China and other parts of Asia for thousands of years.

Understanding how acupuncture works

During acupuncture treatment, the practitioner uses needles to penetrate the dog's skin at specific locations on her body. These locations, called *acupoints,* are believed to communicate with and affect the function of various body organs and tissues. A dog has at least 112 acupoints on her body, which are aligned along *meridians* (groups of acupoints that have similar or complementary effects). The practitioner can stimulate the acupoints by twirling the needles or by applying an electrical or ultrasound stimulus. Water, electrolyte solutions, and other substances can be injected into the site through needles. When several points are stimulated correctly, the effect can be greater than when just one point is stimulated.

Acupressure, in which finger pressure is applied to acupoints on the body, is a related technique. You unconsciously apply a form of acupressure to yourself when you rub your temples to try to alleviate a headache or rub an area you've just bumped. Acupressure isn't used very often in veterinary medicine, but it may be helpful to use it on your dog in between acupuncture visits. Ask your veterinary acupuncturist whether she recommends acupressure and, if so, to show you where and how to press.

The exact biochemical and molecular effects of acupuncture are not yet known. One theory about how acupuncture helps to alleviate pain is that acupuncture stimulates the nerves that send messages to pain receptors in the brain. Some kinds of nerve fibers transmit pain sensation; others don't. Scientists think that the messages from acupuncture stimulation are sent up nerves that do *not* transmit pain impulses. These messages fill up the pain receptors so they can no longer receive pain messages. Another theory suggests that acupuncture stimulation results in the secretion of chemicals called *cytokines,* which reduce pain both in specific areas of your dog's body and throughout the body as a whole. There is evidence to support both of these theories — and they may very well act together.

Knowing whether acupuncture is right for your dog

Many published scientific reports describe the successful use of acupuncture in human and veterinary medicine. It is used most commonly to relieve pain, especially chronic musculoskeletal pain such as arthritis. Traditional veterinary medicine often fails in its attempts to relieve chronic pain because of the frequent inability to identify the exact *cause* of the pain. Painkillers act only temporarily, and most have significant side effects.

Acupuncture often can provide pain relief when conventional therapy has failed. In fact, acupuncture is so beneficial in alleviating pain that if your dog suffers from chronic musculoskeletal pain, such as the kind of pain caused by arthritis, you may want to consider trying acupuncture *before* committing your canine companion to long-term treatment with anti-inflammatory medications.

Acupuncture treatments often need to be repeated, usually once or twice a week for several weeks. There is often no effect at all after the first treatment, but the length of improvement increases with each successive treatment. For chronic painful conditions, such as arthritis, implantation of gold beads at acupuncture sites can help long term.

Some people complain that their dogs initially are worse for the first few days after acupuncture treatment. Such worsening usually occurs because the dog was overtreated — either too many points were used, the wrong needles were used, or the needles were left in place too long. If you decide to pursue acupuncture treatment for your dog, take her to an experienced, IVAS-certified veterinary acupuncturist. Personal recommendations are invaluable in helping locate a skilled acupuncturist as well. As with any veterinary therapy, traditional or alternative, you shouldn't take your dog for acupuncture treatment before an adequate diagnosis has been made.

Finding a veterinary acupuncturist

Veterinary acupuncturists are trained in any of several educational programs and certified by the International Veterinary Acupuncture Society (IVAS), which was formed in 1974. Veterinary acupuncturists are required to undergo at least 120 hours of instruction, submit three detailed case reports, and complete a comprehensive examination. A veterinarian who has gone through this period of rigorous training and evaluation can put the initials CVA (which stand for *Certified Veterinary Acupuncturist*) after his name.

To find a skilled veterinary acupuncturist in your area, contact the American Academy of Veterinary Acupuncture by calling 303-772-6726 or e-mailing them at AAVAoffice@aol.com. You can also visit the AAVA online at www.aava.org, where they have a directory of certified veterinary acupuncturists. After you've identified practitioners in your area, ask your vet or dog-owning friends for personal recommendations.

Aromatherapy

About 50 percent of the time, when I take my dogs for hikes through the old growth forest nearby, one of them will roll in something dead or disgusting. As I drive home with the car windows wide open in an effort to dispel the odor and spend the next half-hour bathing the offending canine, I wonder again what compels dogs to cover themselves with such smelly objects.

Maybe rolling in dead animals is our dogs' version of aromatherapy. The *aromatherapy* that is used to heal, in contrast, is the use of scented oils extracted from plants (like flowers, buds, fruits, peel, leaves, bark, wood, roots, seeds, and resins) in order to heal. These scented oils are readily absorbed through your dog's nose or skin.

Fragrant oils and spices were used thousands of years ago in the Middle East and Egypt, long before the Christian era. Today, the flavor and fragrance industry is responsible for most of what we know about the chemistry of scented oils derived from plants. Anyone who smells the kitchen on Thanksgiving Day knows the effect of odors on mood. Plant oils are thought to have antibacterial properties, promote healing, and contain other properties that remain to be discovered. But the ways in which aromas can affect dogs psychologically and physiologically are largely unexplored. The study of aromatherapy is only in its infancy in humans, let alone in dogs, although interest in aromatherapy is growing. There currently are no formal training or certification programs for veterinarians or lay people in veterinary aromatherapy.

Bach flower therapy

Bach flower therapy is a treatment based on the clinical findings and philosophy of Edward Bach, an English physician. Bach identified 38 English flower essences that were used in the treatment method he identified. So how do these flowers heal? It's theorized that they heal by manipulating the "energy" or natural healing ability of the patient, rather than by pharmacological means.

Bach flower therapy is increasing in popularity among dog owners and veterinarians. However, little research has been performed on the efficacy of these treatments. Plus, there are no standards available that describe how the flowers are prepared and what doses to use for which medical conditions.

Some Bach flower essences, especially Rescue Remedy (which is supposed to have a calming influence on people and animals) have become quite popular. As a homeopathic-type remedy, these essences appear to have little potential for harm, and many people believe they are effective.

As with all forms of therapy, whether traditional or alternative, working with your veterinarian to obtain a diagnosis, and then reading, listening, and discussing with your vet whether this form of treatment has the potential to help your dog, is essential.

Botanical medicine

Have you ever wondered why your dog eats grass? Maybe she's practicing botanical medicine! *Botanical medicine* (the use of herbs, flowers, and other plants for medicinal purposes) is another ancient healing art. Five thousand years ago, Sumerians described uses for laurel, caraway, and thyme in healing certain ailments. Many native cultures have found through trial and error that indigenous plants have healing powers. Specific plants may have the ability to kill infectious organisms, to fight cancer, or to boost the immune system, in addition to many other beneficial effects (see Table 14-1 for some medicinal uses of herbs in dogs).

Table 14-1	Herbs Used in Veterinary Medicine	
Herb	*Scientific name*	*Use**
Astragalus	*Astragalus membranaceous*	To boost the body's immune system
Boswellia	*Boswellia serrata*	To relieve the pain of arthritis
Cranberry	*Vaccinium macrocarpon*	To prevent urinary tract infections in dogs troubled by recurrent ones
Echinacea	*Echinacea purpurea*	To stimulate the immune system
Ginger	*Allium sativum*	To relieve motion sickness
Ginkgo	*Ginkgo biloba*	To alleviate senility and to treat cardiovascular disease and circulatory disorders
Hawthorn	*Crataegus oxycantha*	To treat congestive heart failure or *cardiomyopathy*
Maitake	*Grifola frondosa*	To simulate the immune system in dogs with cancer or immunosuppressive disease
Saw palmetto	*Serenoa repens*	To treat enlargement of the prostate gland
St. John's Wort	*Hypericum perforatum*	To treat depression or anxiety
Valerian	*Valeriana officinalis*	To treat insomnia or anxiety and relax muscles

***Note:** There are no published studies demonstrating the effectiveness of these substances in dogs and they are not FDA-approved for use in animals. In addition, they should not be used in pregnant or lactating bitches.

So why would anyone who can buy a drug to treat an illness want to use a plant for treatment? Veterinarians who practice herbal medicine believe that the use of whole plants or parts of plants, if done appropriately, offer two advantages:

- **The various parts of the plant may actually provide additional therapeutic components that can work with the known active component.**

- **Herbal remedies usually are fairly safe.** In particular, botanical medicine proponents believe that combinations of herbs offer even greater opportunities for *synergy* (two or more botanicals working together) and greatly reduce the potential for toxicity.

Botanical remedies are available without a prescription, but that doesn't mean the remedy isn't potentially toxic.

Many fly-by-night companies are producing and selling herbal products without any external force to ensure quality control. And knowing which dosage is right for dogs is difficult. Plus, dogs may have sensitivities to certain plant components that are not seen in humans.

The best way to use botanical products such as herbs is to contact a veterinary herbalist and get advice about the exact product and formulation you should use for your dog's condition. Ask your veterinarian for a recommendation. You can also do some investigative work on your own by visiting the Internet site of ConsumerLab (www.ConsumerLab.com), an independent company that analyzes a large array of products and rates them as to their adherence with the ingredients as stated on the label.

Chiropractic treatment

Spinal manipulation has been practiced on humans for centuries. The Chinese practiced spinal manipulation as early as 2700 B.C. An important basis of chiropractic therapy is the acknowledgement that spinal cord structure and function is important to the health of the entire body. The spinal cord relays messages from the brain to various parts of the body, not only to the muscles, but also to organs in the abdomen, such as the adrenal glands and the gastrointestinal tract. These messages send important information that modulates their function. For example, when your dog enters her house and sees the cat that your neighbor asked you to care for during his vacation, your dog's spinal cord transmits messages that tell her to chase the cat or to stand very still in case the cat chases her. Other messages tell the stomach and intestine to put digestion on hold until the situation is under control.

Chiropractic treatment is based on the theory that misalignment of bones, particularly those of the spine, can alter some or all of the functions of the spinal cord and the nerves that extend from it. For example, a misalignment of two vertebral bones may cause pressure on the nerves that serve the muscles on one side of the spine, which causes the muscles to tense up. This in turn results in muscle tension on one side and further misalignment of bones, and it sets up a vicious cycle of musculoskeletal pain and musculoskeletal compensation.

Understanding how chiropractic treatment may help your dog

Today's *veterinary* chiropractic treatment has borrowed from the *human* chiropractic profession. Veterinary chiropractors are trained to have a detailed understanding of the structure and function of every bone, muscle, nerve, ligament, and tendon in the body and how they interact and move in relation to each other. To realign the bones, the chiropractic practitioner performs *adjustments,* in which the bones are realigned either manually or using a small impacting device called an *activator.*

Frequently a popping sound is heard during adjustment. This sound is caused by a sudden decrease in the pressure inside the joint space — it's not a cause for concern, nor is it necessary for a proper adjustment. So don't worry if you do — or don't — hear a noise when your dog is being worked on.

Chiropractic adjustment is particularly helpful when a dog has an injury or other musculoskeletal problem that causes her to move abnormally. Perhaps your dog has had an injury and has been limping. Or maybe she has hip dysplasia or arthritis, and she is stiff or favors one leg over the other. These chronic abnormalities in movement can result in an uneven tension of muscles and misalignment of the skeletal system. Chiropractic adjustment realigns the bones, helps relax the muscles, and returns balance to the musculoskeletal system.

You should notice some visible improvement after the first or second chiropractic adjustment. Frequently, however, multiple adjustments are necessary, particularly if the dog has a chronic problem. Combining chiropractic treatment with massage therapy, which can help reduce scar tissue and return the muscles to their normal level of function or acupuncture to control pain and reduce muscle spasms, may be particularly helpful for dogs with chronic problems.

Locating a veterinary chiropractor in your area

Veterinary chiropractors are trained in several educational programs and certified by the American Veterinary Chiropractic Association (AVCA). They are required to take 150 hours of instruction and complete a comprehensive examination. When choosing a canine chiropractor, ask for personal recommendations from your veterinarian or from other dog-loving friends. Because canine chiropractic adjustments require a lot of hands-on work with your dog, the best canine chiropractors are gentle with dogs and give them time to adjust to this new form of therapy.

Some human chiropractors work on dogs without appropriate training. Do not take your dog to a human chiropractor who has not completed a course in animal chiropractic therapy and achieved certification by the AVCA.

Chiropractic adjustment can benefit any dog who has been moving abnormally for a period of time due to chronic pain, lameness, or structural abnormalities. To find a veterinary chiropractor in your area, visit the AVCA Web site at www.animalchiropractic.org or call them at 309-658-2920.

Homeopathy

Homeopathy is one of the most controversial of the complementary and alternative therapies because it flies directly in the face of modern science. *Homeopathy* is based on the theory that disease symptoms are good, because they indicate that the body is defending itself — curing itself of the disease or condition. Homeopathic medicines are designed to augment the body's own defenses, not replace them.

Homeopathic remedies are prepared in a very specific way: The original active ingredient (derived from herbs, minerals, or animal products) is diluted, then violently agitated, then diluted again, then agitated, and so on. This process is repeated until the final preparation is so dilute that it, theoretically, cannot contain any of the original active ingredient. These medicines contain infinitesimal doses of the active ingredient that causes the same symptoms as the disease with the intent of augmenting the body's natural healing mechanisms. In fact, the greater the dilution, the greater the theoretical effect of the homeopathic preparation.

Even using tiny doses of a substance as a cure may not make sense, a number of properly controlled clinical studies in humans and animals have shown that certain homeopathic medicines *are* effective. Homeopathic remedies can be worth considering for specific conditions, after getting a veterinarian's advice and as a supplement to conventional veterinary medicine. If you have doubts as to the effectiveness of homeopathic remedies, keep an open mind and try it. At least with the tiny doses used, you're unlikely to harm your dog. And if it helps, you're ahead of the game.

To find a veterinary homeopathic practitioner in your area, visit the Academy of Veterinary Homeopathy online at www.acadvethom.org. Or call them at 305-652-1590. Be sure to ask your veterinarian or friends for specific recommendations as well.

Magnetic therapy

Magnetic therapy has been used for centuries in other cultures. The first magnets used in medicine were lodestones, which have a natural magnetic field. Lodestones were observed to speed healing of wounds and to relieve pain. In the past decade there has been a resurgence of interest in and use of magnets for alleviation of pain and acceleration of healing. Today, you can purchase magnets of various shapes and sizes from a number of companies. Magnets can be affixed to the injured or painful area and left in place for various periods of time to aid in healing. They also have been incorporated into leg wraps, dog coats, and dog beds.

The biochemical and molecular reasons for the healing powers of magnets are still being investigated. Studies have shown, however, that magnets do increase blood flow and the oxygen-carrying capacity of the blood. Thus, magnets may heal by a mechanism similar to massage, in which increased blood flow brings nutrients to the area of injury and removes waste products from damaged cells.

Magnetic therapy has been used extensively in veterinary medicine with horses, and its use in dogs is growing. Many musculoskeletal conditions are thought to benefit from magnetic therapy including arthritis, hip dysplasia, and spinal disorders. To treat arthritis of the knee, for example, magnets can be placed over the knee joint and the knee wrapped with an ACE brand bandage to hold the magnets in place. Dogs with chronic pain from arthritis can benefit from sleeping on a special pad with magnets sewn under the cover. Magnetic therapy is probably most beneficial in dogs with hip dysplasia or any of the many joint abnormalities that result in arthritis, as well as for relief of pain from degenerative disk disease.

Never place a magnet on a cancerous growth or on an area with a bacterial infection. Don't use magnets on an acute injury such as a laceration or a bruise, on pregnant females, on dogs who suffer from seizures, or on dogs who have pacemakers or artificial cardiac devices.

Massage therapy

In its simplest form, massage involves the healing manipulation of muscles, ligaments, and tendons. The goal of massage therapy is to increase circulation, which removes waste products from that area and brings healing nutrients to the affected area. Massage also stimulates the muscles, nerves, and other tissues to improve their function. It can be very effective in removing excessive scar tissue, in improving and balancing muscle function, and in relaxing a dog. Because anyone can learn to perform the simplest forms of massage therapy with a minimum of training, people sometimes dismiss this form of therapy as unimportant or of minimal effectiveness. To do so, however, is to miss one of the most important forms of healing in which you can participate.

Finding out how massage can help

If your dog has an injury or has had surgery, massage can significantly improve the speed and success of her healing. But massage also is beneficial to healthy dogs. Active larger-breed dogs gain tremendous benefit from regular massage because they put a lot of stress on their bodies. Massage is also an excellent pre-performance warm-up and post-performance therapy. It helps to relax and soothe the sometimes-achy muscles of elderly dogs and helps to reduce some of the scar tissue that the usual wear and tear of life causes. Through massage, puppies learn to accept and enjoy the touch of humans over all the parts of their bodies. And massage helps rescue dogs connect with, accept, and love their new people. So no matter how old your dog is or what her daily life entails, massage can be a great way for you to help her feel her best.

Ask your veterinarian or other canine-loving friends for a referral to a canine massage therapist. Some human massage therapists also work on dogs, so don't be surprised if your dog ends up sitting in the waiting room with a few hurting humans. During your massage appointment, ask the massage therapist to show you some techniques you can perform on your dog daily to improve healing. Practice them in front of the therapist so you know how to do them right.

Discovering massage techniques you can do yourself

If you're familiar with several basic principles of massage, you can use it to help your dog (and friends and family, too!):

- ✔ **Every movement should have a purpose.** Massage is not just random rubbing of the muscles; it is slow and rhythmic strokes designed to warm the tissues and stimulate blood flow to bring nutrients to the area and remove wastes.

- ✔ **When performing a massage, begin gently and be sensitive to any areas of tenderness or spasms.**

- ✔ **Always stroke with an even pressure in the direction in which the hair grows.**

For more information about massage, read *Canine Massage: A Practical Guide,* by Jean-Pierre Hourdebaigt and Shari L. Seymour.

Never massage over an area of infection, where there is broken skin, over a torn muscle, or over an area of bleeding or bruising. Use massage only for chronic or healing stages of disease — it can be detrimental if you use it for acute injuries (those less than a week old).

DOG TALK

When your dog has fallen and can't get up. . . .

A few years ago, I received a call from a woman named Stephanie who lived in California. Her champion Belgian Malinois had fallen off a 25-foot cliff and had landed on his shoulder on a huge rock. A major tendon of the shoulder was irreversibly damaged and had to be surgically removed. This was expected to cause significant scarring and permanent severe lameness. Stephanie wanted advice about how she could help her dog heal and prevent severe lameness if possible. I felt a bit at a loss never having seen the dog, but I described over the telephone how she could use massage to help prevent scarring and to improve healing. I happened to be in California four months later, and Stephanie showed me her dog. I was stunned to see that the dog barely had a limp. I felt the area where the tendon had been removed, and there was no scarring. This miracle of healing was in large part due to Stephanie's vigilance in performing massage on her dog several times a day throughout the months of healing.

Nutraceutical therapy

Nutraceuticals are substances that occur naturally, as opposed to *pharmaceuticals,* which are chemicals designed by humans. A number of oral nutraceutical products are highly effective in reducing the pain of arthritis and even in aiding the repair of damaged joints. These products are derived from naturally occurring substances such as the green-lipped mussel, shark or bovine cartilage, and other sources.

Nutraceuticals come in injectable and oral forms. The injectable form is called Adequan and has been available to veterinarians for many years. The effectiveness of Adequan has been demonstrated in controlled, scientific trials. The oral forms of nutraceuticals are a more recent addition to the market. The most well known oral joint protective nutraceutical is Cosequin, but there are many, many others on the market. Unfortunately, not all the products have the levels of active ingredients that are stated on the labels. Ask your veterinarian for recommendations of the specific products to purchase or go to www.ConsumerLab.com to find out which companies are most reputable.

WARNING!

Avoid nutraceutical formulations that have added calcium. Excess calcium can have an adverse effect on the skeletal system, especially in growing dogs.

Nutraceuticals can dramatically reduce the pain of arthritis, although sometimes it takes six to eight weeks for the oral preparations to take full effect. Antiarthritic nutraceuticals can be helpful for dogs with known arthritis or with conditions that result in arthritis, such as hip or elbow dysplasia. I give oral nutraceuticals daily to my dogs after the age of 8, on the assumption that most older dogs have aches and pains due to arthritis just as most older, active humans do.

Do not administer antiarthritic nutraceuticals to puppies to prevent hip dysplasia and other causes of arthritis. These products have not been shown to be effective in _preventing_ hip dysplasia or other joint abnormalities. Plus, treatment may obscure clinical signs when problems _do_ occur and prevent you from obtaining a timely and accurate diagnosis.

Nutritional therapy

If nutrition is important in the healthy dog, it is doubly so in the ill dog. Proper nutrition can greatly speed healing by providing additional nutrients needed for support and repair of diseased organs.

Nutritional therapy is so important that I devote Chapter 8 of this book to the subject.

Physical therapy

In humans, physical therapy may be considered complementary, but it's certainly not an alternative form of medicine. Anyone who has a sports injury these days undergoes physical therapy. Yet physical therapy has not traditionally been used in dogs. Luckily, this is changing as veterinarians begin to understand how to apply the physical therapy principles that are used in humans to their canine athlete patients.

A primary goal of physical therapy is to relieve pain. Pain relief, in turn, improves movement and allows the body's natural healing mechanisms to operate. Another goal of physical therapy is to return the injured area to full range of movement and strength. Physical therapy in dogs may apply any or all of the following methods: electricity, ultrasound, magnetics (see "Magnetic therapy" earlier in this chapter), heat and cold, stretching (through manual manipulation), and controlled exercise.

Electricity

Electricity frequently is used to stimulate a dog's sensory and motor nerves, which helps to relieve pain, absorb fluid accumulations in tissues, promote wound healing, and produce muscle contraction to help slow _muscle atrophy_ (the loss of muscle strength associated with disuse). Chiropractors use this form of treatment with human patients, too.

Ultrasound

Ultrasound is a heat-producing treatment that is highly effective in chronic injuries, especially those with scarring that impairs function. The principles of ultrasound therapy are the same as those of massage therapy. Heating fibrous structures such as tendons, ligaments, and areas of scar tissue increases their extensibility. This, combined with gentle flexion and extension exercises, helps to remodel scar tissue and prevent excess scar formation.

Heat and cold

Physical therapy also includes the appropriate use of heat and cold. Heat increases circulation to improve nourishment of the tissue; it also helps to reduce pain. Heat is used to help heal chronic injuries. Cold helps to stop bleeding and reduces swelling and other overzealous inflammatory reactions. It is used on acute injuries.

Stretching

Stretching helps to increase *flexibility* — the ability of soft tissues to elongate and then return to their normal length without loss of strength. Stretching exercises are best used therapeutically in combination with heat therapy. Additional benefits of stretching exercises include improved athleticism and reduced chance of injury.

Never stretch an area where there is an acute injury or inflammation. Stretching should be used in chronic injuries or in healthy animals before and after exercise.

Controlled exercises

Controlled exercises can be used to strengthen specific muscle groups. For example, if your dog has a shoulder injury, you can teach her first to shake, where she puts her paw in your outstretched hand. Then you can graduate to asking her to hold her leg in the air for a second (wave) and then for gradually longer lengths of time before you put your hand out to shake. This exercise helps to strengthen the muscles of her shoulder and upper arm without adding any of the impact of weight.

Part IV
Health for the Body and Soul

In this part . . .

Good health isn't just about eating the right diet and fighting off illness; it's also about giving your dog time for exercise and play, so her life is more than just about eating and sleeping. In the chapters in this part, I let you know what kinds of supplies can really make your dog's life, er, a dog's life — everything from beds and crates to toys and treats. I also give you some great tips for helping your dog get the exercise she needs (and loves!). If you and your dog are getting tired of your daily walk around the block, you can always try one of dozens of sports and activities to add some variety to your life. Plus, I let you know how you can train your dog — not just so that she's nice to have around when company is over, but also so that she's challenged mentally. The best part about the things you'll find in this part is that these are activities you and your dog can do together!

Chapter 15

Stocking Up on the Supplies You and Your Dog Need

*J*ust like babies, dogs require lots of supplies — everything from a place for the dog to sleep to brushes and combs that keep him looking and feeling good to tags that identify him if he ever escapes. In this chapter, I let you know what you need to have on hand for your dog in order to keep him happy and healthy for years to come.

Getting the Essentials

In this section, I give you the lowdown on the tools you really must have at the ready. Keep in mind that, as with anything in life, you can get more than you or your dog need, or spend more than you really have to. What you spend and how much you buy is really up to you, but the following items are ones that any dog owner will find helpful in raising a happy and healthy dog.

Crates

Wolves make their homes by digging out a dirt-packed cavity under the roots of a fallen tree, or by finding a hollow formed by large rocks in a sheltered place. This becomes the wolves' *den* (the home base where the pups are born and grow, the gathering area where the adults come with their stomachs full after a kill, and a place where the entire wolf family feels safe and protected). Thousands of years of domestication later, dogs still love to have a safe, protected place of their own. They will sleep under a low table or in a quiet corner of the room. Or we can provide them with a crate to fulfill their need for seclusion and security.

Much of what you can buy for your dog probably isn't necessary for his health and well-being, but if you're making a list of things to buy, a crate should be at the top of it. *Crates* are plastic or metal cages with a door at one end. You can find them in pet-supply stores or catalogs. A crate is your dog's home within your home — a safe place he can go to escape the crowd. It's also a place you can put him when he needs a timeout.

One of the greatest benefits of a crate is that it makes housetraining a breeze. You can use the crate to take advantage of your dog's clean gene. Contrary to popular belief, dogs are quite clean creatures. Mother dogs are particularly fastidious and constantly clean up after their puppies in the *whelping box* (the place where the pups are born). Likewise, if given a large enough yard, your pup will try his best not to soil his home and most dogs will defecate in an area far from the house and away from well-traveled pathways.

When you first bring a new puppy or adult dog home, put some treats in the crate to encourage your hesitant hound to step inside. If you give him his dinner in the crate, he will love being there even more. When he's used to the crate, close the door for gradually longer periods of time. Never put your dog in his crate for punishment. When your dog is comfortable in his doggy den, you can confine him there when you're out of the house or otherwise unable to supervise him. When you return, immediately take your dog outside and praise him when he eliminates, making it clear to him that urinating outside is the only acceptable option. Your carpets will escape the inevitable messy mistakes, and your canine companion will remain safe from accidents, poisons, and other doggy danger.

Do not confine your dog in a crate if he shows signs of intense anxiety when left alone. Locking him in a crate at this time can cause him to panic and injure himself. It also may make his separation anxiety worse. To learn more about what you can do about separation anxiety, see Chapter 17.

What size crate should you get? If your dog is an adult, take him to the store and, using an ample supply of treats, try several crates on for size. Get a crate that allows your dog to lie flat on his side with his legs outstretched and to stand up without having to duck his head. If you're getting a crate for a young pup, get one that will be suitable for him when he is full-grown. If you're debating between two sizes, get the larger one.

While your pup is still growing, you can put a plastic divider inside the dog crate to make it temporarily smaller. Otherwise, he may learn to pee on one end and sleep on the other.

Avoiding accidents

In addition to crate-training your new addition to the family, you can make a few modifications in your environment and habits in order to prevent accidents in the house. Here are a few to get you started:

✔ **Always put your dog outside first thing in the morning, as soon as you arrive home, right after he eats, and last thing at night.** Soon your dog's bodily functions will keep the same routine as you.

✔ **Feed your dog a good-quality food and resist the temptation to give him an** occasional big treat of a food he's not used to, such as a large fatty beef bone, which can make him sick to his stomach.

✔ **Watch your dog's water consumption.** Some dogs need to have their water restricted in the evening because they tend to drink excessively when their people come home after work.

✔ **After your dog has gone for 6 months without having an accident, you can confine him to an easy-to-clean part of the house when he is unsupervised.**

Leashes

Leashes usually are made of leather or nylon or cotton webbing. Many people prefer leather leashes because they are soft on the hands and easy to grip. Leather leashes do stretch over time, however, and they break more easily than nylon or cotton ones do. Plus, when they're wet, the leather dye can stain your dog's fur and your hands or clothes. Nylon webbing is the strongest and most durable material for leashes. It comes in many different colors and widths. Nylon leashes, however, are sometimes difficult to hold onto when a strong dog is pulling. Cotton leashes are easier to grip but they're less durable than nylon.

Avoid leashes made of chain. Although they're strong, they can cause injuries if they inadvertently get wrapped around an arm or a leg. In addition, they usually have plastic or nylon handles that are easily separated from the chain, putting the dog at risk of escaping.

As a general rule, the shorter the leash, the greater your control; the longer the leash, the greater your dog's freedom. Many people find a 6-foot leash a good compromise when taking a walk. It lets your dog wander in a 12-foot diameter around you, but you still can reel him in quickly when necessary. With a little experience, you can learn to hold the leash so your dog won't get his legs tangled in it, and your dog will learn to untangle himself if he does. If you're walking your dog in a high-traffic area or where lots of people are around, you may want to use a 3- or 4-foot leash for better control.

If you're taking your dog out to exercise in a park or another recreation area that requires your dog to be kept on leash, consider using a retractable leash. Retractable leashes are very popular, because they give your dog a great deal of freedom while still providing you with some control. Retractable leashes have a short length of nylon webbing that snaps to your dog's collar. The nylon webbing is attached to a spring-loaded cord that comes out of and retracts into a plastic handle. Pushing a button on the handle causes the cord to be locked in position. So your dog can run out to a distance of 15 feet or more and return to you without getting tangled in the leash. You can control the distance your dog strays by using the locking mechanism.

Never let go of the handle of a retractable leash when it is attached to a dog. The handle will spring towards the snap and can badly injure a human or dog in its way. Projectile retractable leashes have seriously injured or knocked unconscious both dogs and humans.

The *waist leash* is one of the best-kept secrets for comfortable dog walking. It consists of an adjustable belt that fastens around your waist with a sliding snap, and an adjustable leash that snaps to the waist belt at one end and to the dog at the other. Usually, the leash has a loop handle and a quick-release mechanism to quickly disengage it from your waist belt so you can use it as a regular leash when necessary. Being able to freely swing your arms when walking your dog is surprisingly pleasant. Even if your dog doesn't pull, a leash in your hands does affect your balance. If you are a regular dog walker or like to run with your dog, try a waist leash.

Be sure to obey your local leash laws. In more and more areas of the country, dogs are not allowed at all. A major reason for this is the inconsiderate behavior *not* of dogs, but of their people, who let their dogs roam, bothering people and wildlife, and leaving canine messes behind. Be sure you don't contribute to that problem.

Beds

The best dog beds are made of foam, synthetic batting, or cedar chips enclosed in a washable cover. Many dogs like to lie with their heads slightly elevated. If your pooch has this propensity, you can get him a bed shaped like a donut, with a hollowed out center and a raised edge. In the summer, your dog may appreciate the air circulation provided by a cot made of plastic mesh and raised about 6 inches off the ground. Many dog beds and cots are available at pet supply stores. Before you get a dog bed, however, ask if you can bring your dog into the store to test the bed out.

Some dogs, particularly those with thick coats, prefer the cool, hard floor over a soft bed any day. Even if your dog always has scorned beds, however, keep an eye on him as he gets older. Canine senior citizens often appreciate a soft bed to ease some of their aches and pains.

Do dogs dream?

Scientific studies have confirmed what most dog owners know: Dogs do dream. Like their people, dogs have periods of rapid eye movements (REMs) that correspond to dream time.

Next time your dog twitches and yips while sleeping, he's probably dreaming of chasing rabbits or running on the beach.

If you plan to invest in a dog bed, make sure it is big enough for your dog to toss, turn, and lie in any position he wants. Although they are quaint, most wicker beds are not suitable for dogs because their hard, raised sides and rounded shape force a dog to sleep in a curled position.

Brushes and combs

Regular coat care is important, and not just for the sake of appearance. Providing regular coat and skin care is one of the best things you can do for your dog's health. Years ago, people used to believe that dogs didn't need baths, and even that bathing was unhealthy for them. Frequent baths *can* dry a dog's coat and skin, particularly if you use harsh shampoos. An occasional bath and brushing will, however, remove dead hairs that may otherwise mat, potentially causing skin infections. When the dead hairs are removed, new, healthy hair can grow in. And frankly, a bath will remove that doggie smell, making your dog more pleasant to be around.

How often should you bathe your dog? Whenever he smells or his coat looks dirty or feels greasy or dusty.

Breeds differ greatly in the amount of coat care they need. If your canine friend has a short, smooth coat (such as that of a Doberman Pinscher or a Dalmatian), he may just need a quick weekly wipe-down with a damp cloth or a rubber curry comb to clear away dead hairs.

If your dog has a double coat (such as that of a Golden Retriever or a Shetland Sheepdog), he should be brushed from head to toe at least once a week. Have your dog lie on his side and work your way over his whole body, using a pin brush to get through the undercoat to the skin. When you're finished, you'll be amazed at how much hair the brush contains. Better on the brush than on your carpet and clothes!

In spring and fall, double-coated dogs shed copious amounts of hair. During these periods, they need daily brushing to remove the dead undercoat hairs that lie enmeshed in the longer, *guard hairs* (the stiff, longer hairs that give a double coat its shape). The best tool to use at this time is a *rake,* which has widely separated teeth that dig through the dense coat and grasp clumps of undercoat. You can follow up with a slicker brush, which picks up any loose hairs left behind by the rake. Removal of the dead hair allows the skin to breathe and promotes growth of the new coat. Then in six months you can start the cycle all over again!

If your dog has a long, single coat, such as that of a Lhasa Apso or a Bearded Collie, you'll have to be a pretty dedicated groomer. Ideally, these dogs should be carefully *line brushed* at least once a week. To line-brush your dog, follow these instructions:

1. **Place your dog on his side and, using a Greyhound comb, make a part in his hair along his back just above the center of his back.**

2. **Using a pin brush, brush the hair that you have separated against the direction in which it normally lies, carefully removing any knots.**

    If the hair is tangled, start by brushing just the last third of the hair. With each brush stroke, move closer to the skin. If big tangles have formed and you can't work them free, you may have to cut them off.

    When cutting off a tangle that's close to the skin, be very careful. You can very easily nick the skin by accident.

3. **Next make another part ½ inch from the first part and again brush the separated hair against the direction of flow.**

4. **Continue making parts along your dog's side, working your way across his body from his back to his stomach until you have brushed all his hair against the direction in which it normally falls.**

5. **Turn the dog over to his other side and repeat.**

6. **When you are done, let him stand up and gently brush the hair in its normal direction.**

    This process can take quite a while, but it very relaxing to the dog and it's essential if you are going to keep your dog's coat clean and mat-free.

Figure 15-1 illustrates the different grooming tools you may need, depending on your dog's coat.

Some dogs, such as Poodles and Portuguese Water Dogs, require regular clipping. This is best done by a professional dog groomer, but if you want to try it yourself, make sure to get the right tools and proper instruction first (talk to a pro for tips). At the very least, your efforts at dog sculpture may be humorous. At worst, you may seriously injure your dog's skin with the clippers or scissors.

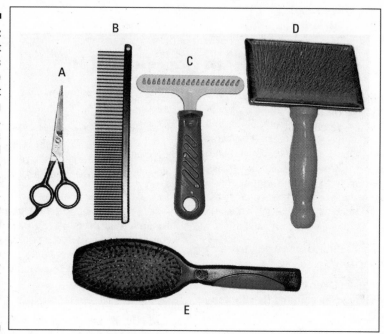

Figure 15-1: Different coats require different grooming tools, including some or all of the following: (A) scissors, (B) Greyhound comb, (C) rake, (D) slicker brush, and (E) pin brush.

Toys

Playtime is essential for a dog's mental and physical health. Young puppies play as soon as they can walk, which helps them grow and develop correctly and teaches them about their environment. It also helps them learn the social skills they need to get along with other dogs and with humans. Most adult dogs like to play, too. Play helps relieve stress and keeps adult dogs physically fit. By selecting your dog's toys wisely and by participating in games with your dog, you can make his play more interesting, you can strengthen your bond with your dog, and you can make sure your dog plays safely.

Scientists believe that, during the process of domestication, the mental maturation of dogs was slowed so that our domesticated dogs behave more like wolf puppies than adult wolves. Part of this behavior includes an intense love of play.

For more information on toys that exercise your dog, turn to Chapter 16.

Making bath time bearable

Every now and then, your white wonderdog will spend some time in the yard digging a hole to China, or your canine hiking companion will decide to roll in some smelly mess. You know your filthy dog should have a bath, but you both hate the mess and the hassle. An expensive solution is to transport your four-legged friend to a professional dog groomer. If you choose the do-it-yourself method, however, here are some ways to make bath time easier on you both:

✔ **Start bathing your dog when he's a pup so he'll get used to it.**

✔ **Place a rubber mat on the floor of the bath-tub to provide some stability for your furry friend's feet.**

✔ **Invest in a noose, an inexpensive loop of plastic or fabric that slips over your dog's head and attaches by a suction cup to the wall of the bathtub.** You can tighten the loop so your dog cannot slip out of the collar, which enables you to have both hands free for bathing.

✔ **An elevated bathtub is a wonderful con-venience if you find yourself bathing your pooch frequently.** If your dog is small enough, you may be able to use the laun-dry tub or even the kitchen sink. If not, con-sider installing an elevated bathtub. Raised

doggie bathtubs also are sold in pet-supply catalogs.

✔ **Give your dog a treat for getting in the tub and periodically throughout the bath, but not at the end.** You want to reward him for the process of being bathed, not just when it is over.

✔ **Use a dog shampoo that doesn't sting when it gets in your dog's eyes.** Don't use human shampoo on your dog. The *pH level* (the level of acidity) of human shampoos is not appropriate for dogs and will dry and irritate their skin.

✔ **Thoroughly towel-dry your dog after the bath.** During warm months, most dogs can air-dry after toweling. In the winter, how-ever, use a hairdryer set on low or a pro-fessional dog dryer so your dog doesn't get chilled.

An alternative to bathing your dog in the family tub is to use one of the "self-serve" bathing areas that are becoming more popular in pet shops. You bring the shampoo, and they supply the elevated bathtub, water, towels, and a blow dryer.

If you want your wet dog to shake the water off himself, blow gently into his face and stand back!

Chew toys

The best way to protect the legs of your mahogany chairs and to keep your other home furnishings intact is to provide a variety of chew toys for your dog. Test your dog with a number of toys to see how aggressive a chewer he is. Frequently, Sporting dogs are gentle chewers because they have been bred to have soft mouths so that they don't destroy the birds they retrieve. Chew toys last a lot longer for these dogs than for more assertive chewers. Tough, latex squeaky toys, stuffed toys with squeakers, and rope toys all are great for passionate chewers.

Dogs who have a fierce desire to chew can gut an expensive stuffed animal in a matter of minutes. To satisfy their desire to chew, you can purchase old children's stuffed animals from secondhand shops or from yard sales. Just remove the eyes, nose, ribbons, and any loose items that your dog can choke on and then let him joyfully tear apart this latest victim. Be sure to supervise him, however, and discard the pieces as soon as he's done.

Rawhide bones, sterilized real *long bones* (the bones of the leg) purchased from pet supply stores or catalogs, and *dental bones* (bumpy, hard plastic bones designed to clean the chewer's teeth) all are excellent outlets for the canine chewer. The chewing motion helps remove plaque and *calculus* (hard mineral build-up) from dogs' teeth, and it also massages the gums.

Dogs should be supervised whenever they chew a new toy for the first time to be sure they don't break off and swallow pieces of it.

Supervise your dog when he is chewing a rawhide bone because he may soften a large piece, try to swallow it, and choke. If your dog has had a fractured tooth, don't let him chew real bones or other hard objects.

You can wash most stuffed toys, but the squeakers generally don't work after a trip through the washer and dryer!

Tug toys

Many dogs (like the one in Figure 15-2) love to play tug-of-war, whether it's with a leash, a stick, or a toy designed for tugging. Rope toys, balls with a rope or bungie cord attached, and rubber toys shaped in a figure eight are all designed to help you satisfy your dog's desire to tug.

How dogs play

Many canine games imitate hunting behavior. Chasing, pouncing, tugging, wrestling, shaking, and chewing are all components of a successful hunt. Dogs often use inanimate objects as prey. With a little imagination, a leaf blown by the wind becomes a dashing bunny rabbit, a stick is transformed into a captured bird, and a plastic bag becomes a piece of skin and fur. One reason so many dogs love toys is because squeaky toys and stuffed chew toys simulate the sound and texture of prey. Hollow objects such as bones or Kong toys stuffed with treats and sealed with peanut butter are like bones with marrow to be sucked out.

Individual dogs often prefer certain games over others. Some dogs will retrieve a ball or a flying disc for hours. Other dogs enjoy playing tug-of-war. Still others prefer to pounce on a stuffed toy and pull its innards out. All these games are good outlets for a dog's energy, as long as the toys are chosen wisely and the playful pooch is supervised.

Toys to avoid

Never give your dog a small toy that can get lodged in his throat, and never give him a toy that has metal parts — particularly lead, copper, or zinc — because they can be toxic when swallowed. Many children's toys fit into these categories, because they have small parts that can break off or that your dog can chew into small parts. If you have small children, be particularly watchful. You may not want to let your dog play in the area where your children keep their toys. Try to have the children pick up their toys after they are finished playing with them (they'll like not having their toys demolished by the dog, too).

Some people mistakenly think they should not let a dog play tug because it may make the dog more dominant and aggressive. But I believe that playing tug is perfectly okay as long as you have control of the game. Teach your dog that he must obey you when you tell him to let go. And make sure you maintain control by asking your dog to stop every now and then.

Figure 15-2:
This Belgian Tervuren is having fun playing tug-of-war.

Toys that educate and occupy

You don't need to feel guilty when you leave for work, knowing that your dog will be alone all day. Instead, give him a toy that will keep him occupied for several hours. A beef leg bone stuffed with peanut butter will keep your dog busy sticking his tongue down the marrow hole, trying to get every last morsel. You also can stuff a rubber Kong toy (which is shaped like a beehive and has an open, stuffable center) with some cookies, seal it with cream cheese or peanut butter, and let him dig out the treasures.

A *Buster Cube* is a 6-inch square (for large dogs) or 3-inch square (for small dogs) cube with a hole in one end into which you can deposit dog food or other small morsels. To release the treats, your dog must move the cube with his nose or paw, tilting the cube just so. The Buster Cube is a great toy to occupy dogs and to hone their problem-solving abilities. This toy can keep a dog occupied for hours, hunting for just the right way to expel the food.

Knowing Which Tools Can Keep Your Dog Safe

Although you may never intend for your dog to be running loose, dogs have a way of sneaking out when you're not looking. So in the following sections, I give you some great suggestions for keeping your dog confined and providing him with identification so that you can be reunited if he does manage to get out.

Confining your dog

Whether your dog sleeps in the lap of luxury or roughs it, he should not be allowed to run free. Loose dogs are likely to be hit by cars, and they frequently chase wild animals. If their chase instinct gets the better of them and they run after sheep or other farm animals, they could be shot. If they haven't been spayed or castrated, they will likely contribute to the problem of dog overpopulation. And small stray dogs frequently are carried off by birds such as eagles or vultures. Because of these hazards, dogs who are allowed to roam free do not live as long and do not remain as healthy as their confined counterparts.

 A walk around a postage stamp-size backyard is not enough exercise for a medium or large dog. Daily exercise helps keep your dog trim, healthy, and happy, and he will live longer, too (see Chapter 16 for more information on exercising your dog).

So what are your options for keeping your pooch on your property? A fence (like the one in Figure 15-3) is the best choice for a number of reasons. A fence provides a visible barrier that not only keeps your dog in, it also keeps other dogs out — a definite advantage in city neighborhoods where dogs often roam loose. A split-rail fence lined by woven wire makes an attractive, effective, and relatively inexpensive fence. Some people prefer solid fences such as *stockade fences* which provide more privacy for a dog who feels the

Playing recess monitor: Knowing which toys require supervision

Some dogs need a little supervision when playing with certain toys. Here are a few general guidelines:

✔ **Always supervise your dog the first time he plays with a new kind of toy.** This way you can be there to make sure he doesn't break off pieces and swallow or choke on them.

✔ **Always supervise your dog when he is chewing a rawhide bone or playing with a toy that has strings or rope attached.**

✔ **Supervise aggressive chewers when they play with stuffed toys.**

✔ **Throw away any bone that becomes small enough to be swallowed.**

need to guard his property from every passerby. This advantage also can be a disadvantage, however. Dogs kept behind solid fences may not be as acclimatized to the sights and sounds of the neighborhood and may be more fearful when they're not on their home turf.

A 4-foot fence adequately confines most dogs. A few dogs can jump a 4-foot fence and require a 6-foot fence. Occasionally, dogs learn how to climb fences. These canine escape artists require smooth-sided, 6-foot stockade fences or kennels with enclosed roofs.

Figure 15-3:
A fence is the best way to keep your dog on your property.

Photograph courtesy of Sheli Rhodes

Don't tie your dog up by a chain or rope. Dogs who are tied often become frustrated as they bark and lunge at passing dogs, people, and wild animals. Typically, chained or tied dogs are more aggressive to strangers and other dogs, even when they are loose.

Unfortunately, many suburban developments prohibit the fencing of property, necessitating the use of other confinement methods. One of the most popular is the *electronic fence,* which uses an electrical circuit buried a few inches underground at the perimeter of the property. The dog wears a battery-operated collar that, when in close proximity to the buried wire, closes an electrical circuit and provides a shock to the dog's neck. The dog initially is trained to recognize the boundary by the presence of small, flagged stakes. After the dog has learned his boundaries, you can remove the flags.

Many people use electronic fences successfully, and in neighborhoods where fences are strictly forbidden, an electronic fence works better than tying your dog outside. Electronic fences are, however, subject to a number of problems. First, it doesn't prevent other dogs from entering your yard, so neighborhood dogs can come over and harass your canine companion. In addition, your dog may play with a visiting dog in your yard or chase a squirrel and accidentally cross the fence. If this happens, the shock then prevents your dog from re-entering your yard. Finally, as with all electronic gadgets, these fences are subject to failure. They may fail because the power has been shut off, because the battery in the dog's collar has not been sufficiently charged, or because the dog was let outside without his collar on (just this once).

Outdoor living

Some people prefer to house their dogs outdoors or in indoor-outdoor kennels. Farm dogs often sleep on blankets or straw in the barn instead of on the quilt in the master bedroom. Many sled dogs live in doghouses and enjoy the great outdoors, even in the depths of winter. In general, dogs who live in cold climes do better living outdoors than those in the tropics. Dogs are designed to deal with cold, but they frequently suffer in the heat.

If your dog is destined to be an outdoorsman, he needs a place to sleep that will protect him from the wind, rain, and cold. The best outdoor doggie digs is a dog house with a thick layer of blankets or straw for your dog to sleep on. The doghouse should be just big enough for your dog to stand up and turn around in. That way, he can heat it with his own body warmth — as long as it's wind- and rain-proof and contains a thick layer of bedding. Do remember, however, that dogs need human companionship. If you decide to house your dog outside, you still need to spend lots of quality time with him every day.

Dogs with short coats do not have enough protection to live outdoors in the winter. In addition, dogs who do live outdoors in the winter need extra food with a higher level of fat to provide the energy they will need to keep warm.

Don't include your front yard in the area surrounded by an electronic fence. Your dog will be more likely to become a nuisance by barking at strangers who walk by. Plus, some dogs develop territorial aggression because of the constant stimulation of cars and children walking along the front of their property. It's best to confine your dog to your backyard.

If you use an electronic fence, don't leave the collar on your dog when he's indoors. In addition, check the area under his collar every day. The collar must be worn tight so the metal prongs contact your dog's skin. If the collar is too tight or the skin gets wet, however, a bacterial infection can develop.

Don't assume your dog is perfectly safe just because you've installed an electronic fence. Check on your dog every few minutes when he's outdoors. Animal-control officers say that many dogs killed on the road are wearing electronic collars.

Making sure your dog can be identified

One of the more important things you can do as a dog owner is give your dog ample identification so that, if he escapes, others will be able to identify him and return him to you right away. You can accomplish this in several ways, all outlined in the following sections.

Tags

Military servicemen call their ID tags *dog tags* for a reason. Both types of dog tags are essential to identify the wearer in case he is lost or injured. The vast majority of dogs in animal shelters were not wearing identification tags when they were found, making it much more difficult for the dogs to be reunited with their owners.

Make sure your dog is always wearing an ID tag (like the dog in Figure 15-4), with your name, address, and telephone number on it. You also may want to include the dog's name on the tag and other pertinent information, such as the name and telephone number of your veterinarian. (Some people prefer not to include their dog's name on the tag because they fear someone will use their dog's name to befriend and steal him. But the way I see it, if a thief is close enough to your dog to read his name on the tag, your dog has probably already befriended him!)

In the U.S. and Canada, the law requires all dogs to be vaccinated for rabies. You can save yourself, your dog, and others a great deal of trouble and worry if you make sure that your dog wears his rabies tag at all times. If your dog is lost and ends up biting a stranger, the veterinarian or animal control officer will know that your dog has been vaccinated against rabies. They also may be able to contact you through the number on the tag.

If your dog's jangling tags drive you crazy, just tape your dogs' tags to his collar with duct tape or purchase a small pocket designed to slip onto your dog's collar and carry his tags.

Figure 15-4:
This dog always wears his rabies tag, as well as an ID tag with his home phone number engraved on the back.

Make sure your dog wears his collar and tags all the time. It can save his life. And you never know when your dog will dash out the door after a squirrel in the yard or when a well-intentioned appliance repairperson will let your dog out. If your dog wears a collar and ID tags at all times, the person who finds him will be able to get in touch with you no matter what.

Tattoos

Many dog owners use tattoos to permanently identify their dogs. Tattoos can be placed on the skin inside the ear, on the lower stomach where the hair is thinner, or on the inside of the thigh (see Figure 15-5). Puppies as young as 7 weeks can be tattooed, a practice very common in Canada where both pure-bred and mixed-breed dogs are required by law to be identified by tattoos. A tattoo usually costs between $10 and $20.

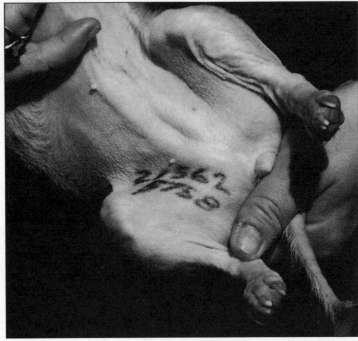

Figure 15-5:
Even the
tiniest of
dogs have
room on
their bodies
for a tattoo.

Get an experienced canine tattoo artist to do the job. Tattooing is a permanent procedure, and you want the tattoo to remain clear throughout your dog's life. Ask your veterinarian or local dog club for a referral.

Before getting your dog tattooed, check with various registries that record tattoo numbers and help reunite lost, tattooed dogs with their owners. Different registries may suggest that you include specific information on the tattoo. The National Dog Registry, for example, one of the foremost registries for dog tattoos, suggests that you tattoo your dog with your social security number, because this is a number you will have all your life. If you decide to use your social security number, add one or more additional digits that are unique to each of your dogs; that way, each of your dogs is identified individually. You also can tattoo your purebred dog with his American Kennel Club (AKC) registration number or use another unique registration number. After your dog has been tattooed, be sure to register him with your chosen registry. You don't need to register your dog with more than one. The following organizations offer registration of tattooed dogs:

✔ National Dog Registry (phone: 800-637-3647; Web site: `www.natldogregistry.com`)

✔ Tattoo-a-Pet (phone: 800-828-8667; Web site: `www.tattoo-a-pet.com`)

Always include the telephone number of your dog's tattoo registry on his ID tag.

I always have the tattooist put a large heart with an arrow through it below my social security number. A simple picture like this is easy to see through the fur and may help the person who finds your dog locate the tattoo number.

Microchips

Thanks to digital technology, your dog can be identified by a tiny microchip the size of a grain of rice. Your veterinarian can insert a microchip with a unique identification number under the skin at the back of your dog's neck, where it will remain for the rest of his life.

As with tattoos, register your dog's microchip number with an organization that reunites lost dogs with their owners. The best and most commonly used organization is the AKC Companion Animal Recovery (phone: 800-252-7894; Web site: www.akc.org).

If your dog is lost, a veterinarian or animal shelter worker can use an electronic scanner to read the ID numbers on the microchip. They then can contact the registry and get your name, address, and telephone number.

Always include the telephone number of your dog's microchip registry on his ID tag.

Chapter 16

Getting the Lead Out: Exercising Your Dog

Thousands of years ago, for better or for worse, dogs linked up with humans. Overall, the marriage has been a great success for both parties. But one of the sacrifices most dogs have made is the ability to go outside and run free any time they want. Wolves often cover 100 miles a day hunting and exploring; with most people leading very busy lives and working outside the home, dogs are lucky to get a mile-long walk on a leash every day, and most don't even get that.

Exercise offers tremendous physical and psychological benefits for your dog (and for you, too). With all the companionship your dog provides you, she deserves to get the exercise she craves. This chapter tells you how to give your dog the hard body she has always wanted — even if you work all day, are disabled, or just plain don't have the energy.

Recognizing the Benefits of Exercise

Exercise provides immense physical and psychological benefits to dogs of all ages. Dogs who exercise regularly live longer, remain healthier, and are more active in their later years. With regular exercise, your dog will become stronger and more coordinated, and her muscles will become more powerful and ready to kick into action any time. Strong muscles stabilize the joints, slowing the progression of arthritis. Exercise strengthens the heart and the lungs as well, improving the delivery of oxygen and nutrients to tissues throughout the body. Exercise also is an excellent way to control your dog's weight; strong muscles are larger and utilize more calories while at rest than smaller muscles do.

Runners and other fitness buffs have long recognized the psychological benefits of exercise. It causes endorphins to be released in the brain. *Endorphins* are biochemical messengers within the brain that induce a feeling of euphoria and overall well-being. So exercise (and the good feeling it brings) can prevent a dog from developing problems such as *lick granulomas* (sores caused by repeated licking or chewing at the skin), destructive behaviors (such as chewing the corners of your new couch or digging up your tulip bulbs), restlessness, or excessive barking. In fact, exercise is so important to a dog's psyche that it's the first line of treatment for most behavioral problems. Dog behaviorists claim that lack of exercise is a significant contributing factor in over 50 percent of all behavioral problems in dogs.

Getting Started

Despite all the benefits of exercise, the majority of dogs in North America do not get enough exercise. If your dog spends so much time lounging that she's starting to look like part of the furniture, it's time to get her on her feet and out of the house. Do it gradually, however. Just as you wouldn't head out the door to run a marathon without any training, you shouldn't expect your dog to be able to exercise for hours without building up to that level.

If your dog is seriously overweight (more than 20 percent over her ideal weight), get the thumbs up from your veterinarian before you start her on a serious exercise program. Your vet should give your dog a physical examination with special emphasis on the heart, lungs, and musculoskeletal system to be sure she's ready to up her activity level.

If you start your dog's exercise program slowly, increase the amount of exercise gradually, and use common sense, so your dog has only minimal risk of injury. To be safe, overweight dogs should not do much running with quick turns or jumping until they have slimmed down.

If your dog shows signs of fatigue such as excessive panting, grimacing, or scuffing the toes, ease up or stop altogether. Dogs who have a tendency to go until they drop definitely need guidance about when to stop.

To remain fit and content, a dog should get a minimum of 15 minutes of exercise a day and should have a longer exercise period two to three times a week. Be creative with your dog's exercise. This is a time when you and your dog can get to know each other better — make the most of it!

Try to provide a mix of both strength-training and endurance-training exercises. Like humans, dogs have a mixture of muscle fibers — some for strength and some for endurance. These fibers use energy differently and are called upon in different circumstances. Exercises such as retrieving and chasing that involve many starts, stops, and turns help build strength. Exercises such as trotting, in which the dog moves continuously for at least 20 minutes, build endurance. Dogs benefit most if you build both their strength *and* their endurance muscles.

If you are a fitness buff, be sure not to over-exercise your dog. During sustained, repetitive physical activity, lactic acid builds up and breaks down muscle cells. And it takes 48 hours for the cells to repair themselves. So if you run with your dog beside you on a leash for more than 30 minutes, give your canine athlete a day off between runs to recover.

Being Creative with Your Dog's Exercise Routine

Does the word *exercise* evoke images in your mind of runners with sweaty shirts, glazed eyes, and sore feet? Don't worry, you can exercise your dog without sweating beside your panting pup over miles of hot pavement. Many more interesting and effective ways of providing your dog with the exercise she needs are at your disposal. With a little imagination, you can invent a variety of exercises and games that will build your dog's strength and endurance and that you'll both enjoy. Exercise takes a little time, but the payoff is enormous in terms of your dog's health and vitality, her confidence and behavior, and your relationship with her. Besides, who among us can't use a few moments of stress-free playtime during the day?

Inject a little variety into your playtimes. After all, too much of even a fun game gets boring. Play different kinds of games in different locales, at different times of the day, and using different treats for rewards.

Instinctive activities

Often the activities that are most fun for dogs (and their humans) are those that imitate the dog's natural drives and instincts. When your dog plays fetch, she imagines herself as a mighty hunter, chasing her prey and bringing it home to the pups. For dogs with herding instincts, such as Shelties and

Collies, it's the chasing part that's fun, not the capture. They bring the ball back so they can chase it again. A pair of dogs will often exercise each other, alternating between being the chaser and the chasee. Terriers and other dogs originally bred to hunt vermin love to play games with a killing theme. Nothing feels quite as good to a terrier as chasing a stuffed toy, capturing it, and shaking it to break its neck.

You can design games around a dog's latent herding instinct by inventing chasing games. One fun game is to have your dog sit and stay in the middle of a soccer field, place yourself approximately three quarters of the way to the goal, release your dog, and start running. See which one of you gets to the goal first (but handicap yourself so your dog wins about half the time).

You also can recapitulate vermin-catching games for your terrier. Drag a bone or a toy over the ground for 25 feet or so and then bury it in an area of the garden that you don't mind if she digs in. Watch your terrier's face beam as you take her to the beginning of the scent trail and encourage her to "find the rat." To a terrier, there's no delight quite like that of finding the prey and digging it out.

Walking

Many people derive great pleasure from a daily walk with the dog. For some, this means an early morning stride through the neighborhood with the dew on the grass and the birds chattering in the trees. For others, it's a chance to put on the headphones, crank up the music, and forget the day's stresses. Most dogs enjoy walks because of their natural curiosity about the environment. They love to be surrounded by new sights and smells. You may find it kind of frustrating, however, to stop at each vertical object along the way so your dog can exchange pee-mail with the other dogs in the neighborhood. I find that a compromise works best. Before going for a walk, I let my dogs into the yard so that they eliminate there. During the walk, I let my dogs stop and communicate only on the first block. After that, I give the command, "Let's go!" They are expected to get moving and not stop again until I say so.

Always carry a plastic bag and pick up after your dog (and remind your dog walker or pet sitter to do so, too). Just slip your hand in the bag, grab the dog poop, and then turn the bag inside out over your hand and tie it in a knot. Find a trash can to deposit your package in, or throw it out when you get home. Your neighbors will appreciate your thoughtfulness and you will feel good knowing that you're doing your part to keep the neighborhood dog-friendly.

Use a *waist leash,* a belt to which your dog's leash can be attached. Walking or running with your dog when your hands are free to swing at your sides is much easier than having to hang on to a leash the whole way.

Trotting

If you want to step it up a bit, take your dog for a run. (Actually your dog trots, while you keep up by any number of means. Trotting is one of the best endurance exercises for dogs.) It's not even essential for you to run alongside. You can try inline skating on a paved high school track with your dog trotting on the infield grass. Or try training your dog to trot beside your bike (like the dogs in Figure 16-1). Be sure to use a device such as the Springer or K-9 Cruiser to attach your dog's leash to the bicycle, leaving your hands free. (One incident with a squirrel running across your path should convince you of the benefits of these attachments.)

Figure 16-1:
Attach a device to your bike so that you don't have to hold on to a leash and try to maneuver the bike at the same time.

Photo courtesy of Todd Jackson

Bicycling with a loose dog is dangerous. Even on country paths, a loose dog can chase wild animals such as rabbits or deer and become lost or injured. Use an attachment that connects your dog to your bicycle.

Skijoring

Skijoring (in which your dog pulls you over the snow on skis) is a great winter variation on taking a walk. If your dog gets a bit carried away or you are a cautious skier, you can also cross-country ski with your dog running beside you.

Running in deep snow is very strenuous, so these activities should be limited to dogs over 2 years of age.

Some dogs get snowballs between the pads of their feet when they play in the snow. This problem can be reduced by trimming excess hair from the bottom of your dog's feet and between her toes. You also can apply petroleum jelly or cooking spray liberally to the skin between her toes before going outside. Another excellent fix for this problem is to have your dog wear booties, which are available at pet supply stores and through companies that sell products for mushing dogs. If your dog runs mainly on packed snow, get booties made of polar fleece. If she runs on mixed snow and gravel or pavement, you'll need to get booties made of a tougher fabric, such as canvas or Cordura nylon. Booties can be an excellent aid for the city dog who feels the sting of salt spread on the streets and sidewalks in the winter as well.

Fetch

Fetch is a favorite game of many dogs. Most people are fond of this game because they can play it while standing still. You can use many different fetch objects, from a simple stick to a ball or a disc. Some balls even glow in the dark or have an internal flashing light so you can use them for a quick game of fetch when you get home from work on a dark winter night.

Bumpers (plastic cylinders that float and have a rope attached to one end) are a favorite fetch toy for many Retrievers, especially for retrieving on water. The rope makes them easier to throw, too. Many dogs like to chase flying discs as well. The way the disc floats in the air and changes directions is very exciting to the canine hunter.

Be careful when playing fetch with a flying disc. Throw the disc just above the ground so your dog doesn't have to leap up to catch it. Dogs can suffer severe injuries by twisting their backs or by landing on their rear legs when trying to catch a disc. If you decide to take up canine disc-catching as a sport, get proper instruction on how to throw the disc to reduce the risk of injury to your dog.

If your dog is not much of a retriever, he may enjoy playing soccer. Use a ball that is too large and too firm for him to pick up in his teeth. Kick it around the yard, encouraging him to chase it. He will eventually get the idea and learn to push the ball around the yard himself. Dogs can have a lot of fun playing with a large ball in the water, too. They use their noses to push the ball back and forth and try to capture it.

If you can't throw a ball very far and your dog is looking at you as if he wished he were owned by a baseball star, try using an aid to throw the ball farther. That way your dog will run farther for each fetch, making it more fun and less risky for her. Use a tennis racket or a bat to whack the ball as far as possible. Another great invention is the Chuckit, a plastic stick that cups a tennis ball at one end while you hold the other end and swing it. When you let it go, the ball flies up to 250 feet, much farther than if you used your arm. The Foxtail is another type of ball that is easy to throw long distances. This ball has a colorful nylon tail that flaps in the breeze as it trails the ball. If you use the tail to swing it before letting go, the Foxtail can fly hundreds of feet.

If your dog is a keen retriever, why not add a few twists to the old game of fetch? First throw the ball as far as you can. Then throw a short one. Then throw your dog a grounder, then toss the ball high into the air for your dog to catch. Praise her just for trying, and give her verbal praise and treats for extra fast or talented retrieves.

You also can make the game tougher by having your dog retrieve an object while running uphill. This increases the amount of weight she has to bear on her rear legs, thus increasing the amount of work the rear legs perform. This in turn strengthens the rear leg muscles, which is especially important as the dog gets older.

Swimming

Swimming is one of the best forms of exercise for any dog. Because swimming is a non-weight-bearing activity, it strengthens the cardiovascular and muscular systems without placing stress on bones and joints. This is especially helpful for dogs with arthritis.

Many dogs, like the one in Figure 16-2, naturally enjoy swimming, and most can learn if they're given encouragement when they're young. The best way to teach a pup to swim is to start by putting your boots on and walking with her in a creek. Creeks have deeper and shallower parts, and eventually, your pup will find herself swimming over a short distance without even realizing it. If your adult dog is reluctant to swim, the best way to teach her is to get wet yourself and encourage her to join you in the fun. If she is hesitant to swim over her head, use the Hansel-and-Gretel principle: Walk slowly out to deeper waters, depositing dog treats as you go (Cheerios float very well) and offering encouragement. Often, your dog's stomach will overcome her fears.

Figure 16-2:
The smile on Tally's face as she leaps into the water is all the proof you need to know that swimming is one of her favorite activities.

If your water-loving canine is going to swim in a pond, make sure to scout the area for broken glass, fishing lines, and other hazards first. If you find broken glass, find another place for your dog to swim, because there's likely to be more where the piece you found came from. If she bounds into the water and steps on broken glass, it can cut the tendons that run across the wrist just under the skin of her legs. Tendons are notoriously difficult to repair and those particular tendons are critical for a dog to be able to walk and run without discomfort, so you definitely don't want to risk it.

If you or a friend have a swimming pool and don't mind a little dog hair in the filter, letting your dog swim there is just fine. In fact, if you want your flabby dog to build a little muscle, you can put her on a leash and walk around the outside of the pool for 5 to 10 minutes while she swims beside you. Throw a few treats in the water every now and then to keep up her interest.

Never let your dog swim in a pool without supervision. Every year, dogs drown in pools after becoming exhausted trying to find their way out, even when stairs are available. Plus, some breeds, such as Bulldogs, aren't built for swimming and can drown in shallow water. Be sure you know your dog's limitations.

Trying Your Paws at Canine Sports

If training and competing with your dog appeals to you, you can get involved in one of many organized performance events in which dogs and handlers compete as a team through novice, intermediate, and advanced levels. You can even obtain championships in many of the performance events. Most canine performance sports are open to all breeds of dogs as well as mixed breeds.

Agility is a very popular canine sport in which the handler must direct the dog over a course of jumps and obstacles within a certain amount of time (see Figure 16-3). Fast thinking and excellent teamwork are the keys to this sport!

Figure 16-3: This dog is obviously having fun participating in agility.

Photograph courtesy of Elinor Lerner

Even if you never plan to compete, consider enrolling your dog in agility classes sponsored by a local dog club. The classes will give her some exercise, boost her confidence, and stimulate her mind while conveniently training her at the same time.

In obedience trials, the ability of a dog to walk at heel on and off leash, to stand while being examined, and to come when called is tested. At the higher levels, a dog must be able to differentiate between a dumbbell scented by the handler and eight others scented by a stranger. She also must be able to jump and retrieve, among performing other tests. Obedience training, in addition to being a fun sport, has the added advantage of making your dog easier to live with.

Flyball is a very popular sport in which a dog runs down a 50-foot mat, jumping over four jumps on the way, presses a pedal that releases a ball, catches the ball, and runs back over the jumps. Four dogs on a team race as a relay against another team of four dogs.

Dogs of specific breeds can also show off their particular instincts at events such as hunting tests for the Sporting breeds, herding tests for the Herding breeds, lure coursing trials for the sighthounds, and go-to-ground tests for the Terriers.

For more information about canine sports, go to www.dog-play.com. This Web site lists every type of canine sport you can imagine and has links to organizations that offer those sports. It is a veritable smorgasbord of canine-play Web sites.

Exercising Indoors

When the weather is bad or the days are short, you and your dog can still exercise together in the comfort of your home. Indoor exercises can strengthen your dog's muscles, improve her coordination, and relieve some of the stress of being confined. Crawling strengthens the spinal and rear leg muscles, rolling over improves coordination, and waving one front leg strengthens the shoulder muscles. You can teach your dog all these exercises by using food to lure the dog into position and then encouraging her to try it on her own. Be sure to praise the dog every time she gets closer to doing what you want her to do. Many other stationary exercises can be devised by an inventive coach or by anyone who enjoys teaching dog tricks (see Figure 16-4). Check out *Dog Tricks For Dummies* by Sarah Hodgson (Hungry Minds, Inc.) for more information on training your dog to perform tricks.

For people with disabilities, for the fitness-challenged, or after a tiring day when you just want to rest, use a little creativity to devise other ways to exercise your dog. An elderly neighbor of mine solved an exercise problem in a unique way. She used to exercise her tiny Maltese senior citizen by sauntering along the sidewalk that encircles a nearby school, her nose in a book. When her canine companion died, she went to an animal shelter and came home with, believe it or not, an adolescent American Pit Bull Terrier. Within 24 hours, it became evident that her previous dog-walking technique wasn't going to work anymore. The next day, I saw her sitting on a park bench on a hill above a schoolyard reading a book. I watched as she threw a ball down the hill then rested her upturned hand on the bench while her dog ran down the hill, snatched the ball, and returned to drop the ball into her hand.

Figure 16-4:
This
Australian
Shepherd
has been
taught to
spin for
exercise
and as a
stress
reliever.

Doggie play groups in parks are a great way to let dogs exercise each other while the owners watch and chat. Just make sure you monitor the dogs to be sure there isn't a canine bully in the group.

A friend of mine who lives near a school has devised an excellent way to exercise her ball-crazy dog. She has a Border Collie who needs a lot of exercise, but with a recent knee replacement she hasn't been very active herself. So she tapes a piece of Velcro (the side with the hooks) to the goal post at one end of the school's football field and then sticks 12 tennis balls to the Velcro. She and her dog then go to the other end of the field. She unfolds a lawn chair and relaxes while her dog runs to get each tennis ball and bring it back. The possibilities are limited only by your imagination.

Always watch for signs that your dog is becoming fatigued. Don't depend on your dog to restrict her own activity when she is tired. Many dogs will literally exercise until they drop because they enjoy it so much. Signs of fatigue include stumbling, an anxious look, excessive panting, and widening of the end of the tongue.

Exercise for dogs with physical problems

Even if your dog has a physical condition such as hip dysplasia or arthritis, she still needs exercise. It's important to keep her muscles toned so they take over some of the work of the weakened joints. Moderation is the key here. Give your dog a little bit of exercise every day. Don't let her be a weekend warrior, overdoing it on the weekend and spending the rest of the week on the couch.

As your dog gets older, be extra sensitive to signs that she is tiring when she's out playing.

Continue to exercise her daily but reduce the length and intensity of her exercise enough to prevent her from becoming fatigued.

Remember: Dogs with disabilities can play, too. Deaf dogs and blind dogs can play in familiar, safe areas. Deaf dogs enjoy toys that blink with lights, and blind dogs can retrieve toys that make continuous noise. Dogs who have had a leg amputated can get around almost as well as a dog with all four legs, and they enjoy exercise just as much as other dogs.

Paying Attention to the Heat When You Exercise Your Dog

The ideal air temperature for a sedentary dog is 65 to 75 degrees with low humidity. At this temperature, a resting dog's body neither gains nor loses heat. The dog doesn't have to expend any energy to maintain her body temperature. (The normal body temperature for dogs is 100.5 to 102.8 degrees.)

Dogs have limited mechanisms for coping with overheating. Panting is their main mechanism for dealing with heat. Muscles in the tongue allow it to expand to approximately twice its normal size, increasing the surface area for heat exchange. In addition, blood vessels in the tongue dilate to bring more blood up to the surface of the tongue to be cooled. Humidity inhibits the evaporation of moisture on your dog's tongue and in her mouth and lungs, contributing to the potential for heatstroke.

Although dogs don't have sweat glands like we humans do, dogs do perspire on the pads of their feet. If you walk your dog over a shiny floor on a warm day, you can see the imprint of each foot as she leaves a sweaty paw print on the smooth surface. Dogs also try to lower their body temperature by seeking cool places, by not eating (therefore producing less internal heat), and by reducing their activity level.

Be sensitive to the possibility of your dog becoming overheated. Our own mechanisms for coping with heat are far superior to those of our dogs. So if *you're* uncomfortable, you can figure that your dog must be *very* uncomfortable. ***Remember:*** Your dog can't communicate verbally and tell you how warm she feels. Provide her with access to drinking water at all times, let her wallow in a pond or wading pool, or cool her by applying ice packs to her groin. If the temperature outside is hot, forget exercise and let your dog stay cool.

Signs of heatstroke include rapid, noisy breathing; a red, enlarged tongue; thick saliva; a body temperature above 106 degrees; staggering; and weakness. A dog with heatstroke should be wrapped in towels that have been soaked in cold water and transported to a veterinarian or emergency clinic as soon as possible. There she will be given further treatment, such as intravenous fluids and perhaps cool water enemas, as well as treatment for shock if necessary.

Getting Your Puppy the Playtime She Needs

Puppies need proper exercise for growth and development. Studies have shown that puppies who are prevented from exercising are not as physically developed and coordinated as those who get adequate exercise.

An exercise program for a puppy should not include strenuous exercises or long play periods. The *growth plates* (soft areas at each end of the bones) do not harden until a puppy is 10 to 14 months of age. These soft areas are susceptible to fractures, and even though the bone will heal, it is likely to grow unevenly, resulting in a deformity of the bone. Puppies also are more likely to injure themselves because of their lack of coordination and muscle strength. In addition, puppies are more susceptible to the stresses of heat and cold than adult dogs.

Activities for puppies should mix moderate exercise and lots of play. Provide abundant variety and opportunities to visit new environments and meet new people and other dogs. When a puppy is under 12 weeks of age (like the one shown in Figure 16-5), play lots of fun games, letting her climb over and crawl under your lap and chase a toy-on-a-string. Give your puppy cardboard boxes, bricks, and other safe objects to step on and explore. At that age, you also can go for a five-minute walk or play in a shallow creek.

Puppies under 6 months of age need only moderate exercise. After 6 months of age, provide strengthening exercises such as games of fetch and chase, but don't add endurance exercises until your dog's bones are fully mature (18 months for tiny dogs, 24 to 30 months for big dogs).

As your pup grows older, she'll be able to trot for greater distances and play for longer periods of time without needing a rest. Throughout her adolescence, your puppy will have lots of energy and will want to be busy all the time. When her body reaches adult size, you may be fooled into thinking she has adult stamina. The trick at this stage is to give her abundant exercise, play lots of games, and give her many intellectual challenges — without overdoing it.

Figure 16-5:
This young puppy plays with her dad every day.

Photograph courtesy of Marcia Halliday

Giving Your Dog Things to Do While You're Away

Exercise is an important part of your dog's day, but if you're like most people, you're probably only home for a few hours every day. So providing activities for your dog while you're gone is a great way to help her get the exercise she needs.

Occupying busy paws

Always give your dog the opportunity to play with or chew a safe toy while she is alone. Several products on the market are designed to keep your pooch's paws busy while you're away.

Don't stay away too long! As a rule, dogs should not be left alone for more than ten hours at a time. Puppies and some older dogs may need potty breaks every two to four hours.

One of the best objects to keep an active dog occupied is the Buster Cube, which is a tough plastic cube into which you pour a little dry dog food. Using a dial, you regulate the speed at which the pieces of food drop out of a hole in the cube. Your dog pushes the cube with her nose or turns it over with her feet. When the cube is positioned just right — voilà! — out drops a piece of food. When your dog realizes that this toy really is a food dispenser and that she is in control, she will keep working away at the cube until every last morsel is gone.

Note: The Buster Cube has only two small disadvantages. First, some dogs move the cube around so aggressively that it bangs into the walls and the legs of nearby furniture. So it's best not to play this game in the room with Aunt Martha's valuable antiques. Second, this game involves food and some dogs don't appreciate the assistance of other dogs in their quest. So the Buster Cube is best played alone or among (the rare) dogs who play cooperatively when food is involved.

Another way to keep your dog occupied during the day is to stuff the center cavity of a real bone with soft cheese or peanut butter. You can even hide some broken cookies or pieces of kibble in the core of the bone. You can stuff other toys such as Kong toys with food and seal them with peanut butter or cream cheese. Getting to the good stuff can occupy your dog for many hours.

If your dog's personal area has a window looking out over a quiet place such as your backyard, place a couch or a safe table in front of it so she can watch the birds and other wildlife while you're away. It's usually better if your dog isn't able to see the activities on the street in *front* of your house, however, because if she sees the mail carrier bringing the mail to the house, for example, she may bark and carry on, sensing that she should guard the house in your absence. When the carrier leaves after delivering the mail, your dog becomes convinced that her barking has driven him away. If this scenario is repeated day after day, your dog may become quite aggressive toward the mail carrier — and others who come on the property, which is why tens of thousands of mail carriers and delivery people are bitten by dogs every year. Your dog doesn't need this kind of experience, you don't, and the mail carrier certainly doesn't either.

A dog door can be a real boon for a dog who is home alone all day. Whenever she likes, she can go outside into her fenced-in yard, eliminate, catch some rays, chase a squirrel or two, and then go back in to sleep some more. Dog doors are especially helpful for older dogs who may have trouble holding their urine for a full day. If you use this convenience, however, your yard *must* be completely safe for your dog. She shouldn't be able to escape by climbing the fence or by digging under it. It's also best if your dog can't see the comings and goings of children and delivery people. A dog door works best if it is used in a quiet neighborhood and it opens to an enclosed kennel or to a secluded yard with a secure fence.

Doggie daycare

Doggie daycare is a booming industry because more and more people are away at work during the day, sometimes leaving their canine companions at home for long periods of time. If you want to give your furry friend an outlet for her energy during the day, consider doggie daycare facilities, which offer a variety of services including boarding, play groups, dog walking, obedience training, and even hiking or swimming.

The best way to find a reputable doggie daycare establishment is to ask dog-owning friends and neighbors if they know of any. If you come up empty, call a local dog club, a dog-training facility, or your veterinarian for a recommendation.

When you've found a doggie daycare, inquire about their interview process. Good daycare facilities interview prospective clients and their dogs just as a children's daycare would. They will want to know whether your dog is properly immunized against communicable diseases so she won't catch or spread any infections while she's there. They will also be interested in what activities your dog enjoys and whether she plays well with other dogs so she can participate in doggie play groups.

During your interview, find out what activities are available and how your dog's day will be structured. Here are some important questions worth asking:

- ✔ **Where will my dog stay when she is resting?** The kennel area should be clean and should have bedding and safe toys available for the dogs.

- ✔ **What does the owner do if there are tiffs between dogs over playthings?**

- ✔ **How does the owner handle a dog who is aggressive or dominating around others?**

- ✔ **How long do the dogs play each day, how much rest time do they have, and how much one-on-one interaction do they get with daycare personnel?**

- ✔ **What veterinary facilities does the facility use if one of the dogs has an accident or becomes ill?** Make sure the owner has insurance to cover his facility.

As of this writing, no organizations oversee or accredit doggie daycare facilities. Be a good consumer and make sure that all your questions are answered and all your concerns are laid to rest before you enroll your canine family member.

Doggie daycare costs a little more than boarding a dog overnight in a kennel. It can be quite expensive if your dog attends every day, but it is an excellent solution for single people and busy families.

Dog walkers

Exercise is very important to dogs, and with the busy lives most of us lead these days, giving your dog the exercise she needs each and every day can be difficult. So dog walking is a great way for your dog to get some activity while you're away. Dog walking also provides a great opportunity for neighborhood kids who have a love for animals and a desire to make a few bucks the old-fashioned way.

Depending on the size of your dog (which dictates how much he pulls when he sees a squirrel) and his level of obedience, a responsible child as young as 11 or 12 years old can be a good dog walker. Just make it clear to the young entrepreneur how he is to walk your dog — including which leash and collar to use, where he can go, how long he should walk him, and so on. Always post the phone number where you can be contacted as well as other emergency numbers such as another contact person and the telephone number of your regular and emergency veterinarians.

If you hire a child to walk your dog, always meet with the child's parents first. They generally are involved in scheduling your dog's walk around the child's other after-school events. Their concern for the child's safety means they're keeping an eye on your dog, too.

Adult or professional dog walkers are an excellent option, particularly if you have multiple dogs who may be too much for a child to handle. Many professional dog walkers are bonded and insured, giving you a little more security than you have with a neighborhood kid. Again, try to get a personal recommendation and have a thorough interview before you trust your dogs to a stranger.

Don't hire a dog walker who walks several dogs together when the dogs are strangers to each other. This experience can be tremendously stressful to the dogs.

Pet sitters

Pet sitters can make a huge difference in your dog's life. They let your dog stay in her familiar environment when you have to be away for extended periods of time, making your absence much less stressful for your canine companion than a kennel full of strangers.

The best way to find a dog sitter is to obtain a referral from someone who has used the dog sitter extensively and has been pleased with his work. You can also go to the Web site for Pet Sitters International (www.petsit.com) to find a reliable and responsible pet sitter in your area.

Always interview a new dog sitter before hiring him. Introduce your dog to him and make sure they connect with each other. The dog sitter should not be hesitant to handle your pooch, and your dog should show acceptance of his touch. He should appear genuinely interested in your dog and her welfare while you are away. He should ask specific questions about how you want your dog cared for. If you see any red flags such as hesitance to interact with your dog or evidence of a short temper, the applicant probably isn't a good match for your dog.

Some dog sitters stay at your home while you're away; others visit three to four times a day for a predetermined amount of time to let your dog out, feed her, and walk or play with her. Either option can work well. Just be sure you are comfortable with your decision.

Before your new pet sitter starts her first assignment, make an appointment for her to spend some time with you learning your dog's obedience commands and other house rules. For example, I have a dog who, unless commanded to wait, always barges out of the door, knocking the other dogs over like bowling pins. My pet sitter also makes my dog wait, which strengthens her obedient behavior while I'm away.

Be sure to leave complete written instructions for your dog sitter. They should include the following information:

- The address and telephone number where you can be reached.
- The address and telephone number of an emergency contact near where you live.
- Your veterinarian's name, address, and telephone number.
- The name, address, and telephone number of an emergency veterinarian who is available after hours.
- Complete feeding instructions (including the type of food, the amount, when and where your dog should be fed, and whether she needs to go out right away after she eats).

- ✔ Instructions for exercising your dog (including what activities she likes, for how long, and how often).

- ✔ Instructions for picking up the yard, if necessary.

- ✔ Notes about any medication your dog needs.

- ✔ Any other habits or needs specific to your dog.

- ✔ Whether the dog sitter should answer the telephone or let it ring.

Chapter 17

We Want You!: Enrolling Your Dog in Basic Training

*Y*our dog's emotional health is inextricably linked to his physical health. He is a much happier and healthier dog if you appreciate and love him, and that's a bit easier to do when your dog is familiar with basic obedience training, because you're able to spend more time loving your dog and less time saying, "No."

For a dog, a little bit of training goes a long way. Gentle, consistent training can make the difference between your dog living a long life as a treasured family member or getting divorced from your family because of irreconcilable differences.

Most dogs, when left to their own devices, will jump up, bark, chew on the furniture, run in front of cars, and generally do whatever they please. But dogs who are given consistent, clear guidance about what kind of behavior is acceptable are more secure of their place within the family "pack" and make better companions.

In this chapter, I show you how to have the trained dog of your dreams — without too much work.

DogSpeak 101: Figuring Out How to Communicate with Your Pet

Communication is the give and take of information. Every relationship needs good communication, including the relationships we have with our dogs. In fact, an essential part of training your dog is knowing how to communicate with him. If you can figure that out, you're well on your way to having a well-trained animal on your hands.

In the following sections, I let you know how to go about communicating with your dog, tell you how your dog interprets what you say, and give you some tips for communicating better.

Knowing how your dog communicates

Researchers have found that human communication is 55 percent body language, 37 percent tone of voice, and only 8 percent the meaning of the words themselves. That's why a simple phrase such as "I'll be fine" can have very different meanings, depending on your body position when you say it and the tone of voice you use. If we depend so much on body language, think how much *more* our dogs, who have very limited verbal skills, must depend on it.

Body language is the language of dogs. Because they speak body language, dogs also are great observers. Your dog reads slight shifts in your posture and the position of your arms, legs, and hands. He observes the position of your eyebrows, the turn of your mouth, and the expression in your eyes. From all this information he understands your likes, your dislikes, your needs, your wants, your moods, and your thoughts.

Try this experiment, and you'll discover how observant your dog is. Next time your canine friend disobeys you, don't say anything. Instead, put your hands on your hips and frown. Your brows should be furrowed, your eyes angry, and your mouth down-turned. Your dog will get the message that you aren't happy with his behavior, even though you haven't spoken a word.

Even though our dogs are always observing (or listening to) us, we frequently are not very good at listening to them, mainly because we're much more dependent on verbal language. If you take a little time to learn the canine language, however, you'll reap the rewards of a stronger bond with your dog.

The key to the canine language is that dogs use a combination of body posture, facial expression, and tail position to represent phrases. To be fully versed in the canine language, you need to observe *all* parts of your dog's body. If you concentrate only on one part, such as the tail or the face, you may make a significant language blunder. Most people believe, for example, that a wagging tail means the dog is happy. Depending on the dog's facial expression and body posture, however, that wagging tail can be a sign of intense anger or a warning of impending aggression.

Some dogs actually smile by lifting their lips up and exposing their teeth. You may initially mistake this smile for aggression. But if you look at the rest of a smiling dog, you'll see relaxed ears, twinkling eyes, and a wagging tail. If you have a dog who likes to smile when greeting strangers, be sure to explain to your guests that he's baring his teeth in laughter, not anger.

Some people theorize that dogs who smile live with families who laugh a lot and that the dogs have simply learned to imitate their people. One of the funniest people I know has had many dogs of many different breeds, and they always start to smile between 1 and 2 years of age.

Here are just a few of the most common canine phrases. As you become a better observer, you'll become quite fluent in the canine language:

English	Dog
I'm happy.	Ears relaxed, tail wagging gently, head held high.
I'm ecstatic!	Ears floppy, tail wagging vigorously, rear end wiggling with effort.
Let's play!	Ears forward but relaxed, eyes bright and teasing, lips pulled back slightly but relaxed, tail up.
Who's that?	Ears erect and forward, eyes wide open, neck out-stretched, tail still.
I'm afraid.	Ears back but stiff, tail tucked under, head down, eyes closed a little and shifting back and forth.
Watch out or I'll bite!	Ears forward and stiff, lips raised exposing teeth, hair on shoulders raised, tip of tail lashing back and forth.

Giving your dog an A for effort

The key when training your dog is to make it very clear what he should and should not do. Let your dog know when he's doing the *right* thing. In the language of *behaviorism* (a theory that says that dogs make a connection between their behavior and the consequences of that behavior), telling your dog when he's doing something right is called *reinforcement*. When you give your dog reinforcement for a certain behavior, he will want to repeat that behavior. The best reinforcements are your praise, food treats, and toys or games. If you give your dog a tasty treat when he comes when called, he is more likely to come when you call him the next time.

How dogs understand your language

Although dogs are adept readers of body language, they also learn many of our words and phrases. Most dogs have a pretty good idea what "Do you want a treat?" means. And "Want to go for a walk?" will send most dogs running for the door.

Dogs learn these phrases by *association* (you say the same phrase every time you offer him a treat or go for a walk, and eventually he understands that that phrase signals the event he

likes so much). Here's a common example. Your dog may appear to be sleeping nearby as you talk on the telephone. As soon as you say "Okay, bye," your dog leaps up, ready to see what's going to happen next. This is because your dog has noticed that, when he hears those words, you usually get up and maybe even pay some attention to him. He has made an association between a word and your actions.

Be careful of dogs who show signs of fear. Many more dogs bite because of fear than because of aggression. Learn to read the warning signs that show a dog is afraid, especially when you're meeting a new dog. If you see signs of fear or aggression, give that dog a wide berth.

Reinforcing your dog's good behavior and correcting the bad

Just as with kids, you won't get very far with your dog if all you ever do is yell at him when he's done something wrong, and he won't learn what's wrong if all you ever do is praise him when he's done something right. Training is a delicate balance between praising good behavior and correcting bad behavior.

Do that again!: Letting your dog know when he's on the right track

Your dog will be able to learn more easily if you teach him a specific word that means that he's right. You can use any word such as *nice, great, yes,* or *good* to communicate to your dog that he's on done what you wanted. Choose a one-syllable word that doesn't sound like your dog's name and won't be confused with a command word such as *sit* or *down*. Personally, I like the word *yes* (so I use it as an example in this section, but you can substitute it with another word of your choosing).

Start by showing your dog that when you say "Yes!" you mean, "What you just did is right." And the best way to help your dog make that connection is with food. Essentially, you'll be making a link in your dog's mind between the food and the word "Yes!" With a few treats in your hand, say "Yes!" and then immediately give your dog a treat. Repeat this exercise 8 to 10 times, making sure that your dog is not always in the same position (so he knows it's not that particular position you're rewarding) and that he isn't barking, jumping up, or doing anything else you don't want to reward. Over the next few days, repeat this exercise in a number of different locations both in the house and outside. When you see that your dog perks up (expecting food) when you say "Yes!" you'll know he understands the meaning of the word. Now you have a tool you can use in training to mark the correct behavior. You don't have to have food always at the ready. You can just say "Yes!"

In the last few years, using a *clicker* (a box with a metal strip that makes a clicking noise when pressed) instead of a word like "yes!" to tell the dog he's just done the right thing has become popular. Some people argue that the clicker more accurately defines the moment at which the dog has behaved correctly. Clickers have been used to train many species of animals, most particularly marine mammals like dolphins and killer whales to perform complicated acrobatics.

Stop right there!: Being sure your dog knows what's bad in your book

To give your dog the complete picture of what correct behavior is, you need to let him know when he's doing the wrong thing. This is called *correction*. A correction is something that makes your dog want to stop a behavior. One of the best ways to correct your dog is to say "At!" Although it may not make a whole lot of sense to say the word *at* as a correction, most dogs instinctively dislike the sound, and that's all that matters.

Show your dog exactly what "At!" means by putting a treat in the palm of your hand and showing it to your dog. If he tries to get the food, say "At!" and close your hand around the food. Look away, ignoring him. Then try again. If he sits still, waiting for you to give the word, say "Yes!" because he's got it! Just as you will say "Yes!" when your dog is doing something right, you now can say "At!" when he's doing something wrong. This is the foundation of teaching your dog right from wrong.

Physical punishment rarely lets any dog know the difference between right and wrong. Unless you can be right beside your dog at the second he makes the mistake, chances are that, by the time you strike him, he will have moved on to another behavior and will have no idea why you've just hit him. Plus, striking a dog is an expression of anger. And emotions such as anger interfere with your dog's ability to learn the difference between right and wrong. Instead of correcting the behavior, you're teaching your dog to be afraid of you. Finally, some dogs react aggressively to physical punishment. (After all, how do you think you'd feel if someone hit you?) Bottom line: Don't use physical punishment to get your point across, and don't let anyone else do that to your dog either. The risk is far greater than any possible benefit.

Are you concerned that you may hurt your dog's feelings by verbally correcting him? If so, keep in mind that dogs are much happier when all the rules are clear and everything is black and white. Uncertainty makes dogs unhappy; so it stands to reason that knowing what *not* to do is as important as knowing what *to* do. And this is the purpose of corrections.

Putting it all together

So how do you use reinforcement and correction together to train your dog? Here I use training your dog to sit as an example. (Training your dog to sit is extremely useful. If he is sitting, he won't be jumping up on your guest's white dress, and he's more likely to stay still while you clean his teeth or check inside his ears.)

Here are the steps you take to get your dog to sit quickly each and every time:

1. **Arm yourself with an ample supply of treats and toys.**

   Fanny packs are great for holding treats. They allow you to carry more than you can in your hand. Plus, they keep the treats out of your dog's sight.

2. **With your dog standing beside or in front of you, and while holding his collar gently, position a treat slightly above your dog's head and move the treat slowly backward.**

   This causes your dog to raise his head and lower his rear to follow the food. Holding his collar prevents him from jumping up for the food.

3. **As soon as your dog sits, say "Yes!" and give him the treat.**

   You have just reinforced that good behavior.

4. **Repeat this exercise four or five times.**

   Before long, your dog probably will be plopping his butt down as soon as you get a piece of food out of your fanny pack, and he'll be looking very pleased with himself. That's because he already has made an association between his behavior and its consequences (food). Give him a few more short lessons over the next week or so, saying "Yes!" and giving him a treat each time he sits.

5. **Next time you play this game, say "Sit" as you place the food above his head (see Figure 17-1). Continue to say "Yes!" and give him a treat when he sits.**

   This exercise teaches your dog that he should perform the behavior not just when you hold the food above his head, but also when you say "Sit."

6. **When you're sure your dog knows what the word "Sit!" means, start giving him the treat randomly, not every time you ask him to sit.**

   You don't need to give your dog a treat each time he sits correctly after he has learned the behavior. Studies have shown a dog is more likely to obey a command if he doesn't know whether he'll be reinforced or not. Be sure to always praise him, however, even if you don't give him a treat.

Figure 17-1:
Treats are a
great way to
train your
dog to sit.

At some point, your little Einstein will ignore your request to sit. He may ignore you because he is distracted by something more interesting, or perhaps he'll just look at you and say, "I don't have to." (What child hasn't said that?) At this point, you need to show him that ignoring you isn't an option. It's time for you to administer a correction:

1. **Take his collar and gently and unemotionally pull up and back to move him into a sitting position.**

2. **When he is sitting, say "Yes!"**

3. **Move him and ask him to sit again.**

   If he sits, say "Yes!" and give him a treat. He'll respect you for insisting and will be more likely to comply next time.

If your dog doesn't sit on your first request, don't repeat the command unless you want your dog to learn not to sit until you say "Sit! Sit!" or even "Sit! Sit! Sit!" The first command should be enough. Teaching your dog that you only ask once is a big part of being consistent in your training. *Remember:* Dogs recognize and appreciate consistency.

How do you know when your dog needs correcting? When he makes mistakes but is still learning your command, use only rewards. After he completely understands a command, you can correct him if he is distracted or deliberately refuses to obey.

Enrolling your dog in school

If you have a puppy, you don't need to wait until your precocious pooch grows up to teach him his ABCs. A young puppy is like a notebook on the first day of school — clean and ready to be written in. You can fill that notebook with some very clear lessons, appropriate to your pup's age and understanding. But if you let your pup doodle in the notebook for a few months or a year, you may have a harder time getting him to obey when he gets older.

Puppy kindergarten is one of the best training environments for your canine youngster. Many dog clubs hold puppy classes for dogs from 3 to 6 months of age. These classes usually are very relaxed with an emphasis on *socialization* (becoming used to greeting and relating to new humans and strange dogs). Typical lessons include teaching the pups to come when called, to enjoy a grooming session, to allow his nails to be clipped, and to be examined all over by a stranger.

Remember: Keep your eye out to make sure that all puppies are playing well together. If there is an aggressive puppy, or if you're concerned that your small pup will be hurt by a clumsy larger one, by all means take your puppy out of the play group.

If you're new to dog training or you haven't trained a dog in years, consider taking your dog to obedience school for a semester or two. You can learn lots of helpful techniques from a talented instructor, and it will motivate you to progress with your dog on your own.

Private lessons have a number of advantages over group classes. You can learn at your own speed, and your teacher can gear your sessions to your dog's individual needs and to your personality. Private lessons are expensive, however, so some people start with private lessons to learn the basics and then go to group lessons with some experience under their belt.

Group lessons are much less expensive, and they do have one major advantage: socialization. You have much less time to ask questions in group lessons, however, and you may have trouble getting personal attention for a problem dog. Try to find a class with no more than five or six dogs per instructor. Ask the instructor what her philosophy of training is. Look for an instructor with a positive attitude who seems to genuinely love dogs. If the instructor at your dog-training class asks you to do something you aren't comfortable with, just say you'd prefer not to do that. You can train a dog in many ways, and you don't have to do something that makes you feel uncomfortable.

The quality of obedience lessons can vary greatly. To find an obedience instructor near you, ask your veterinarian or contact one of the following associations:

Association of Pet Dog Trainers
P.O. Box 385
Davis, CA 95617
Phone: 800-738-3647
Web site: www.apdt.com

The National Association of Dog Obedience Instructors
Corresponding Secretary
729 Grapevine Highway, Suite 369
Hurst, TX 76054-2085
Web site: www.nadoi.com

What Every Dog Should Know: Teaching Your Dog the Basics

Every dog should know the basic obedience commands. When you're able to control your dog's actions, you can live together much more easily. Wouldn't you rather have your dog lie down in an adjacent room during dinner than crawl around under the table looking for food? Wouldn't it be great if your dog could join the party when you have guests instead of whining and scratching at the door because you had to ban him from the room for being a pest?

Obedience training is not just for our convenience, though. Dogs crave a structured environment. They feel much more secure when they know where they are supposed to be and what they are allowed to do. Dogs need rules to be enforced firmly and consistently. So have a family meeting and decide what your dog will be allowed to do and where he will be allowed to go in the house. Then work together to fairly and consistently enforce the rules so that every family member is telling the dog the same thing. Otherwise, your dog will be confused as well as disobedient.

Come

Come is the single most important command you can teach your dog. It can even save your dog's life. For example, if you're walking with your dog in a park, and you see a loose dog who is aggressive, you quickly call your dog, put him on a leash, and walk away. You have just averted a disaster (or at least a messy, stressful confrontation).

Start teaching your dog to come when called as soon as you get him. In an enclosed area, crouch down and call him with a happy voice. When he comes to you, give him a treat and lots of praise. Repeat this exercise often. Begin to give him the treats on a random basis, but always remember to praise him. Bring a stash of dog treats whenever you go for walks with your dog. Call him every now and then and say "Yes!" as soon as he turns towards you, then reward him as soon as he gets to you.

Never call your dog if you are going to punish him. He'll quickly learn to think twice before coming, or he may stop coming altogether. When you call a playing pooch, use an upbeat voice to encourage him to obey.

Sit

Sit is a very useful command. If your dog is sitting, he won't be able to jump up on a friend you meet on your walk. And you can also clean your dog's teeth and check his ears when he is sitting. Your veterinarian will appreciate the fact that your dog can sit still when she needs to take a blood sample. For instructions on training your dog to sit, turn to the "Putting it all together" section earlier in this chapter.

Down

The best way to teach your dog to lie down is to have him start from a standing position. Take a treat and bring it toward your dog's chest. He will bend his head down to get the food and will tend to rock backward. From there, a little encouragement and perhaps a little push on his shoulders will soon have him comfortably in a down position (see Figure 17-2). The second he's all the way down, say "Yes!" and give him a treat.

If you want to make sure he stays down, it is best if he tips over onto one hip so it takes a little more trouble to get up. You can do this by taking a piece of food and placing it against the side of your dog's hip. As he turns his head to get the food, he'll find it easier to roll onto the other hip.

Stay

The easiest way to train your dog to stay is by doing it in a sitting or down position instead of when he's standing. Start with your dog on a leash. Bring the palm of your hand to a position in front of his face and say "Stay!" If your dog starts to move, use the leash to gently place him back in position. When he is in place, say "Yes!" and give him a treat. He'll soon get the idea.

Figure 17-2:
If your dog knows the down command, you'll be able to use it when company arrives at your door or when you're eating dinner.

You can make the stay exercise easier by giving him a place where he is to remain. Just as kindergartners have their own mats for nap time, you can give your pup a rug of his own. Train him to go to the rug and stay on it. Your dinnertime will be more relaxing with your pup lying in his place and your family eating in theirs. After dinner, you can give your pup a treat for staying on his own rug.

Let's go

Dogs usually pull on a leash because they are eager to get going. The best way to teach your dog to walk without pulling is to show him that the more he pulls, the longer it will take to get where he's going.

Start walking with your dog on a 6-foot leash. When your dog pulls, stop and stand very still, ignoring your dog. When your dog stops and turns to look at you, as most do, continue walking. At first, you won't get very far, but most dogs quickly learn the advantages of not pulling.

Training Your Dog to Eliminate on Command

Teaching your dog to eliminate on command is very helpful: Imagine that you're on a road trip and you'd like your dog to go potty at a rest stop. It's cold outside and freezing rain is spattering your parka. Wouldn't it be great if your dog urinated right away?

Here are simple tips for teaching your dog to go on command:

- ✔ **Take your puppy outside on the following occasions:**

  - Whenever he wakes up from a nap

  - Whenever you take him out of his crate

  - Just before you put him in his crate

  - Immediately after he eats

  - Approximately every hour while he is loose in the house under supervision

- ✔ **Take him on a leash to a predetermined potty area and tell him, "Do your stuff."** You can use any command. Some people say, "Hurry up" or "Find a spot." Some people whistle a specific tune. These words or sounds eventually become a cue for your dog to urinate on command.

Stay there until your puppy urinates. If it seems like he'd rather play than pee, just repeat your "go potty" command and ignore his antics. After your puppy urinates, praise him generously and give him a treat.

✔ **If you also want him to defecate, you can teach him a separate command for that.** Make sure he urinates first, before you ask him to defecate, because that order is easier for the dog. When your dog knows the command to defecate, he won't be able to defecate on command just any time of the day, but he will go faster during the morning and evening when he usually has to eliminate.

✔ **If he wants to stay outside afterward and play after eliminating, humor him.** Otherwise, he may learn that delaying tactics will allow him to have a little fun first.

Avoid choosing embarrassing commands! I made the mistake of using the commands "Go pee" and Go poo." When I'm at a rest stop surrounded by a bunch of truckers, having to repeat these commands several times while my dog searches for just the right spot is kind of embarrassing!

Knowing Why Dogs Misbehave

Most of the time dogs want to please their people, but sometimes they act up or make mistakes in judgment. Sometimes they can't seem to help themselves. Your dog may be convinced that he hears the garbage can calling, just begging him to dip in for a snack while you're out of the room; or his hidden fears and instincts may emerge, making your dog fearful of thunderstorms, for example.

Often misbehavior is simply a case of your dog just doing a doggy thing at the wrong time or in the wrong place. For example, you may be glad that your dog barks a warning when a stranger comes to the door. But if your dog barks continuously while you're away, your neighbors may not be happy at all.

In this section, I let you know why behavioral problems develop so you can be better prepared to deal with them.

Knowing why they do those things they do

Solving problems with your dog is difficult (if not impossible) if you don't understand what's causing it. Keep in mind that a dog who is behaving badly is usually being *rewarded* for his behavior in some way. After all, dogs learn by association. If an action produces positive results, the dog is more likely to repeat that action again. Rewards are powerful motivators to dogs, and a dog can be rewarded for bad behavior in many ways (even ways you may not be aware of initially). Here are some common ways that your dog's behavior (or misbehavior) is rewarded:

- ✔ **It meets an instinctual drive.** Sometimes your dog's activity is rewarding because it fulfills instinctual needs. For example, if your dog loves to chase cars, it may be because he was bred to herd sheep or cattle and finds movement highly stimulating. So even though he knows you don't want him chasing cars, he does it anyway because he gets tremendous joy from the chase — so his bad behavior is still rewarding.

- ✔ **It offers rewards your dog can see and feel.** Often bad behavior presents its own very tangible rewards. A dog who digs is rewarded by some cool dirt to lie in and interesting smells to enjoy. A dog who jumps the fence gets to visit the interesting female next door.

- ✔ **It makes your dog feel like he has accomplished something.** A dog may be rewarded just by circumstances. When the mail carrier approaches the house, the dog starts barking. His barking increases in volume and intensity as the person deposits the mail in the box. Then the mail carrier leaves. Your dog thinks, "Yes! I have driven that intruder away!"

- ✔ **It gives him the results he wants.** You may even be inadvertently rewarding bad behavior by helping your dog get what he wants. For example, if your dog is outside your screen door and wants to come inside for a little action, he may bark a couple of times. You ignore him. And he barks a little more insistently. You look up and tell him to be quiet. He barks again and scratches at the screen. You sigh, get up, and let him in because you don't want him to damage the screen door. You've just told him, "If you scratch the screen door, I'll let you in." You've given him exactly the message you wanted to avoid — and he's learned that misbehaving gets him what he's looking for.

You can be at least partly responsible for your dog's behavior problems. Examine your interactions with your problem pooch to make sure you are not inadvertently rewarding his unacceptable behavior.

As you deal with your dog every day, think about the associations you are creating in his mind. Here are a few common associations that every dog recognizes:

Dog's Action	*Your Reward*
Your dog sticks his nose under your arm.	You pat him.
Your dog paces back and forth at 6:00 p.m.	You feed him.
Your dog scratches at the door.	You let him in.
Your dog jumps up on you.	You give him attention by pushing him off.

I often hear people say that their dogs *know* when they have been bad. For example, your dog raids the garbage can while you're out and he's rewarded with a delicious pile of dinner leftovers. When you come home and see the trash strewn about the room, your dog's body language says, "I'm sorry." His tail is down, his ears are back, his head is bowed — he is the picture of apology. It sure looks as if he knows he has misbehaved. You may angrily think, "He knows it's wrong, but he did it anyway."

Dogs are great at making associations. While you're away, your dog succumbs to his ancient urge to scavenge any food he can find. He has a wonderful time examining every piece of garbage and licking up the leftovers. In the past, you've been angry when you arrived home to find garbage on the floor. Now, when you open the door, he remembers that you get angry when there is garbage on the floor, and his submissive body language reflects that anticipation. He doesn't recognize that you really are angry because he raided the garbage. Certainly, when he is delightedly sifting through the trash, he doesn't think, "If I do this, my person will be angry." This is because the trash is rewarding his behavior with leftovers. Your dog later associates your anger only with the trash on the floor, not with the actions that caused it.

People often believe that their dogs disobey out of spite or to "get back" at them. Most canine behaviorists, however, believe that dogs aren't even capable of deliberate, spiteful behavior.

Being the leader of the pack

Preventing behavioral problems is much easier than trying to fix them after they've already started. The key is to establish routines around the house that make it clear that *you're* the leader of the pack. You don't have to lord it over your dog all the time, but you do need to set clear boundaries from the beginning as to what is acceptable behavior and what is not. ***Remember:*** Your dog wants you to be his leader. He would rather not have the responsibility.

One way to demonstrate your leadership is by controlling the food bowl. You decide when your dog eats, not the other way around. Feed him at approximately the same time every day, but don't let him push you into feeding him on *his* schedule. A good way to remind your dog that you are in charge is to make him sit and stay while you prepare the family's dinner. Prepare his food at the same time but don't give it to him. Leave his food bowl on the counter until you and your family have eaten for a few minutes. Then release your dog from his stay and give him his food.

Another way you assert your leadership is by winning at games. Playing tug games can be great fun, but the game must be played on your terms. Practice asking your dog to release the tug object to remind him that you are in control.

Knowing when to compromise

After my Golden Retriever was housetrained, I let her sleep loose in my room at night. For several nights in a row, I awakened feeling crushed as she lay on top of me. I told her to get off, and she always did. A little while later, however, I would wake up with her on top again.

I decided to put an end to this war by tying her to the leg of the bed with a rope that was just short enough to prevent her from getting on the bed. For three weeks, she slept beside my bed. Then one morning I awakened to find the rope chewed through and Stripe asleep on the bed but plastered against the wall where she took up no space at all.

I was concerned that the bed would again become a battleground, so I got a new piece of rope and again tied her to the leg of the bed. Again she chewed through the rope and slept through the night at the very edge of my bed. I decided that this was an acceptable compromise, and she has never again taken advantage of my generosity.

You can also use grooming to confirm that you are the leader. Your dog should stand still while you brush him.

Make sure your dog knows that you are in charge of the home territory. If your dog is allowed on the furniture, ask him to get off every now and then. If he lies in front of a doorway, ask him to move. (A gentle push with your foot may help convince him.) You don't have to constantly assert your dominance, and sometimes compromises are in order. You should, however, gently make it clear that you are the leader.

Whether you let your dog sleep on your bed is a personal choice. Some people enjoy it; some don't. I let my dogs sleep on the bed because it gives them some extra quality time with me, and they keep my feet warm. A dog who knows his place in the home hierarchy usually is fine sleeping on the bed. But if your dog shows signs that he is planning a palace coup, the first thing you should do is ban him from the bed.

One of the best ways to confirm your leadership is by training your dog. Basic commands such as come, sit, stay, down, and let's go (covered earlier in this chapter) will help you control your dog at home, on walks, and when visiting others. They are the keys to developing a harmonious relationship with your canine companion.

Set up your environment so your dog has his own personal area. Every dog needs a place to go for some peace and quiet. This may be his crate or a dog bed in the corner of a room, but it should be a place of his own where family members don't disturb him. Provide your dog with toys to occupy him when he is alone and be sure to give him plenty of exercise. Idle paws often find mischief.

Coming up with a plan to solve problems

Solving established behavioral problems usually requires a multipronged approach. Terry Ryan, a talented canine behaviorist and trainer of dog trainers, has devised the following eight tools that can be used alone or in combination to repair problem behavior in dogs. To make them easier for you to remember, put the first letters of each tip together and it spells out the words "yes train."

- **Yield a little.** Sometimes the best solution is a compromise. Does your dog want to lie in your favorite chair? Give him a chair of his own.

- **Eliminate the cause.** If you can eliminate the cause of a problem behavior, this may be the easiest and certainly the most permanent solution. Is your dog escaping by jumping over the fence? Make the fence higher. Is your dog chewing on a corner of the carpet while you are away? Put a piece of furniture over the tempting corner.

- **Systematic desensitization.** Desensitizing your dog is a good way to deal with canine fears and insecurities. Expose your dog to the source of his fear in ever-increasing amounts so he gradually becomes used to them. Here's an example of systematic desensitization: Sandy was pregnant and wanted to be able to take her baby and her dog for walks together, but her dog was afraid of children's strollers. Over several weeks, Sandy gradually desensitized her dog to strollers. First she placed the stroller in the living room. She gradually moved the stroller a few inches and then a few feet with her dog in the room. Then she took the stroller outside, put her dog in a down-stay position on the front lawn, and moved the stroller back and forth on the sidewalk (hoping that her neighbors weren't looking). Over time, she was able to move the stroller right past her dog without him even flinching. She then walked a few feet pushing the stroller with one hand and holding her dog on a 6-foot leash with the other. Just in time for the baby's arrival, the dog graduated desensitization training by happily walking around the block beside the stroller.

- **Take away the reward.** Dogs are more likely to repeat a behavior if the behavior is rewarded. If your dog surfs the kitchen counters and happens upon a roast left out to thaw, he is more likely to surf again. You can remove his reward by thawing the roast in the refrigerator.

- **Reward an incompatible behavior.** This is where obedience lessons come in handy. Does your dog jump up on guests? Having him sit is an excellent solution (and one he can be rewarded for). Does your dog bark uproariously when the doorbell rings? Have him lie down and reward him — for some reason, many dogs won't bark while they're in the down position.

- **Acclimate the dog.** This is a great way to make sure your dog can deal with new and unusual circumstances. For example, if you're planning to go camping with your dog, and you're worried about how he'll deal with sleeping in the tent. Set up your tent in the back yard and let your dog go in and out. Maybe lie in there with him and read for a while so he gets used to the environment.

✔ **Improve the association.** A popular and easy way to deal with problem behavior is to reward a different behavior. For example, if your dog always barks at another dog behind a fence on your walks, just before you get to that property, pull out a ball on a rope and play tug with your dog as you go past the property in question.

To cure a dog of a fear, use a two-pronged approach. Desensitize him by gradually increasing exposure to the object of his fear and improve his association with the object of fear by rewarding him for being bold.

✔ **Negatives.** If your puppy is playfully chewing on your hands in his mouth, for example, apply some taste deterrent (available at pet-supply stores) to your hands. If your dog barks continuously while you are away, have him wear a collar that automatically sprays a distasteful scent when he barks. Just make sure negatives aren't your tool of choice.

Never use negatives to deal with aggressive behavior. Negatives are more likely to increase aggression than decrease it.

Finding solutions to common problems

Identifying the reason behind your dog's problem behavior is important. Understanding the cause will help you know which tools to use to stop the behavior.

Illness or pain is at the root of many behavior problems. Always check with your veterinarian to rule out health issues when a problem behavior arises.

Barking

Dogs bark for many reasons. They bark when they sense danger ("The doorbell is ringing!"), they bark because they are bored ("I hate being alone all day!"), they bark to get attention ("Let me in!"), and they bark for fun ("Let's play!"). Barking can be a great stress reliever for dogs, so I like to let my dogs bark a little when the circumstances allow. I even teach them to bark on command as a game.

No one likes a dog who barks outside in the middle of the night, and many people find a barking dog frightening. For these reasons, you do need to control your dog's barking. One great way to control barking is to teach your dog to bark and, as part of the lesson, teach him to stop. That way, when he barks at the wrong time or in the wrong place, you can control it.

Controlling a dog who barks while you are away is much more difficult. For a dog who's bored alone at home, you may try giving him more exercise before you go to work. You also may want to leave him with several problem-solving toys such as a Buster Cube or a Kong toy stuffed with treats. You may even take him to a doggie daycare to give him something better to occupy his mind.

For a dog who barks an alert at every noise outside, try playing the stereo so he can't hear the sounds of people outside. If your dog barks to get attention, make sure you studiously ignore him. When you remove the reward (the attention) he will stop.

If your dog barks because he is happy, be happy, too! If only all our dogs could be so pleased with themselves and with life!

Wanderlust

The solution to a dog who wanders away is simple — if your dog is wandering off, you need to confine him better. For his safety, you should confine your dog whenever he is alone and supervise him whenever he is with you. Build a fence or fortify your existing one. Make sure the gate is locked at all times. (Children, gardeners, and visitors all forget to shut a gate.) Don't put your dog's life in jeopardy by failing to keep him secure.

Chasing cars

Herding dogs in particular tend to be stimulated by moving objects — and if that object is a car, all the better! The solution to this problem is to reward your dog for an *incompatible behavior* (one he can't do while he's chasing a car, such as coming to you).

Train your dog to come on your first command, no matter what. When he understands that "Come!" means "Come right now!," you set up a series of distractions of increasing intensity. For example, you may walk your dog near another dog or a cat; then have a family member walk past, eating and dropping food; then have a child throw a ball near your dog. Each time the dog looks at the distraction, say "Come!" and if he doesn't come immediately, correct him by pulling on the leash. If he does come, praise him effusively and give him a treat. Then ask someone to drive a car by and again say "Come!" and correct or praise depending on your dog's reaction. Practice this "Come!" game often. ***Remember:*** Car chasing can cost your canine companion his life.

Some dogs have a kind of reverse car-chasing behavior. When they ride in the car, they get very excited when they see oncoming cars. They may jump back and forth in the car, wanting to chase the approaching vehicles. The solution to this problem is to remove the cause. Put the dog in a crate and cover it with a blanket so he can't see the movement of the cars. If you want, you can desensitize the dog by gradually removing the blanket. In any case, for their safety, it's always best to keep dogs in crates when they're in the car.

Fear of thunder

Fear of thunder can be really debilitating, especially in areas where summer storms whip in and out several evenings a week. Your dog may start to pace up and down and pant hours before the storm arrives. To solve this problem, you may try desensitizing him by playing a recording of thunder softly at first and then gradually louder and for longer periods of time. Just make sure not to reward any nervous behavior.

Don't try to soothe your dog if he shows signs of fearfulness. If you do, you will be rewarding his fearful behavior. Wait until he acts a little more calmly, then reward him.

Some dogs feel better if they are loose in the house when it thunders. Others prefer to be confined in a room or a crate. Melatonin can relieve fear of thunderstorms in some dogs. Ask your veterinarian for the correct dose for your dog.

Licking

Some dogs get in the habit of licking themselves. They lick their front legs most often, but sometimes they lick their rear legs or flanks. The licking sometimes starts with an irritation, such as allergies, that causes the feet to be itchy.

If there's no medical reason for the licking, your dog may be licking out of boredom. If so, remove the cause by giving him lots to do — games to play, extra exercise, and doggie daycare all may be in order. You also can give him a bone to chew when you see him start to lick. Perhaps use a negative by applying a taste deterrent to his favorite lick spot.

If your dog licks his front legs, make sure to thoroughly wipe his legs after he chews a bone, especially if it is a rawhide or beef-basted bone. If his legs are flavored, he'll be more likely to lick and chew on them.

Biting

For dogs, the mouth is a very useful tool. Not only does it have the ability to sense like a hand, it also can taste things! If your dog is exploring some of your furnishings with his mouth (and teeth), use a taste deterrent on the object to make him think twice.

House soiling

When a young dog urinates or defecates in the house, make sure he has graduated from housetraining school. During the early stages of housetraining, you must accommodate your schedule to your dog. Make sure you let him out when he wakes up, after he eats, and about every hour while he is free in the house and supervised. By the time your pup is 3 to 4 months of age, you may think he is housetrained and begin to supervise him less. If he begins to have accidents in the house, it may be that you were the one who was trained, not your dog.

If your adult dog suddenly begins to have accidents, or if your pup is having trouble with housetraining, make an appointment with your veterinarian. Viral and bacterial infections, diabetes, and kidney disease all can cause changes in your dog's bladder or bowel habits.

Sometimes young dogs, particularly females, will urinate submissively when you arrive home or if a stranger pets them. This problem requires a multi-pronged attack aimed at reducing the dog's submissive feelings. First, eliminate the cause by kneeling down to pet your dog instead of bending over her. Avoid reaching over the top of your dog to pet her and ignore her for the first ten minutes after you arrive home. You also can reward an incompatible behavior by teaching your dog to sit when you greet her. Another way to improve the association is by carrying a tug toy and playing with her when you get home. Let her win the game sometimes by pretending she has pulled the toy from your hand or by falling over as she tugs the toy. This will build her confidence. Luckily, most dogs outgrow submissive urination.

For more information on submissive urination and other problems caused by fear and shyness, turn to *Help for Your Shy Dog: Turning Your Terrified Dog into a Terrific Pet* by Deborah Wood (published by Hungry Minds, Inc.).

If your male dog urinates on the walls, the sofa, other vertical objects, he may be marking his territory. This dominance behavior is most common in unneutered males, and castration solves it in the majority of cases. Whether or not you castrate him, a marking dog usually will benefit from being reminded who exactly is the leader of this pack (that's you!). Feed him *after* you eat, and practice his obedience exercises. Make sure he is not dominating your space by occupying your favorite chair or by taking up all the room on the bed.

An ingenious product called MarkOut can help you put the kibosh on marking behavior in male dogs (the vast majority of dogs who mark are male). MarkOut is a belly wrap that you tie around your dog's abdomen, covering his penis. The dog who wears one learns that the only thing he marks is himself.

Digging

Digging is a deeply ingrained behavior in many dogs. After all, the Terriers were bred to dig up vermin, and female wolves dig a den for their family members. One solution to unwanted digging is to reward an incompatible behavior. Find something, such as playing with a soccer ball or chewing on a big bone, that your dog likes even better than digging. The Buster Cube can be a great asset here because working to get the food reward is somewhat like digging to find a surprise.

For the inveterate digger, you may need to yield a little by making your dog his very own sandbox in which to dig. Hide a few toys in the sandbox for him to discover on one of his archaeological outings.

Eating stools

Although this activity seems disgusting to us, it often is totally delightful to our dogs. In fact, eating stools is one of the most common behavioral problems reported. Yet we really don't know exactly why dogs do this. The behavior is more common in female dogs, perhaps because bitches clean up their puppies' feces to keep the den or whelping box clean. Some people believe that dogs eat feces because of a deficiency in their diets, but there is no solid proof of this. Others believe that dogs may eat stools to get attention from their people. Dogs often eat stools when they are on a weight-loss diet. Eating stools usually is not a problem for the dog, but it certainly is an aesthetic problem for dog owners. No one wants to get close to a dog with poop-breath!

You can try one of many different approaches for solving this problem. It is worth trying several of these fixes with the hope that one will make a difference.

Many people try eliminating the cause by changing the dog's food or by supplementing his diet. Green vegetables, alfalfa, barley, and yeast all have been suggested as supplements to reduce stool eating. Some people have found that adding digestive enzymes to their dogs' food helps as well. Other people believe that negatives should be used for this problem, and they sprinkle a taste deterrent such as Tabasco sauce on feces in the yard. The problem with this suggestion is that it's hard to catch all the stools in the yard. If your dog eats some of the stools with the taste deterrent but happens upon one normal stool, he will be intermittently rewarded and will be more likely to eat stools in the future. Besides, if you are going to go around sprinkling the stools with something nasty, you might as well pick them up, which in the end is probably the best solution to this problem.

Separation anxiety

Dogs who suffer separation anxiety usually are overly bonded to one individual. They get panicked when their person leaves, and they pace around, pant, and often bark frantically. One of the best solutions is to eliminate the cause by reducing the dog's overdependence on you. Try making your departures very boring. Start to ignore your dog 20 minutes before you leave. When you return, ignore your dog for the first ten minutes you are home.

Another approach is to improve the association by giving your dog some delectable treats when you leave. A toy stuffed with food is best because it will take some time for him to get all the food out, and separation anxiety is strongest right after the dog's person leaves.

You also may want to try desensitizing your dog to your departures by starting the car, jingling your keys, cleaning up the kitchen counter, or doing any of the other things you habitually do before you leave in the morning. Leave for just a few seconds, return, leave for a few more minutes, return, and keep this going for longer and longer periods of time. Your dog will gain a sense of security that you'll return no matter how long you're gone.

In extreme cases, it may be beneficial to schedule an appointment with a veterinary behaviorist to discuss your dog's problem. She may prescribe anti-anxiety medication that can assist in making your behavior modification efforts more successful.

Aggression

Any sign of aggression toward humans is unacceptable. Your dog's aggression may seem to surface suddenly, but if you look back, you'll probably see some hints that the behavior was developing. Your dog may have started chasing the neighbor's cat, grumbling when you asked him to get off your chair, or growling when you took his food bowl away.

Aggression, whether toward other dogs or people, is a potentially dangerous situation best left to professionals. Any time you are dealing with an aggressive dog, get the assistance of a canine behaviorist. Until you can get help, avoid situations that will provoke the dog. Look for a behavior consultant who mainly uses positive methods and who, during the interview with you and your dog, seems to enjoy working with dogs.

Giving an aggressive dog to a shelter or a "home in the country" is not an acceptable solution. You have not solved the dog's problem and may be endangering other people and dogs at the dog's new home. Sometimes euthanasia is the most responsible solution for an aggressive dog when all other avenues have failed.

Determine whether your dog is truly aggressive toward other dogs or just wants to maintain his personal space. Many bitches, for example, don't want obnoxious male dogs sniffing their butts and will give a quick snap at the male to tell him, "Back off!" This behavior may startle you if you've never seen it before. But it's an acceptable mode of communication for female dogs, as long as the male was truly being a pest and the female doesn't escalate her message.

Your aggressive dog actually may be in pain, ill, or otherwise uncomfortable, particularly if this behavior starts suddenly. Dogs with cataracts, for example, may be startled when you approach and lunge out. Always be sure to have an aggressive dog examined by a veterinarian to rule out medical problems.

Early socialization is important to help prevent aggression. But you can (and should) continue to socialize your dog as an adult. Don't pull your dog toward you every time another dog approaches with another person. Let the two dogs communicate a little in the way dogs do — end to end. If you're always fearful of other dogs, your dog will pick up the message, and he likely will become more fearful, too.

Where to get help

The following organizations can help you find a behavioral consultant for your dog:

Animal Behavior Society
Indiana University
2611 East 10th Street #170
Bloomington, IN 47408-2603
812-856-5541
E-Mail: aboffice@indiana.edu
Web site: www.animalbehavior.org

American College of Veterinary Behaviorists
Dr. Bonnie Beaver, Executive Director
Dept. of Small Animal Medicine and Surgery
Texas A&M University
College Station, TX 77834-4474
409-845-2351
E-Mail: bbeaver@cvm.tamu.edu

American Veterinary Society of Animal Behavior
Steven Feldman, D.V.M.,
Secretary/Treasurer
9414 Brandywine Road
Clinton, MD 20735
E-Mail: avsabe@yahoo.com
Web site: www.avma.org/avsab

If two of your dogs are having occasional tiffs such as growling over toys, get control of the situation immediately. Don't try to determine who is the good dog and who started the argument. You won't be able to understand all the subtle nuances of canine body language to determine who started the fight. Just because one dog has a bunch of the other's hair in his mouth, it doesn't mean the other dog didn't provoke him. The best solution to these occasional skirmishes is to remind both dogs who the real boss is. I find it helpful to tell each dog to lie down and stay in opposite corners of the room. I supervise them for about ten minutes and then gently release them. This works like a timeout for children. Usually, by the time they are released, the dogs have forgotten what the argument was all about in the first place. If the battle was over a toy, be sure to remove it.

Part V
Caring for the Canine Senior

The 5th Wave By Rich Tennant

"Well, someone's starting to show his age. Look at how Rusty has to hold his chew-toy at arm's length now to see which one he's got."

In this part . . .

Getting old is a part of life — whether you're a dog or a person — and the chapters in this part help *you* help your *dog* through the last years of his life. I let you know how you can help your aging dog get around more easily (by using ramps up to the couch, for example) and how you can make his rest more restful (by making sure his bed offers the cushioning his aching joints may need). I also let you know about cancer in dogs, and what you can do if your dog develops it. Finally, I offer a helping hand through the difficult decision of knowing when the time is right to let your dog go to that big park in the sky.

Nothing in this part is something you'll be eager to face — but when the time arrives, the information you'll find here will help you face it with grace, so that your dog is as free of pain as possible.

Chapter 18

Helping Your Dog Age Gracefully

• •

In This Chapter

▶ Knowing what to expect as your dog ages

▶ Dealing with the difficulties dogs sometimes face as they age

▶ Keeping your older dog healthy and active

• •

*O*ne of the most difficult parts of having a canine friend is that we must watch them age. As they age, dogs experience many of the same physical and mental changes that humans do. They find it a little more difficult to get around, their vision deteriorates, and they get a little hard of hearing. Happily, dogs are living longer than ever before. With some help from you, your dog may enjoy added years of health and vigor.

You can slow these aging changes to some extent by providing your dog with a healthy diet, by making sure she gets regular exercise, and by watching for the early signs of illness so you can get her appropriate veterinary care. This chapter details the most common effects of aging in dogs and provides pointers on how you can keep your senior dog active and happy even when she is very old.

Knowing How Old Is Old

You're only as old as you feel. At least that's what most people over 40 say. Older people have widely varying levels of physical ability and drive. Some may have serious health problems; the lucky ones may have none at all.

Because of breed differences in longevity, dogs vary even more than people in terms of the age at which they can be considered senior citizens. As a general rule, smaller dogs tend to live longer than larger dogs. Most of the giant breeds begin to show aging changes at 5 or 6 years of age; the majority of medium-size dogs are young until 8 or 9 years of age; and lots of tiny dogs are still going strong at 10 to 12 years of age. As with anything in life, there are exceptions to this trend. Cavalier King Charles Spaniels, for example, tend to have a shorter life span than the other Toy breeds. Scottish Deerhounds, on the other hand, are said to live longer than most other giant breeds.

You probably have heard the guideline that, if you multiply a dog's age by seven, you'll get her age in human years. But this is only a very rough estimate. It doesn't factor in the tremendous variation in longevity of the different breeds. A giant dog such as a Newfoundland is a senior at 7 years of age, while at the same age, a tiny Papillon is in his prime.

Recognizing the Signs of Old Age

One of the first signs that a dog is getting older is the graying of hair on her muzzle and her face (as in the dog on the right in Figure 18-1). In some dogs, this begins to happen quite early. In most dogs, however, a few gray hairs begin to sprout around the age of 6 to 8. Much older dogs often have white hairs on their back, legs, and tail, too. Occasionally, a dog will gray very early, especially if she has a life-threatening illness.

My Golden Retriever Cajun went gray in the face after recovering from a devastating case of pneumonia at the age of 3. For the rest of his life, people would smile and say, "Oh look at the old doggie! How old is he, 14?" Most people think these coat color changes are endearing — the sign of a dog who has given many years of pleasure to his people.

Figure 18-1:
Even though a gray face betrays Tuffy's age, at 14, she still enjoys the Alaskan countryside with her friend Joey (left).

Photograph courtesy of Dee Geisert

Older dogs often have physical problems associated with the inevitable deterioration of tissue and organ function that occurs with advancing years. One of the first things you may notice is that your dog doesn't seem to have the endurance she had in the past. Maybe she can't run as fast or as far as she used to, or perhaps she seems to suffer more when it's hot and humid than in the old days.

Many old dogs are a little stiff when they arise after a nap. This may be due to loss of muscle strength, arthritis, or both. When you look into an old dog's eyes, you'll often see a bluish tint — a sign that her vision isn't what it used to be. You may begin to notice that when you call your old friend in from the yard, she sometimes doesn't hear you. Some old dogs even develop a hoarse or gravelly voice. These are all normal signs of aging and are not always something for which you need to make a specific appointment with the vet.

Handling the Problems of Old Age in Your Dog

Because older dogs tend to have more medical problems, you should have some extra tests done during your senior dog's annual physical examination.

Always bring a morning urine sample. Collect a midstream sample (let a little urine flow first before collecting) in a very clean or sterile container the day of your appointment. Try to get the sample to your veterinarian within two hours after the time of collection. Your veterinarian will perform a *urinalysis,* which tests for kidney malfunction, bladder infections, and other problems of the urinary system.

Also ask your vet to take blood for a *serum chemistry panel,* which provides information about the function of the liver, kidney, pancreas, and other organs. By doing these screenings in addition to a thorough physical examination, you may be able catch some old-age problems early enough to slow the process.

Arthritis

Arthritis is a common malady in older dogs. After all, your dog's joints have flexed and extended millions of times as she ran after balls and tumbled with her human and canine buddies. Arthritis isn't inevitable in older dogs, however. It is much more common in dogs who have hereditary disorders of the joints such as hip or elbow dysplasia and in dogs who have injured a joint (for example, by tearing or rupturing ligaments). In addition, if a dog is overweight, increased stress is placed on her joints, accelerating the progression of arthritis. This is a good reason to keep your furry friend fit and trim, even in her senior years.

Make sure your elderly canine has a soft bed on which to lie. It'll help ease her aching joints.

If your dog is very stiff when she stands up, if she avoids stairs, if she hesitates to jump on the couch or into the car, or if she limps when she first starts moving, ask your veterinarian to check for arthritis. He will feel your dog's joints, flex and extend her legs, and probably take some x-rays.

Many products on the market today relieve the pain of arthritis in dogs and even soothe and heal the joint cartilage. Start by giving your dog one of the joint-protective nutraceuticals (see Chapter 6 for more information). If your dog's arthritis pain is severe, your veterinarian may suggest that you also give your dog a painkiller every day or just on days when she is especially in pain.

A little carpentry can make it much easier for your arthritic dog to get around. If you have steps leading to the backyard, make a ramp for her to walk up and down. Some people even make a small ramp so their old dogs can get on and off the bed at will. Make sure you apply a non-slip surface to the ramp. Use some of the woven rubber mats made to prevent carpets from sliding on wood floors, or sprinkle some sand on the surface after you have painted it. You may also find carpeted ramps for sale in pet supply catalogs.

Obesity

Obesity is a common problem in canine senior citizens. If your older dog isn't exercising as much, cutting back on her food rations is important so she maintains her youthful figure. Obesity increases the incidence and severity of arthritis, makes exercising less fun, and increases the risk of injury during exercise. This can set up a vicious cycle of less exercise, more weight gain, and less desire to exercise.

Most people have an understandable tendency to overindulge their older dogs. I *never* give my dogs human food while I am eating. Well, except for my 14-year-old dog, who gets French fries when we go to McDonald's and the crusts when I eat a sandwich, and. . . . If this sounds familiar, try to temper your treat-giving tendencies by dispensing healthy snacks such as carrots, other vegetables, and fruit. In other words, do as I say, not as I do when it comes to French fries.

Vision problems

Have you ever noticed that older dogs have a bluish tint to their eyes? This is a sign that the dog has *lenticular sclerosis* or *presbyopia* (old-age eyes). Just as most of us have trouble reading the phone book after the age of 45, older dogs also have trouble focusing up close. Luckily, they don't need to read the phone book very often, so this vision decline is quite subtle. It occurs because the lenses harden a bit and thus don't accommodate as easily to differences in focal length. Dogs (and humans) with lenticular sclerosis don't see as well in the dark. They aren't actually night blind, but everything is a lot clearer if there is an adequate amount of light to penetrate those hardened lenses.

If your dog loses her vision to the point where she bumps into furniture or can't find objects you place on the ground, have her eyes examined by a veterinary ophthalmologist. She may have glaucoma or another treatable ocular disease. If her vision loss is permanent, she won't be as devastated as a human who loses his vision would be. Blind dogs do very well at home as long as you don't move the furniture. They also learn to take a certain route in the yard when they go out to exercise so they can find their way back to the door. If you want to find out more about making a blind dog comfortable in your life, read *Living with Blind Dogs: A Resource Book and Training Guide for the Owners of Blind and Low-Vision Dogs,* by Caroline D. Levin.

Deafness

Have you ever noticed that your older dog can't hear you call her to get her nails clipped, but she can hear a potato chip bag open in the next room? Before you blame her for deliberately ignoring you, consider the fact that dogs first lose their ability to hear low sounds like voices. They usually retain the ability to hear high-pitched sounds for much longer. If your older dog is having trouble hearing you, you can either speak louder, which helps for a while, or speak in a normal volume but with a higher pitch to your voice.

Wake your dog with vibrations rather than touch. Older dogs often sleep very soundly because they don't hear low-pitched sounds. If you try to wake an older dog by touching her, she may be very startled and even frightened for a minute. I've found that the best way to wake a sleeping senior is to stomp on the floor beside her, just as hard as is necessary to wake her up.

Another way to prepare for the deafness that is almost inevitable in old dogs is to teach your dog hand signals for the most common commands while she is young. I teach my dog that a hand raised above my head means "down," a hand raised in front of me as if I were carrying a tray means "sit," and a hand motion as if I were first reaching forward and then crossing one hand over my heart means "come." These few commands are tremendously useful in communicating with a deaf dog.

One problem with older dogs is that they go out in the yard at night for one last pee, but they don't hear you calling them back in. When you notice your dog beginning to lose her hearing, flick the outdoor lights when you call her. She soon will learn that the flickering light is a signal to come in at night.

For more information about helping a deaf dog live a full life, read *Living with a Deaf Dog: A Book of Advice, Facts, and Experiences about Canine Deafness,* by Susan Cope Becker.

Incontinence

Many older dogs suffer from *incontinence,* the inability to hold their urine. If your dog starts to leak a little urine while she is sleeping or if she can't seem to make it through your workday without having an accident, a visit to the veterinarian is in order. Be sure to bring a urine sample collected first thing in the morning.

Incontinence can be caused by many things. Some of the causes of incontinence can be cured; some just have to be managed. In older dogs, kidney failure and urinary tract infections are the main reasons for incontinence. With age, the filtering mechanisms of the kidneys get clogged, and instead of retaining water, they let more of it out into the urine. When the dog expels more urine, she needs to drink more water to replace the water lost in the urine. In veterinary talk, this is called *polyuria* (frequent urination) and *polydypsia* (frequent drinking). These two conditions often occur together in older dogs and are referred to as *PU/PD.* If your dog begins to drink and urinate more frequently, a veterinary exam should reveal the reason. If kidney failure is the cause, a low-protein diet may help slow the kidney's degeneration. Your veterinarian also will have other recommendations specific to your dog's needs.

If your older dog can't make it through the day while you're at work, try giving her a doggie-litter box. Fill a plastic wading pool with an inch or two of kitty or doggie litter. Use the kind of litter made from pelleted sawdust or old newspapers — they're safer than clumping cat litter and cleaner than clay litter. Cut openings in opposite sides of the pool, leaving just enough of a lip to retain the litter. This makes it easier for your canine senior to get in and out of the litter box. Teach her to use the litter box by taking her to the box when she needs to urinate and praising her when she uses it. She'll get the idea, and you will both be relieved.

Digestion problems

Some older dogs suffer from constipation, especially if they aren't eating as much as usual. Constipation can also be aggravated by arthritis, which can make it difficult for a dog to assume or maintain the posture for defecation.

Try increasing the fiber in your dog's diet while still providing nutritious and palatable meals. I've found that many canine seniors like canned, solid packed pumpkin added to their diets. They like the flavor, and it provides vegetable fiber to bulk up the stools a bit without causing diarrhea.

Many older dogs suffer periodic bouts of diarrhea and/or gas. Veterinarians theorize that this may occur because older dogs don't digest their food as well as when they were young. If your canine senior has an occasional tummy upset, you may try jump-starting your dog's digestion processes by adding pancreatic enzymes to her food before she eats it. Ask your veterinarian to suggest the product that is best for your dog.

Gingivitis

Gum disease is a very common problem in older dogs. Not only can gingivitis make eating painful for your dog, but the bacterial infection in the gums sometimes spreads to other tissues. Gingivitis eventually causes the teeth to loosen and drop out. It also can cause a tooth *abscess* (infection). Good tooth care is important throughout your dog's life, but it is especially so in her older years when a little bit of comfort can make such a difference in the quality of life.

Throughout your dog's life, whenever she has to be anesthetized for any reason, have her teeth cleaned. In addition, try your best to regularly brush your dog's teeth, especially those of your older dogs. Check your senior's teeth regularly. If there is a buildup of plaque or swollen gums, talk to your veterinarian about a dental visit. Having healthy teeth really does a lot to bolster an older dog's spirit.

Cognitive problems

Sometimes older dogs develop an Alzheimer's-like condition called *cognitive dysfunction syndrome*. Dogs with this condition become disoriented and may not recognize where they are or who they are with. They also sometimes experience changes in their sleep patterns and develop housetraining problems. This condition is thought to be caused by chemical alterations in the nervous system that can occur during old age. If your older dog fits this description, visit your veterinarian to learn about new drugs that can treat this condition.

Feeding Your Canine Senior

Older dogs have special nutritional needs. In the past, many people routinely fed older dogs lower-protein diets under the assumption that this protected the kidney from degeneration. We now believe that healthy older dogs don't necessarily need low-protein diets. Most older dogs with normal kidney function do well on 22 to 25 percent protein. The protein in an older dog's diet should be highly digestible so that it can readily be absorbed from the intestine and used by the body to repair tissues, which are undergoing degeneration at an increased rate during the older years.

Talk to your veterinarian about giving your older dog supplements. Older dogs sometimes benefit from the addition of digestive enzymes and antioxidants to their food to help them absorb all the nutrients in their diet. Seniors also can benefit from vitamin supplements, particularly B-complex vitamins, vitamin C (250 to 1000 milligrams per day) and vitamin E (100 to 400 IU per day). If your old dog has dry skin, you may want to add 250 to 1000 milligrams per day of fish oil and 1 to 15 milligrams per day of zinc.

For more information on nutrition, turn to Part II of this book.

Making Sure Your Older Dog Stays Active

I am convinced that exercise is the key to canine longevity. It helps control weight and keeps muscles toned so they can take over some of the work that the now-arthritic joints used to do. By getting your senior out for several walks each day, you'll keep her interested in her surroundings. She'll be excited to see all the squirrels and to smell the scents at every vertical object.

Exercise has proven effects on transmission of nerve impulses in the brain, resulting in a feeling of well-being. See Chapter 16 for ideas on ways to exercise your dog. If your older dog is fit (like the dog in Figure 18-2), she'll be able to participate in more of your family's activities, and you'll remember her twilight years with fondness rather than frustration.

Figure 18-2: Even at the age of 9, Tally enjoys vigorous exercise.

Chapter 19

Coping with Cancer

• •

• •

*W*ith the growth in scientific knowledge, dogs are living longer than ever, and many remain healthy well into old age. The downside to improving our dogs' longevity, however, is an inevitable increase in the incidence of diseases associated with old age, especially cancer. Luckily, the same medical advances that have helped your dog age gracefully also can help us diagnose cancer early and can increase the chances of treating it successfully.

In this chapter, I let you know what cancer is and what signs you should look for to detect cancer early. I also describe the most common kinds of cancer and how you can get the best treatment for your canine buddy.

What Cancer Is

The words *cancer, neoplasm,* and *tumor* all mean essentially the same thing: an abnormal growth of cells that results in the development of a mass. Normal cells communicate with each other. When they recognize that there are other cells nearby, they stop growing, which is referred to as *contact inhibition.* Without contact inhibition, your body and all the organs within it would continue to grow bigger and bigger. In cancer, something stops contact inhibition, and cells continue to replicate and pile up on one another.

Tumors can be *benign* (non-cancerous) or *malignant* (cancerous). Benign tumors are abnormal growths of cells that don't spread within a tissue or *metastasize* (spread) to other tissues. Warts and the fluid-filled cysts many dogs get on their skin in older age are examples of benign tumors. Malignant tumors spread either by invading deep into the tissues nearby or by penetrating blood vessels and traveling to distant organs where they set up shop and produce another tumor mass. The term *cancer* usually refers to malignant tumors; the terms *neoplasm* and *tumor* are more general and can be used to refer to a mass that is either benign or malignant.

Why Older Dogs Are More Likely to Get Cancer

Probably 99 percent of canine cancer occurs in middle to old age. One reason for this increase in the cancer rate among older dogs is that, for cancer to develop, there usually must be more than one event that alters the cells' ability to replicate. For example, cancer rarely develops after exposure to just one toxin. In order for cancer to develop, a combination of events has to take place, such as exposure to a toxin or radiation such as the sun, genetic susceptibility, and perhaps even chance mistakes in the way the cell works. Because it takes time for these multiple alterations to occur, cancer develops more often in older dogs.

The newly developed cancer cells also must be able to survive the dog's immune system. Healthy dogs have immune cells called *natural killer cells* that circulate throughout the body and act as guards against cancer. When these natural killer cells detect an abnormal cell or mutated cell, they kill it on the spot. So the majority of cancer cells that are made never grow into a tumor mass. During old age, however, the effectiveness of your dog's immune system declines, and more cancer cells are able to escape detection.

Another factor in the development of cancer is genetics. Some breeds of dogs, such as Boxers, Golden Retrievers, and Flat-Coated Retrievers, have a much higher incidence of cancer than other breeds. Although we don't know for sure, this increased risk in certain breeds is probably due to selective breeding that has resulted in the inadvertent selection of genes associated with cancer.

Cancer can strike any purebred or mixed-breed dog, although some breeds and lines within breeds have a higher incidence of cancer. When looking for a puppy, ask the breeder about the incidence of cancer in the puppy's ancestors.

Every day we identify new genes associated with cancer in people. Comparable studies in dogs are just around the bend. When we've identified the genes for various forms of cancer, we will be able to test dogs before breeding them and, hopefully, reduce the incidence of canine cancer.

Common Cancers and Their Symptoms

Be familiar with the most common kinds of cancer so you can watch for the earliest signs in your dog. Early detection can mean the difference between the cancer being curable or not. My dog Bannor, for example, developed a painful abdomen around the time of his 14th birthday. Because I knew that tumors of the spleen are very common in dogs, I rushed him to an emergency clinic instead of waiting to see if he was better the next day. Sure enough, there was a mass on the spleen, and his spleen was removed immediately. If I had waited, the mass may have ruptured and caused him to die.

Skin tumors are among the most common tumors in dogs, and there are literally dozens of types. Most skin tumors are benign and don't spread to other tissues nearby or metastasize to other tissues via the blood stream. Some skin tumors can be malignant, however, causing serious pain and even death.

Your veterinarian is the best person to determine whether a tumor is benign or malignant, but here is a handy guideline: If you find a lump, part your dog's hair and take a look at it. If it is small and round, it may be a fluid-filled cyst, which are very common in middle-aged and older dogs. Next, grasp the mass and try sliding it over the tissue below. If it seems to be attached to the skin, is small, and moves easily over the tissues below, it's probably benign. But if the mass is large, shaped irregularly, grows rapidly, or is attached to the tissue below, it may be malignant. In either case, however, take your dog to the veterinarian to get the lump checked. Vets see lots of skin tumors in dogs and draw on their experience to decide whether a tumor needs to be removed and sent for a definitive diagnosis.

Cysts, the most common tumors of the skin, can be filled with clear fluid or thick white or yellow material, and they usually are benign. Another common benign skin tumor is the *histiocytoma,* which usually occur in dogs under 2 years of age and are most common on the head, neck, and front legs. If you wait, these tumors almost always regress, but many people have them removed just to make sure. *Lipomas,* benign masses of hardened fatty tissue under the skin, also are very common in dogs. They often are very large, even 3 inches or more in diameter, and they may look worrisome even though they're benign. Dozens of other benign tumors of the skin are derived from hair cells, cells of the glands in the skin, and cells from the surface of the skin.

Small skin tumors often can be surgically removed using a local anesthetic. Larger masses require general anesthetic, which gives the veterinarian the time to be sure they are removed carefully and entirely.

The most common malignant tumors of the skin are *mast cell tumors, melanomas, fibrosarcomas,* and *lymphocytic tumors.* These tumors generally are fast growing and are attached to the tissues below. Malignant tumors also are quite common in the mouth, so be sure to check your dog's mouth during your weekly once-over. If you see a mass in his mouth, always have it checked by your veterinarian.

If a tumor on the surface of the skin is black, it can be a *melanoma,* a form of skin tumor that often is malignant.

The most common internal cancer is probably *hemangiosarcoma.* These tumors are caused by uncontrolled replication of the cells that line the blood vessels. Hemangiosarcomas consist of large blood-filled vessels and cavities. They are usually found in the spleen or the heart, but they can also occur in the skin and other tissues. If these swollen blood vessels rupture in the spleen or heart, enough blood can escape to cause sudden death.

Another common internal cancer is *lymphoma,* cancer of the lymph nodes. This cancer often affects dogs in middle age. The cancerous cells are present in lymph nodes, and the lymph nodes all over the body become enlarged. If you feel any firm mass under your dog's skin, especially if you find multiple masses, have your dog checked by a veterinarian.

Table 19-1 provides common characteristics of benign and malignant skin tumors.

Table 19-1	Characteristics of Benign and Malignant Skin Tumors	
	Benign	*Malignant*
Size	Usually small	Any size
Shape	Uniform	Any shape, often irregular
Growth	Grows slowly	May or may not grow rapidly
Spread	Remains at local site	Invades locally or metastasizes to other tissues

Cancer Prevention

What can you do to reduce the chances of your dog developing cancer? Because we can't even begin to know all the causes of cancer, the answer isn't simple. But here are a few places to start:

✔ **Prevent prolonged exposure of your dog to the sun, especially if he is white or light-colored (see Figure 19-1).** Radiation from the sun is known to cause skin cancer in dogs just as it does in humans. Use SPF 15 sunscreen on your dog's nose, ears, and face if he has a very short coat. On longer coats, the sunscreen is messy, and the hair provides protection.

✔ **Feed your dog a good-quality dog food with ingredients that are as natural as possible.** Supplement your dog's diet with washed vegetables, especially broccoli and other greens.

✔ **Supplement your dog's diet with vitamins C and E.**

✔ **Avoid exposing your dog to herbicides or pesticides whenever possible.** Don't let your dog play on a lawn that has been treated with fertilizers or chemicals to kill weeds.

✔ **Don't smoke.**

✔ **Spay or neuter your dog.** Female dogs who are spayed before their first heat are much less likely to develop breast cancer than those who have even one heat period. Male dogs who are castrated obviously won't have to worry about testicular tumors. In addition, the incidence of *perianal gland tumors* (tumors of glandular tissue around the anus) declines greatly in castrated dogs.

✔ **Give your dog adequate exercise to keep him fit, not fat.**

Figure 19-1:
This light-colored dog wears sunscreen on his nose, face, and ears, because he trains and competes outdoors frequently.

Photograph courtesy of Lauren Tapyrik

Cancer Treatment

Dogs have benefited immensely from cancer research for humans. There are many forms of cancer therapy today, and more are being discovered all the time. If your dog has malignant cancer, get a referral to a veterinary internist or, better yet, an *oncologist* (cancer specialist). An oncologist will be familiar with the latest treatments for your dog's specific kind of cancer and will have treated other dogs with the same kind of cancer. She will be able to give you a realistic idea of the likelihood of successful treatment for your dog's form of cancer, and she'll know the cost and side effects of treatment as well. Advances in chemotherapy, radiation therapy, and immunotherapy mean your dog may not have the side effects that used to be associated with cancer treatment. If the biopsy reveals a malignant tumor, don't give up yet. Get the facts from a veterinary specialist and then make your decision.

Derby (shown in Figure 19-2) is proof that dogs can and do survive cancer. When he was 2 years old, his owner, Kelly Armstrong, noticed a lump on Derby's tail, which turned out to be a very malignant tumor. Thanks to Kelly's observation and excellent veterinary care, Derby is still healthy and having fun at the age of 6.

For more information on canine cancer, you can read *Pets Living with Cancer: A Pet Owner's Resource* by Robin Downing D.V.M. (published by the American Animal Hospital Association).

Figure 19-2: Derby is living proof that dogs can and do survive cancer.

Photograph courtesy of Kelly Armstrong

Living Every Day

Some day you may learn that your dog has incurable cancer. You can do a lot in his last months, weeks, and days that will comfort you both. Enjoy every extra day you have and do things you both find fun. Here are some pointers:

- ✔ **If your dog likes to be groomed, spend some time brushing and massaging him each day.** A gentle brushing makes most dogs feel better, especially when they are ill.

- ✔ **Spoil your furry friend just a bit.** Give him teeny treats of ice cream, cheese, or other special goodies.

- ✔ **Visit a place where you have enjoyed spending time together.** Have a romp in the snow or a picnic and just enjoy your time together.

- ✔ **Take lots of pictures.** You'll treasure them later as you remember what fun you had and how you celebrated life those last few days.

And then, when all the pills and potions no longer work to ease his pain, hold him 'til the end and tell him how much you love him.

Chapter 20

Making the Difficult Decision to End Your Dog's Life

● ●

In This Chapter

▶ Knowing when the time has arrived

▶ Being comfortable with how euthanasia works

▶ Allowing yourself the time you need to grieve your loss

● ●

Making the decision to have your pet *euthanized* (put to sleep) is one of the most difficult things you will ever have to do. There are so many difficult questions to consider: When is it time to euthanize your canine friend? When it is, how can you make the process as gentle and stress-free as possible? What will she feel? How will you feel? In this chapter, I explore the answer to some of these questions and try to help ease your pain.

Knowing What a Gift a Pain-Free Death Can Be

Several years ago, my best friend, Fran, lay dying of cancer. She was only 45 years old, and every day I had known her she was like sunshine in my life. Fran's cancer had spread and was affecting virtually every organ in her body, and she was in tremendous pain. Even though she was on painkillers, they only dulled the pain and, during her last few days, they kept her from being aware enough to talk to us. Fran's husband, Chuck, and I stayed with her all night. Then, in the early morning, it seemed Fran wouldn't live much longer. She was having trouble breathing, and she had an oxygen mask on her face. She kept pushing the oxygen mask off, and we kept replacing it only to watch her push it off again. Chuck and I looked at each other across the bed and silently agreed to leave the mask alone. Fran died just a few minutes later.

If you have ever accompanied a loved one on his last journey, you know that when people die of an incurable disease they don't just slip away. The days before death often are full of tremendous physical and emotional pain. The law prohibits euthanasia of our most cherished human loved ones, but we can still give the gift of a pain-free death to our canine family members. There is no reason for our dogs to suffer when there is no chance of saving their lives or relieving their pain.

The word *euthanasia* comes from two Greek words: *eu,* which means "good," and *thanatos,* which means "death." This means that, when you choose euthanasia for your dog, you are choosing a good death.

Deciding When It's Time

Saying goodbye to a treasured canine friend and family member is heartbreaking. Most people find it extremely difficult to have to be the one to choose the time when their dog will die. Still, euthanasia is *always* better than allowing a dog to suffer. As a final gift, you can speed your dog's departure from this world rather than let her die on her own after a prolonged period of suffering.

So how can you decide when your dog has suffered enough. Although it's never an easy decision, I try to look at life through the eyes of my dog. Here are some of the questions I ask myself:

- **Is she still having more good times than bad (see Figure 20-1)?** Does she enjoy seeing the birds outside or getting a massage? Does she still wag her tail when she sees or hears you? If the answers to these questions are yes, it may not be time just yet.

- **Does she still enjoy eating, even if she eats less than she used to?** When dogs are in pain or are under extreme stress, they usually stop eating altogether.

- **Can she still perform her bodily functions?** Most dogs have been housetrained all their lives. Losing control of their bladder and bowels is very distressing to them and may be a sign that it's time.

Your dog will most likely tell you when it is time. You will see it in his eyes.

Understanding How It's Done

When you've decided that it is time to have your dog euthanized, arrange to take some vacation time from work. You'll need time for the veterinary appointment, to arrange for the disposal of your dog's remains, and most of all, to grieve.

Figure 20-1:
When trying to decide whether your dog has suffered enough, look at life through her eyes. Is she still having fun like Bannor was on this summer day?

You can have your dog euthanized at a veterinary clinic, and many people do. But I usually try to see if the veterinarian will euthanize my canine friend at home, especially if my dog is fearful of the veterinary office or if moving her is difficult or causes her pain. Regardless of where you decide to euthanize your dog, make sure you stay with her as she receives the injection. As she falls asleep, stroke her gently and tell her how much you love her. Comfort is a last unselfish gift you can give your dog. It will make the grieving process smoother for you, too.

If you've ever had surgery, you know that, as the anesthesiologist puts you under, you feel yourself floating peacefully away into sleep. This is exactly how dogs experience euthanasia. In fact, *barbiturates,* which are often used to induce anesthesia in humans, are the same drugs used to euthanize dogs. The only difference is that the dog is given an overdose. The veterinarian will insert a needle into your dog's vein to inject the drug. Your dog will first fall asleep. A few seconds later, her breathing will stop and then her heart will stop as well.

Ask your veterinarian to euthanize your dog using a catheter placed in a vein of a rear leg or an extension to a catheter placed in the front leg. That way, you can comfort your dog and can hold her head without watching or being in the way of the injection.

Taking Care of Your Dog's Remains

You can dispose of your canine friend's body after she is gone in several ways. The first choice to make is whether you want to dispose of your dog's body yourself or whether you want the veterinarian to dispose of it. Many people like to bury their dogs on their property (see Figure 20-2). I like to plant a tree each time one of my dogs is buried. Every time I enjoy the tree as it grows, I think about my canine friend. Some people like to have their dogs buried in a pet cemetery. This is a practical option for people who want to be able to visit their pet's grave but don't own property on which they can bury their friend.

Figure 20-2:
This is a small canine cemetery on a friend's property, where many dogs who played together when alive now rest.

Photograph courtesy of Sue Armstrong

Make all the arrangements ahead of time, preferably the day before your dog is euthanized. Tell the veterinarian whether you want to take the body home to bury it or have him dispose of it. Pay the veterinarian ahead of time. That way, you won't have to deal with details such as signing credit card receipts after having just said goodbye to your friend.

Another option is to have your dog cremated. You can bury the ashes, keep them in an urn, or sprinkle them in a place where your dog loved to play. I sprinkled my dog Cajun's ashes on a friend's pond where he loved to swim. Keep in mind that cremation can be quite expensive (several hundred dollars), particularly if you want your dog's ashes returned.

You also can ask your veterinarian to dispose of your dog's body for you. The body usually will be kept frozen for a while and then cremated.

Any way you decide to dispose of your dog's body is acceptable. This decision is a very personal one, and you should make the arrangements with which you feel most comfortable.

One of the best ways to memorialize your canine friend is to give a donation to a veterinary school or to a national veterinary research fund, such as the Morris Animal Foundation (see the Appendix for contact information for several excellent organizations you may want to donate to). Many schools have funds set up explicitly for the remembrance of departed pets. These funds are used to improve companion-animal medical and surgical facilities or to sponsor a faculty member who helps clients deal with pet loss and grief. Ask your veterinarian for information about canine memorial funds to which you may want to contribute.

Grieving for Your Friend

Grieving is the process of dealing with a loss. And every loss has to be dealt with eventually. Many people mistakenly think that the best way to deal with the loss of a loved one is to be strong and composed and to stay busy so they won't think about their loss. But we now know that these methods of grieving often just prolong the process.

Grieving is an intensely personal issue. Everyone has his own ways of dealing with loss. The most important thing you can do to help yourself through the grieving process is to give yourself time away from the pressures of work and daily life to let yourself feel your feelings.

Grieving can be particularly difficult if your dog dies suddenly and unexpectedly. In the case of a sudden death, you have no time to mentally prepare, which usually means that the grieving process takes longer.

Grieving takes many different forms. You may find yourself crying a lot, feeling tired, and having trouble eating or sleeping. You may spend a lot of time reminiscing about your canine companion, remembering the circumstances of her death — and you may have trouble concentrating on other aspects of your life. You may feel a variety of emotions including depression, guilt, relief, loneliness, and sadness when your dog dies. People often feel like withdrawing from others for a while. They may even try to understand why death is necessary at all and wonder if there is an afterlife where they will be reunited with their dogs. All these thoughts and feelings are a normal part of the grieving process. What's important is to give yourself the time you need to grieve your loss, and remember that there's no one right way to grieve. You don't have to face the grief over the loss of your four-legged family member alone. Many cities have pet-loss support groups, where people meet to reminisce and grieve. There are many excellent books on the market as well, including *The Loss of a Pet,* by Dr. Wallace Sife (Hungry Minds, Inc.). The Internet provides a community of people to speak with if you feel alone. A good place to start looking for resources or pet loss support is www.petloss.com.

Part VI
The Part of Tens

The 5th Wave   By Rich Tennant

"Actually, sitting on top of their doghouse during inclement weather is normal for some dogs. Catching snowflakes on the tongue, however, seems unique to our particular pet."

In this part . . .

Here I offer up some short and sweet chapters, jam-packed with information on everything from handling household hazards to keeping your canine companion healthy. I also steer you to some great Web sites on canine health and nutrition, so you know where to go to find even more information. And I let you know what signs of illness you should watch out for in your dog. If you're in a hurry, but you want to get some great information to go, you've come to the right part.

Chapter 21

Ten Great Dog Health and Nutrition Web Resources

● ●

In This Chapter

▶ Using the Internet to find out more about your dog's health

▶ Researching your dog's diet online

▶ Surfing the Web to find information on games you can play with your dog

● ●

*T*he World Wide Web has exploded with information in the last few years. But that explosion has a negative side — how do you know where to go to find the information you want? In this chapter, I take some of the guesswork out of finding dog health and nutrition information on the Internet by giving you my ten favorite Internet resources on dog health and nutrition.

These sites provide hundreds of links to other sites and those link to yet others. If you spend a little time on these Web sites, before long, you will be a walking encyclopedia of knowledge on dog health and nutrition. But as with everything on the Internet, remember that anyone can put anything on a Web site. Be sure to check with your veterinarian before you use information gleaned from a Web site to treat your dog.

PetEducation.com

www.peteducation.com

This large and comprehensive site for dog health care includes hundreds of informative articles on canine health written by experts. Turn to this Web site first for information about doggie diseases. The site also includes many other features, such as directories, a veterinary dictionary, and answers to frequently asked questions.

Great Dane and Canine Health

www.ginnie.com/gdlinks4.htm

Don't let the name fool you: This site is not just for Great Dane enthusiasts. It contains the most comprehensive set of links to online canine health information I've ever seen. The Web site has almost 300 links (at last count) to pages that provide information on everything from adrenal glands to Von Willebrand's Disease. Go to this site whenever you want to broaden your information base about a canine disease.

Vetinfo

www.vetinfo.com

Vetinfo has an incredibly comprehensive listing of dog diseases — including symptoms, causes, and treatments. What makes this site unique is that it's set up in an easy-to-read, question-and-answer format, with questions from the public answered by Michael Richards, D.V.M., in a very caring, nonpatronizing way.

AltVetMed

www.altvetmed.com

AltVetMed is the most comprehensive and inclusive Web site on complementary and alternative veterinary medicine. You can find links to sites on the various aspects of holistic veterinary medicine, including acupuncture, chiropractic, herbal medicine, nutritional therapy, homeopathy, and other complementary and alternative treatments. In addition, the site has articles on many subjects from arthritis to weight problems, written from an alternative veterinary medical perspective. If you're looking for more information, you can turn to AltVetMed for an excellent book list as well.

NetVet

netvet.wustl.edu/vetmed

NetVet has over 200 links to just about everything you would ever want to know about animal health and disease on the Internet and beyond. The site isn't exclusively about dogs, but most dog owners are interested in broader disease issues and this site is a great place to start. You can find lots of links to canine connections and Web pages on various canine diseases.

Dog Owner's Guide

www.canismajor.com/dog/alltopic.html

This site contains articles on canine health and veterinary medicine as well as food and nutrition. It also contains articles about other subjects, like dog training, choosing the right dog, and dogs at work and play. One page you'll definitely want to visit is the Survival Kit for Dogs page (www.canismajor.com/dog/alltopic.html#Tsurvive). I discover something new every time I visit.

Earl Wolfe's Dog Food Comparison Chart

home.hawaii.rr.com/wolfepack/foodcht3.html

Don't be put off by the lack of compelling visuals on this site — it contains a wealth of information on dog foods presented in a way that is like no other site on the Internet. The meat of the site, so to speak, is the dog food comparison chart, which tells you the contents of every canine food under the sun and lists the name, address, telephone number, and Web site of each manufacturer. This site contains everything you would want to know to be able to compare dog foods. If you're thinking of changing dog foods or are just curious about how your dog food compares to others, this is where you want to be!

ConsumerLab.com

www.consumerlab.com

The mission of ConsumerLab.com is "to provide consumers and healthcare professionals with results of independent tests of products that affect health and well-being." ConsumerLab.com arranges for independent tests of the quality of various health products and report them on this well-organized and visually appealing Web site. The home page starts you off with summaries of the results of their latest studies. You'll want to visit this site often, especially if you use a homemade diet for your dog or are planning on supplementing his prepared diet.

The Dogpatch

www.dogpatch.org

The Dogpatch is the most comprehensive Web site about active dogs. The site contains comprehensive information on agility, obedience, Frisbee, and herding for dogs. There's also a bookstore, a bulletin board, and links to sites on dog activities, doggie products, online magazines, and just about any information you can imagine for active dogs. To get to the Dogpatch page with links to canine health Web sites, go to www.dogpatch.org/dogs/ dogweb.cfm#A1 (or just choose "The Best Canine Links" from the drop-down menu on the home page).

Dog Play: Having Fun with Your Dog

www.dog-play.com

This Web site has links to pages describing everything you may want to know about more things to do with your dog than you can accomplish in a lifetime! The site is not visually complex, which means it loads fast and gets you right to where you want to go. Want to go to dog camp this summer? Check this page for links to 15 different dog camps. Want to find out more about where and how to take your dog for a hike? This site lists nine links on the subject.

Chapter 22

Ten Signs of Illness to Watch For

In This Chapter

▶ Observing your dog's habits and being familiar with what's "normal" for her

▶ Knowing when to take your dog to the vet

As a dog person, you're probably very observant. You love to watch your dog play, run, eat, and even sleep. And you're probably very good at recognizing when something is wrong. But sometimes you may notice a change in your dog's attitude or behavior and wonder whether she's ill or whether you are just imagining things and worrying for nothing. This chapter describes the ten most common signs of illness in dogs and what those signs may mean.

Lack of Appetite

Eating is very high on the priority list for most dogs. If your dog normally devours her dinner but seems to have lost her appetite, it's usually a sign that all is not well inside. She may just have a little gastrointestinal upset, which is usually accompanied by vomiting and/or diarrhea. Many illnesses can make your dog turn her nose up at food, including fever, a localized or generalized infection, or liver or kidney disease, to name just a few. When your dog stops eating, it usually means that something is wrong, so if she misses two meals in a row, get her to a veterinarian for tests.

Weight Loss or Weight Gain

Weight loss or weight gain is to be expected when you change the amount you feed your dog or the amount of exercise she gets. Unexpected changes in weight, however, can be a sign that she's not well. For example, a dog with a hormone imbalance can gain weight while eating very little. Dogs may also lose weight when they're suffering from cancer or when they're eating a food that doesn't provide them with the proteins and energy they need. Dogs also lose weight during prolonged illnesses if they aren't eating. (That's why encouraging your dog to eat just a bit when she's ill, as long as she doesn't have a digestive upset, is so important.)

Short Temper

When you're ill, you probably feel pretty grouchy — and dogs are no different. Dogs who suffer chronic pain may seem to be trying to bite, but they may actually be trying to keep people and other dogs away so that they won't bump into them and hurt them more. That's why the new joint-protective nutraceuticals and non-steroidal anti-inflammatory drugs can make such a difference to the life of a dog with arthritis (see Chapter 10 for more information). So if your dog suddenly becomes grouchy, take her to your veterinarian to see if there's a medical reason.

Lack of Energy

Dogs who are acutely ill frequently act dull and depressed. They may be unwilling to participate in family activities or to interact with their people in the usual way. They may even leave the room and find a quiet place to lie down away from the bustle.

If you have a busy family life, you can easily miss this sign of illness. This happened to me just recently with my dog Stripe. She is always hanging around, leaning against my leg as I prepare dinner, and lying against my feet as I sit writing in the evenings at home. Because she is around so much, I tend to forget that she's always attached to me. One day, Stripe began to have a very severe bout of diarrhea. I remember thinking how suddenly those symptoms appeared — until I remembered that for the previous 24 hours, she hadn't been hanging around underfoot nearly as much. Instead, she had been curled up in one of the dog beds in the corner of the room.

Fever

Fever is one of the classic signs of illness. Your dog won't always have a fever when she's sick. But when you *do* detect a fever (a body temperature over 102.8 degrees), you can be sure your dog is ill. Fever is usually indicative of an infection, because the body's response to the presence of a foreign invader such as a virus or bacteria is to stoke the furnace, which keeps the organisms from replicating.

If you're measuring your dog's temperature right after she has exercised, her temperature may be higher than normal. A dog's temperature can rise to 105 degrees or higher during vigorous exercise, so make sure you check your dog's temperature at rest.

Excessive Shedding

During times of illness, or more particularly the stress that accompanies illness, dogs shed more profusely than usual. This hair loss is a result of the secretion of stress hormones. If your canine companion is shedding more than usual, especially if she has flaky skin and excessive dander, she may be ill. Look for other signs of illness before you rush to the vet, however, because excessive shedding does occur seasonally in the spring and fall and also can be a sign of inadequate nutrition.

Vomiting

Dogs are smart: They don't leave in their stomachs anything that doesn't feel good. In fact, they have voluntary muscle fibers in the esophagus that allow them to vomit almost at will. If your dog vomits over a period of greater than 12 hours and refuses to drink water, take her to the vet. If she vomits for more than 24 hours but is still drinking water, take her to the vet, too.

Dry or Loose Stools

As gross as it may seem, your dog's stools are an important indicator of her health. They should be firm and formed and should hold together when you pick them up with a shovel or a plastic bag. They should not be so dry that they come out in multiple small pellets — dry stools indicate that your dog is constipated. At the other extreme, if the stools are loose so that they form cow-patty-shaped piles or liquid pools, then your dog has diarrhea. Diarrhea is a sign that the intestine is unable to reabsorb and recycle the water that's in the intestine, and this can lead to dehydration.

If your dog has diarrhea for more than 24 hours, take her to see your veterinarian.

If you are observant, and if your dogs are as naughty as mine, you also may see objects in your dog's stools, such as that paper towel your dog ate the day before, or the carrots she stole off the counter when you were preparing dinner last night. In fact, just a few weeks ago, I was bragging to a friend that my Golden

Retriever, Stripe, would pick up anything I asked her to. To demonstrate, I threw a dime on the ground. And yes, she picked it up, but she also swallowed it. I had to watch for a couple of days to make sure it came out!

Drinking Too Much or Too Little

Your furry friend needs access to clean water at all times. But dogs vary in the amount of water they drink. My Golden Retrievers drink much more water than my Border Collie. Knowing how much water your dog drinks and monitoring her intake a bit is important. You don't have to actually measure how much water she drinks, but you should just note in the back of your mind when she drinks and how often you have to refill the water bowl. Dogs who are ill may refuse to drink water — but this is usually accompanied by a loss of appetite and possibly vomiting. Dogs may refuse to drink when they're excited or stressed, such as when they are traveling, but they should begin to drink again when the stress is removed. Increased water consumption, on the other hand, can be a sign of fever, kidney failure, of hormonal disturbances, so if your dog has started drinking a lot more than she normally does, take her for a vet check.

Limping

Dogs often bang into each other and suffer minor injuries during vigorous play. They tear ligaments, stretch muscles, get bruises, and even break bones, just like people do. A dog who is lame will try to get the weight off the painful leg by reducing the amount of time she spends on that leg. To accomplish this, she will raise her head and/or alter her gait.

If your dog becomes lame, you may have trouble figuring out whether it's serious enough to take her to the veterinarian or whether you should wait. Here is a general rule I use myself: If my dog becomes lame, I give her rest for 24 hours — no running loose, no playing, no roughhousing. She goes outside only to eliminate and only on leash. If she is still lame after the 24-hour rest, I schedule an appointment with the vet.

Don't wait several days after an injury to see a vet, however, because your dog may begin to use the leg again despite significant damage to bones, ligaments, or muscles. Months or years later your dog may develop chronic arthritis as a result of the injury, which should have been surgically repaired when it first happened.

Chapter 23

Ten Ways to Keep Your Dog Healthy

● ●

In This Chapter

▶ Working with a vet to maintain your dog's health

▶ Paying attention to your dog's emotional well-being

● ●

*T*his book is chock-full of detailed information on dog health and nutrition. It provides you with many pages of suggestions for keeping your dog healthy. But sometimes it's easier to just have an easy-to-remember list to tell you what to do. That's what I've provided in this chapter.

Get Your Dog Vaccinated

Years ago, many dogs died from infectious diseases such as distemper, infectious canine hepatitis, leptospirosis, and rabies. During the 1950s and 1960s, veterinary researchers went to work studying these viruses and designing effective vaccines. As a result, they saved hundreds of thousands of canine lives. Take advantage of their hard work by having your dog vaccinated. Work with your veterinarian to ensure that your young pup gets the correct series of vaccinations to build a strong immune response to these viruses. Then make sure that your dog remains immune by getting vaccinations annually (or on a schedule recommended by your vet).

Don't use *nosodes* (homeopathic preparations that are used in place of vaccines to boost immunity) and think that your dog is protected. No good evidence proves that these products protect dogs against deadly viral infections. In fact, pretty strong evidence shows that nosodes are ineffective.

Take Him to the Vet Regularly

A veterinarian is one of the first strangers your puppy ever met — but hopefully she didn't stay a stranger for long. The relationship you have with your dog's veterinarian is a critical factor in your dog's health and longevity. Choose your veterinarian wisely. She should be someone with whom you can talk frankly, who will listen to you, and who, in turn, will educate you. When you've found a vet you like and trust, nourish that relationship. Send her pictures of your puppy as he grows, when he completes his first obedience class, and as he sits beside the Christmas tree. She'll proudly post those pictures on a bulletin board in her office — after all, she studied hard though veterinary school and works in private practice because she cares about animals.

Bring your pooch to your veterinarian every year and she will give him a complete examination, looking carefully for anything that may be amiss. She will test him for heartworm, check his immune status against viral infections, and tell you about the latest products for flea and tick control. This annual checkup is a great opportunity for you to ask her questions about your dog's health and routine maintenance. When your dog is older, bring a morning urine sample when you visit, and get blood work done to keep a closer check on your canine companion's health. And follow your veterinarian's suggestions to the letter.

Feed Your Dog Right

Give your dog the best diet you can afford. Good nutrition will help your pup grow properly, keep him active as an adult, heal hurts, and help ward off old age. Read the chapters in Part II of this book so you know what the dog food labels really mean and what your dog needs. Then you can pick the best diet for your dog when he is a puppy, an adult, and a senior.

Don't Let Your Dog Gain Too Much Weight

Every day as you prepare your dog's meals, assess his daily activity and feed him accordingly. Taking weight off is a whole lot harder than preventing your dog from becoming overweight in the first place (just as is the case in humans). Don't let the pounds creep on in old age, either. There is no reason for older dogs to be fat. Obesity impairs mobility, increases the risk and severity of arthritis, and forces the heart to work harder.

Spay or Castrate Your Dog

This simple operation should be considered an essential part of a dog's healthcare program. Dogs who are spayed or castrated live longer because they have less risk of infections and a lower incidence of cancer. They also fit better into our families because they have fewer objectionable behaviors. And to top it off, they are better citizens because they have done their part to help control the pet population.

Give Your Dog Lots of Exercise

Every dog needs daily exercise. With a few exceptions, generally the larger a dog is, the more exercise he needs. At a minimum, your dog should have an opportunity to run free in a safe area or be taken for a walk twice a day for 15 minutes. Dogs who get sufficient exercise not only live longer, they are less likely to be overweight, they are less likely to suffer injuries, and, if the experience of human runners and joggers is anything to go on, they just feel better.

Take Care of Those Pearly Whites

Regular tooth care is as important for dogs as it is for humans. Without regular tooth care, a high percentage of dogs develop *periodontal disease,* which results in bacterial infections in the gum, loosening of the teeth, and the potential for spread of bacteria throughout the body. Get a doggie toothbrush and gently train your dog to allow his teeth to be brushed. Then brush his teeth regularly. If you see tartar on your dog's teeth, make an appointment to have it removed. The risk of problems with anesthesia is much lower than the effects of gingivitis and eventual tooth loss. Regular canine tooth care pays for itself many times over in health and longevity (and lower veterinary bills).

Do Routine Maintenance on Your Dog

Make sure that you provide your dog with routine preventive maintenance. Just as you get the oil changed in your car every several thousand miles, you need to give your dog a regular check about once every three to four weeks.

Sit down with a big pile of treats and trim his toenails. Give a little treat after each nail so he won't mind as much. While he's chewing, you can quickly clip the next nail. (If he eats too fast, give him a spoonful of peanut butter to slow him down.) And while you're at it, trim excess hair off the bottoms of his feet, take a peek down his ears to be sure they are clean, and run your hands over his entire body to feel for lumps, bumps, and other abnormalities. Give your pooch a bath whenever his coat gets dusty or oily or he begins to get that doggy smell. Preventive maintenance is the best way to stay in touch with your dog's health status.

Take Advantage of Joint-Protective Nutraceuticals

When your dog is about 8 years old, start giving him daily doses of joint-protective nutraceuticals (see Chapter 6 for more information). Nutraceuticals are derived from natural sources, are very safe, and have been shown in numerous studies to increase the *viscosity* (friction-reducing property) of joint fluid, repair worn cartilage, and reduce the pain of arthritis. Because arthritis is so common in older dogs, and because dogs are living longer than ever, these products have been an incredible boon to their health and longevity.

Give Your Dog a Job

In the morning, I walk my dogs to the end of the driveway and tell the younger ones to sit and stay while I send my 11-year-old, Tally, to fetch the morning paper. She bounds over to it and snatches it up with such pride! Then she trots back down the driveway with the paper held high in her mouth, glancing at the other dogs to be sure they notice that she is the one with the paper. What a joy it is for her to do this job every day! All my dogs have their own jobs. Stripe is in charge of putting the toys in the toy box before we go to bed, while Fate sits holding her plush tiger in her mouth, ready to carry it to the bedroom. I train all my dogs in obedience, agility, tracking, retrieving, herding, and other doggie games.

At the very least, take your dog to a basic obedience class. It will make him more comfortable around other dogs and will help him become a true family member and a good citizen. Who knows, maybe some day he will bring joy to older people in a retirement home, or plaster delight on a child's face with his tongue.

Chapter 24

Ten Household Hazards

In This Chapter

▶ Knowing which substances can harm your dog
▶ Keeping your dog from danger

ogs are great explorers, ever curious to see what new scents and tastes they can find in the environment. Like toddlers, they put everything in their mouths to see what tastes good, what has an interesting texture, and what may be used to practice their chewing techniques. As a result, dogs frequently are exposed to toxic or hazardous items. People with children are careful to place dangerous items out of the reach of children, but dogs frequently go places where children don't (like the garage) — and some things that aren't toxic for children are quite dangerous for dogs (like chocolate). Dog-proofing your house and being vigilant about how you store household products after you use them is very important. In this chapter, I let you know about the ten most common household hazards.

Foods

Not all foods that taste good to you are good for your dog. Some, if eaten in enough quantity, can even kill your canine companion. The toxic foods discussed here are the ones deemed most dangerous to dogs by the National Animal Poison Control Center.

For some of these toxic foods, I have provided *approximate* amounts that are toxic, but avoid feeding *any* of these foods to your dog, even in small amounts.

✔ **Onions:** A toxic component of raw onions can cause the red blood cells to burst, resulting in severe anemia and even kidney failure. A medium-sized raw onion can cause illness in a 40-pound dog.

- ✔ **Chocolate, cocoa, coffee, or tea:** Chocolate, coffee, and tea all contain caffeine and theobromine. These toxins can cause vomiting, diarrhea, increased thirst, hyperactivity, increased heart rate, and even seizures. Milk chocolate is less toxic than semisweet chocolate, which, is in turn, less toxic than baker's chocolate or cocoa. The toxic dose of milk chocolate is 1 ounce per kilogram of body weight, which translates to about 1½ pounds of milk chocolate for a 50-pound dog.

- ✔ **Alcohol (ethanol):** Alcohol can cause vomiting, staggering, weakness, and even coma in dogs. One ounce of ethanol (100-percent alcohol) is enough to cause illness in a 65-pound dog.

- ✔ **Yeast dough:** There are two problems associated with ingestion of yeast dough. The first problem is that the yeast can ferment and produce alcohol, producing the same illness as alcohol toxicity. The second problem is that the yeast can swell in a dog's stomach and cause obstruction or even rupture of the stomach.

- ✔ **Salt:** Salt can cause illness in a dog, especially if the dog doesn't have access to water. Dogs with salt toxicity stagger and wander aimlessly, eventually developing seizures that progress to a coma and death.

- ✔ **Macadamia nuts:** About 10 ounces of macadamia nuts can cause soreness, stiffness, listlessness, and rear leg weakness in dogs.

- ✔ **Hops:** Hops are used for beer making, and dogs sometimes eat used hops that have been thrown out by home brewers. Affected dogs develop a very high temperature and eventually go into shock when their body temperature reaches 107 to 108 degrees. If you brew your own beer, be sure to dispose of used hops in such a way that your dog doesn't have access to them.

- ✔ **Green or unripe tomatoes or potatoes and their leaves and stems:** The level of toxicity of these vegetables and their plant parts depends very much on the soil, the temperature and humidity when they are grown. They can cause slowing or complete cessation of digestion, increased heart rate, and signs of excitability such as shaking, panting and pacing. If you are feeding fresh greens to your dog, make sure these items aren't included.

- ✔ **Moldy foods:** Moldy foods can have a variety of toxic fungi and bacteria growing in them. Never give old food from the refrigerator to your dog.

Medications

Animal poisoning by drugs is very common, accounting for over 75 percent of toxin exposures reported by animal poison control centers. Never give human prescription or over-the-counter medications to your dog unless specifically prescribed by your veterinarian, and keep all drugs out of your dog's reach. Many human medications are lethal to dogs, even in small doses. Here are some of the most common toxic human medications that dogs get into:

- ✔ Analgesic and anti-inflammatory drugs (aspirin, ibuprofen, acetaminophen, naproxen)
- ✔ Cold medicine or decongestants
- ✔ Creams and ointments in tubes
- ✔ Antidepressants
- ✔ Vitamins
- ✔ Diet pills

Plants

Hundreds of plants are potentially poisonous to dogs. Here's a list of the most dangerous and common household and garden plants:

- ✔ **Azalea and rhododendron** are members of the same family of plants. If eaten, they can cause weakness, upset stomach, drooling, depression, heart failure, and coma.
- ✔ **Oleander** can cause stomach upsets, heart failure, and excitability or lethargy.
- ✔ **Castor bean** is the most toxic plant we know. Even *one* bean, if chewed, can kill a dog. A dog with castor bean toxicity will have abdominal pain accompanied by vomiting and diarrhea.
- ✔ **Sago palm** is another very toxic plant. Any part of the plant is potentially lethal, but the seeds have particularly concentrated toxins. The plant causes severe liver damage, which may take days to weeks to develop but is irreversible.
- ✔ **Yew** causes vomiting, abdominal pain, and diarrhea in dogs.
- ✔ **Deadly nightshade and Chinese lantern** can cause dilation of the pupils of the eye, loss of voice, extreme agitation, and excitation.

Other plants may be irritating to the mouth and throat if a dog chews on them. Some of these are:

- ✔ Dieffenbachia
- ✔ Begonia
- ✔ Philodendron
- ✔ Calla lily

For a comprehensive list of toxic plants, go to www.barkandwag.com/ healthtips.htm. For more details, order the Household Plant Reference from the National Animal Poison Control Center, 1717 South Philo Road, Suite 36, Urbana, IL 61802.

Flea Control Products and Other Insecticides

I can't possibly list all the insecticides you might have around your home, but I can tell you that all are potentially toxic to your canine companion. Almost all topical anti-flea preparations (dips and sprays) are toxic to dogs, given enough exposure. When applying a flea-control product to your dog, be sure to use it *exactly* as recommended and apply it directly to the dog's skin. When using household insecticides, read the label carefully and use the product exactly as recommended. Keep ant and roach baits out of areas your dog frequents and remove them when they have expired.

Mouse and Rat Poisons

Mouse and rat poisons are highly toxic to dogs. After all, they are designed to kill small animals. Try to avoid chemicals whenever you can: Try a mousetrap rather than poison, beer rather than slug bait, non-chemical lawn products rather than chemical ones — and only go to the chemical weapons if all else fails.

If you put out mouse or rat baits, be sure to place them in a location to which your dog has no access. Put a sign on the entrance to that area stating that there is rodent bait inside and that dogs are strictly forbidden to enter. That way, a guest, delivery person, or cleaning person won't accidentally give your dog access to the area. Keep track of the baits and remove them when they are no longer needed.

Household Chemicals

Many household chemicals are toxic if ingested by animals. Cleaning materials can cause digestive upsets if your dog eats them. Some products, such as those containing lye, can cause burns to the mouth. Here are the most common dangerous household chemicals:

✔ Moth balls

✔ Potpourri oils

✔ Fabric softener sheets

✔ Dishwashing detergent

✔ Batteries

✔ Cigarettes

Gardening and Lawn Care Supplies

Never use garden or lawn care chemicals in the presence of your dog. Keep your dog away when you apply fertilizers to help your roses grow and your grass stay green throughout the summer. Never give your dog access to an area where you have used slug bait, and store those products in a place to which your dog does not have access.

I use the "double-safe" rule for storing toxic products in the home. First, I store the items in a room to which my dogs are forbidden access. Plus, I store the items in a location within that room (for example, high on a shelf) that my dogs couldn't reach if they were somehow able to get into the room.

Automobile Care Supplies

Like household cleaning solutions, car cleaning compounds are also toxic. In fact, frequently they are more dangerous because they are more concentrated. Antifreeze is extremely toxic to dogs; less than 1 tablespoon can kill a 10-pound dog. Windshield washer fluid is also toxic, though less so. Restrict your dog's access to the garage as much as possible, so you can ensure that your dog stays away from these dangerous items.

Several brands of nontoxic antifreeze are on the market, so consider using these instead of the traditional variety.

Furniture Refinishing Chemicals

When you are performing construction or refinishing furniture, keep your dog well away from the area. Varnishes, stains, and caulking compounds all have toxic potential.

Garbage

Never let your dog have access to decaying garbage or road kill. Rotting meat is contaminated with bacteria and toxins produced by bacteria that can be toxic to your dog. Keep your dog properly confined at home and store your garbage in an area to which your dog does not have access.

Appendix

Resources

• •

Canine Sports Events Governing Organizations

American Kennel Club
260 Madison Avenue, Fourth Floor
New York, NY 10016
Web site: www.akc.org

United Kennel Club
100 East Kilgore Road
Kalamazoo, MI 49002-5584
Phone: 616-343-9020
Web site: www.ukcdogs.com

United States Dog Agility Association
P.O. Box 850955
Richardson, TX 75085-0955
Phone: 972-231-9700
Web site: www.usdaa.com

North American Dog Agility Council
HCR 2 Box 277
St. Maries, ID 83861
Web site: www.nadac.com

Veterinary Groups

American Veterinary Medical Association
Public Information Division
1931 North Meacham Road, Suite 100
Schaumburg, IL 60173-4360
Phone: 847-925-8070
Web site: www.avma.org

Canadian Veterinary Medical Association
339 Booth Street
Ottawa, Ontario
Canada K1R 7K1
Phone: 613-236-1162
Web site: www.crma-acmv.org

American Animal Hospital Association
P.O. Box 150899
Denver, CO 80215-0899
Web site: www.aahanet.org

American College of Veterinary
Internal Medicine (Cardiology)
1997 Wadsworth Boulevard, Suite A
Lakewood, CO 80215-3327
Phone: 303-231-9933 or 800-245-9081
(toll-free)
Web site: www.acvim.org

Orthopedic Foundation for Animals
2300 Nifong Boulevard
Columbia, MO 65201
Phone: 573-442-0418
Web site: www.offa.org

PennHip
c/o Synbiotics
11011 Via Frontera
San Diego, CA 92127-1702
Phone: 619-451-3771
Web site: www.synbiotics.com/html/pennhip.html

Canine Eye Registration Foundation
1248 Lynn Hall
Purdue University
West Lafayette, IN 47906
Phone: 765-494-8179
Web site: www.vet.purdue.edu/~yshen/cerf.html

Magazines and Newsletters

American Kennel Club Gazette
260 Madison Avenue, Fourth Floor
New York, NY 10016
Web site: www.akc.org/pubs/index.cfm

Dogs in Canada
89 Skyway Avenue, Suite 200
Etobicoke, Ontario M9W 6R4
Phone: 416-798-9778
Web site: www.dogsincanada.com

Dog Fancy
P.O. Box 6050
Mission Viejo, CA 92690-6050
Phone: 949-855-8822
Web site: www.animalnetwork.co/dogs/

Dog World Magazine
500 N. Dearborn, Suite 1100
Chicago, IL 60610
Phone: 312-396-0600
Web site: www.dogworldmag.com

Good Dog!
P.O. Box 10069
Austin, TX 78766
Phone: 800-968-1738
(toll-free)
Web site: www.gooddogmagazine.com

Your Dog
Belvoir Publications
75 Holly Hill Lane
Greenwich, CT 06836
Phone: 800-829-5116

Front and Finish
P.O. Box 333
Galesburg, IL 61402-0333
Phone: 309-344-1333
Web site: www.frontfinish.com

CleanRun Magazine
Clean Run Productions, LLC
35 North Chicopee Street
Chicopee, MA 01020
Phone: 413-532-1389 or 800-311-6503
(toll-free)
Web site: www.cleanrun.com

Pet Supply Sources

Drs. Foster & Smith Pet Supply
2253 Air Park Road
P.O. Box 100
Rhinelander, WI 54501
Phone: 800-381-7179
(toll-free)
Web site: www.drfostersmith.com

KV Vet Supply
3190 N Road
David City, NE 68632
Phone: 800-423-8211 (toll-free)
Web site: www.kvvet.com

Dogwise
P.O. Box 2778
Wenatchee, WA 98807-2778
Phone: 800-776-2665 (toll-free)
Web site: www.dogwise.com

Cherrybrook Pet Supplies
Route 57, Box 15
Broadway, NJ 08808
Phone: 800-524-0820 (toll-free)
Web site: www.cherrybrook.com

J-B Wholesale Pet Supplies
5 Raritan Road
Oakland, NJ 07436
Phone: 800-526-0388 (toll-free)
Web site: www.jbpet.com

Petco.com
Phone: 877-738-6742
Web site: www.petco.com

PETsMART.com
35 Hugus Alley, Suite 210
Pasadena, CA 91103
Phone: 888-839-9638
Web site: www.petsmart.com

R.C. Steele
P.O. Box 910
Brockport, NY 14420-0910
Phone: 888-839-9420
Web site: www.rcsteele.com

Dog Training Organizations

Association of Pet Dog Trainers
66 Morris Avenue, Suite 2A
Springfield, NJ 07081
Phone: 800-738-3647
Web site: www.apdt.com

North American Dog
Obedience Instructors
PMB #369
729 Grapevine Highway, Suite 369
Hurst, TX 76054-2085
Web site: www.nadoi.org

Animal Charities

American Kennel Club Animal
Health Foundation
251 West Garfield Road, Suite 160
Aurora, OH 44202-8856
Phone: 330-995-0807
Web site: www.akcchf.org

American Veterinary
Medical Foundation
1931 North Meacham Road, Suite 100
Schaumburg, IL 61073
Phone: 800-248-2862, ext. 600 (toll-free)
Web site: www.avmf.org

Canine Companions for Independence
P.O. Box 446
Santa Rosa, CA 95402-0446
Phone: 866-224-3647 or 800-572-2275
(toll-free)
Web site: www.caninecompanions.org

The Delta Society
289 Perimeter Road East
Renton, WA 98055-1329
Phone: 425-226-7357
Web site: petsforum.com/
deltasociety/default.html

Dogs for the Deaf
10175 Wheeler Road
Central Point, OR 97502
Phone: 541-826-9220
Web site: www.dogsforthedeaf.org

Guide Dogs for the Blind
P.O. Box 151200
San Rafael, CA 94915-1200
Phone: 800-295-4050 (toll-free)
Web site: www.guidedogs.com

Guiding Eyes for the Blind
611 Granite Springs Road
Yorktown Heights, NY 10598
Phone: 800-942-0149 (toll-free)
Web site: www.guiding-eyes.org

Morris Animal Foundation
45 Inverness Drive East
Englewood, CO 80112-5480
Phone: 800-243-2345
Web site:
www.morrisanimalfoundation.org

AKC Companion Animal Recovery
Phone: 800-252-7894
Web site: www.akc.org/love/car/index.cfm

National Dog Registry
Phone: 800-637-3647
Web site: www.natldogregistry.com

Tattoo-a-Pet
6571 S.W. 20th Court
Ft. Lauderdale, FL 33317
Phone: 954-581-5834 or 800-828-8667
(toll-free)
Web site: www.tattoo-a-pet.com

Other

Pet Sitters International
418 East King Street
King, NC 27021-9163
Phone: 336-983-9222
Web site: www.petsit.com

Index

attitude, 9, 81, 332
Australian Shepherd, 267
autoimmune disorders, 30, 140
autonomic nervous system, 135
azalea, plant hazard, 341

• B •

baby teeth, lifespan, 127
Bach flower therapy, 227
Bach, Edward, 227
bacitracin, 182
bacteria, 170–173, 209–211
bacterial infection, 138
bad breath (gingivitis), 144
balanced dog foods, 68
bald spots, 141
balls, fetch activity, 263
banner statement, 71
barbiturates, euthanasia, 321
barking, 132, 293–294
Basenji, tightly-coiled tail, 129
Basset Hound, ear function, 128
baths, 11, 31–32, 246
bats, rabies carrier, 167
batteries, hazard, 343
Beauceron, dewclaws, 123
bed sheet, flea detection, 30–31
bedding, flea treatment, 31–32
Bedlington Terriers, 81
beds, 242–243
beet pulp, fiber source, 58
begonia, plant hazard, 341
behaviorism, 279
behaviors
  compromise, 291
  correcting bad, 280–283
  dog/people associations, 289–290
  pack theory, 290–291
  problem solving, 292–293
  reasons, 288–289
  reinforcing good, 280–283
Belgian Malinois, 21
Belgian Tervuren, 11, 248
Benadryl, 182
beneficial nematodes, fleas, 32

benign (non-cancerous) tumors, 311
Bernese Mountain Dog, 150–151
best used by code, 79
BHA, food preservative, 79
BHT, food preservative, 79
bicycling, exercise concerns, 261
bioflavonoids, 90
biotin, water-soluble vitamin, 60
biotransformation, 207
birth, female shedding issues, 11
bitches. *See* females
biting, 295
black stools, 13
bladder infections, 162–164
blanket, 183
bleeding, 191–192
bloat, 121, 143
blood chemistry, 37
blood, serum chemistry, 305
Bloodhound, ear function, 128
blow dryer, flea detection, 30–31
blue-colored Doberman, 130
blunt-ended scissors, 183
body language, 278–280
body temperature, 13–14
body weight. *See* weight
bone meal, diet concerns, 62
bone structure, 119–123
bones, 24, 121, 98–100, 192
bootie (stockinet), 183
Bordatella bronchiseptica, 168–169
Border Collie, 130
boric acid, flea prevention, 32
Borrelia burgdorferi, 33
Borzoi, 124, 128, 143, 150–151
botanical medicine, 228–229
bottle-feeding, weak puppies, 38
Bouvier Des Flandres, 150–151
Boxer, 128, 130, 312
brachycephalic head, 124
breath, 132, 187–188
breath rate, measuring, 185

breeders, 15, 17, 39
breeding, 37–39
Briard, 123, 150–151
broad-spectrum antibiotics, 24
broken bones, 192
brown dog tick, ehrlichiosis, 33
brushes, 243–245
Brussels Griffon, 152–153
Bulldog, 124, 128
Bullmastiff, 150–151
bumpers, fetch activity, 262–263
bumps, skin ailment, 141–142
burns, 193
Buster Cube, 249, 271, 296
buyers, puppy packets, 39
by-products, 75

• C •

cadmium, trace mineral, 64
Cairn Terriers, 138
calcium, 62, 88
calculus (tartar), 23–24, 247
calla lily, plant hazard, 341
caloric requirements, 77–78
cancer, 112–113, 311–317
canine behaviorist, 298–299
Canine Eye Registration Foundation (CERF), 15
Canine Genome Project, PRA, 16
canine parvovirus enteritis, 28, 167–168
canine sports, 265–266
canine teeth, 126
canned dog foods, 68
car chasing, 294
carbohydrates, 57–58
cardiac cachexia, 113
cardiac problems, 15
Cardigan Welsh Corgi, 153–154
cardiomyopathy, 15
cardiovascular collapse, 219
cardiovascular system, 131–132
carnassial teeth, gingivitis, 144
carnassial, 126
carpal joint, 120–121

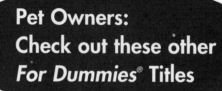

Pet Owners:
Check out these other
For Dummies® Titles

Aquariums For Dummies®	ISBN 0-7645-5156-6	$21.99
Birds For Dummies®	ISBN 0-7645-5139-6	$21.99
Boxers For Dummies®	ISBN 0-7645-5285-6	$15.99
Cats For Dummies®, 2nd Edition	ISBN 0-7645-5275-9	$21.99
Chihuahuas For Dummies®	ISBN 0-7645-5284-8	$15.99
Choosing a Dog For Dummies®	ISBN 0-7645-5310-0	$21.99
Dachshunds For Dummies®	ISBN 0-7645-5289-9	$15.99
Dog Training For Dummies®	ISBN 0-7645-5286-4	$21.99
Dog Tricks For Dummies®	ISBN 0-7645-5287-2	$15.99
Dogs For Dummies®, 2nd Edition	ISBN 0-7645-5274-0	$21.99
Ferrets For Dummies®	ISBN 0-7645-5259-7	$21.99
German Shepherds For Dummies®	ISBN 0-7645-5280-5	$15.99
Golden Retrievers For Dummies®	ISBN 0-7645-5267-8	$15.99
Horses For Dummies®	ISBN 0-7645-5138-8	$21.99
Iguanas For Dummies®	ISBN 0-7645-5260-0	$21.99
Jack Russell Terriers For Dummies®	ISBN 0-7645-5268-6	$15.99
Labrador Retrievers For Dummies®	ISBN 0-7645-5281-3	$15.99
Pit Bulls For Dummies®	ISBN 0-7645-5291-0	$16.99
Puppies For Dummies®	ISBN 0-7645-5255-4	$21.99
Retired Racing Greyhounds For Dummies®	ISBN 0-7645-5276-7	$15.99
Rottweilers For Dummies®	ISBN 0-7645-5271-6	$15.99
Siberian Huskies For Dummies®	ISBN 0-7645-5279-1	$15.99
Turtles and Tortoises For Dummies®	ISBN 0-7645-5313-5	$21.99

From the Pet Experts at Howell Book House, Titles of Interest to Dog Lovers:

TRAINING GUIDES

DOG BEHAVIOR: AN OWNER'S GUIDE TO A
HAPPY, HEALTHY PET
By Ian Dunbar
ISBN 0-87605-236-7 • $12.95

DOG-FRIENDLY DOG TRAINING
By Andrea Arden
ISBN 1-58245-009-9 • $17.95

DOGPERFECT: THE USER-FRIENDLY GUIDE TO A
WELL-BEHAVED DOG
By Sarah Hodgson
ISBN 0-87605-534-X • $12.95

DOG TRAINING IN 10 MINUTES
By Carol Lea Benjamin
ISBN 0-87605-471-8 • $14.95

PORTABLE PETSWELCOME.COM
ISBN 0-764556-426-9 • $19.99

TRAIN YOUR DOG, CHANGE YOUR LIFE
By Gary and Maureen Ross
ISBN 0-7645-631-9 • $23.99

ACTIVITIES/GENERAL

ALL ABOUT AGILITY
By Jacqueline O'Neil
ISBN 1-58245-124-0 • $12.95

CANINE GOOD CITIZEN: EVERY DOG CAN BE ONE
By Jack and Wendy Volhard
ISBN 0-87605-452-1 • $14.95

THE COMPLETE DOG BOOK, 19TH EDITION, REVISED
By The American Kennel Club
ISBN 0-87605-047-X • $32.95

THE DOG OWNER'S HOME VETERINARY
HANDBOOK, 3RD EDITION
By James Giffin, M.D., and Lisa Carlson, D.V.M
ISBN 0-876605-201-4 • $29.95

HOLISTIC GUIDE FOR A HEALTHY DOG, 2ND EDITION
By Wendy Volhard and Kerry Brown, D.V.M
ISBN 1-58245-153-2 • $16.95

To order these and other titles, call 1-800-434-3422 or visit our Web site at www.wiley.com

Behavior...Training...Grooming...Health...Nutrition...Performance...

Learn From the Experts on Your Favorite Breed!

The American Kennel Club invites you to try our official magazine, the *AKC Gazette*. Every month, you'll discover more about the sport of purebred dogs. From the pulse-pounding excitement of agility competition

to obedience trials and the finely groomed world of dog shows, lots of new activities are open to you. The official *AKC Events Calendar* book comes to you free every month with the *AKC Gazette!*

Subscribe now! A full year, 12 big issues, is just $29.93. **Call toll-free: 1-800-533-7323**

AKC guarantees your satisfaction. Cancel at any time, for any reason. The AKC will refund your money for any and all unmailed issues. *(For all other AKC services, please call 919-233-9767)*